PROJECTING THE PAST

The New Ancient World

a series published by Routledge

The Constraints of Desire
The Anthropology of Sex and Gender in Ancient Greece
John J. Winkler

One Hundred Years of Homosexuality
And Other Essays on Greek Love
David M. Halperin

Torture and Truth
Page duBois

Games of Venus
An Anthology of Greek and Roman Erotic Verse from Sappho to Ovid
introduced, translated, and annotated by
Peter Bing and Rip Cohen

Innovations of Antiquity
edited by Ralph Hexter and Daniel Selden

PROJECTING THE PAST

Ancient Rome, Cinema, and History

Maria Wyke

Routledge
New York and London

Published in 1997 by
Routledge
29 West 35th Street
New York, NY 10001

Published in Great Britain by
Routledge
11 New Fetter Lane
London EC4P 4EE

Photo copyright information: photos on page 66 and 69 are ©1960 by Universal City Studios, Inc., used courtesy MCA Publishing Rights, a Division of MCA, Inc. Page 99 ©1934 by Universal City Studios, Inc., used courtesy MCA Publishing Rights, a Division of MCA, Inc. Page 111 ©1951 Turner Entertainment Co. All rights reserved. Page 136 ©1944 by Universal City Studios, Inc., used courtesy MCA Publishing Rights, a Division of MCA, Inc. Page 138 ©1932 by Universal City Studios, Inc., used courtesy MCA Publishing Rights, a Division of MCA, Inc. Page 141 ©1951 Turner Entertainment Co. All rights reserved. Page 174 and 179 ©1935 RKO Pictures, used courtesy Turner Entertainment Co. All rights reserved. Page 186 ©1964 by Universal City Studios, Inc., used courtesy MCA Publishing Rights, a Division of MCA, Inc.

Library of Congress Cataloging-in-Publication Data

Wyke, Maria.
Projecting the past : ancient Rome, cinema, and history / Maria Wyke.
p. cm.
Filmography: p.
Includes bibliographical references and index.
ISBN 0-415-906130X (hb). -- ISBN 0-415-91614-8 (pb)
1. Historical films--History and criticism. 2. Civilization,
Ancient, in motion pictures. 3. Rome in motion picutres.
I. Title
PN1995.9.H5W95 1997   96-35995

Contents

Illustrations

Acknowledgments

I am first and foremost indebted to Mary Beard, who gave me every possible encouragement to begin my research into the Romans on film when I was teaching at the University of Cambridge. During the course of 1990 to 1994, Somerville College, the British Academy, the British School at Rome, and the Wingate Foundation generously (and in some cases repeatedly) provided me with grants to visit archives in both Italy and the United States. Both Newnham College, Cambridge, and the University of Reading also gave me periods of leave in which to pursue my project.

My interest in the subject of classics and film was first stimulated by working alongside Ken MacKinnon while he was teaching a course on Greek tragedy into film at the University of North London. I am extremely grateful to Peter Bondanella for discussing my project with me in its very earliest stages and for introducing me to resources in Rome. Many archivists helped me track down film texts, production records, and press reviews at the following institutions: in the United States, the University of Southern California, the University of California at Los Angeles, the American Academy of Motion Pictures, the Library of Congress, and the New York Museum of Modern Art; in Rome, the Centro Sperimentale di Cinematografia; in London, the British Film Institute. I would like to express my great thanks in particular to Giancarlo Concetti of Cineteca Nazionale for his assistance in my research on the Italian film industry, and to Ned Comstock of the USC Cinema and Television Library for giving me considerable help in sifting through clipping files and campaign manuals, and for sending me a stready stream of additional materials for years after my one visit to the USC archive.

In the later stages of my project, a number of people have been kind enough to read and comment on earlier versions of my chapters on Nero and Pompeii, or have supplied me with copies of their forthcoming works: Richard Dyer, David Forgacs, Duncan Kennedy, Duncan Petrie, Norman Vance, and Christopher Wagstaff. David Mayer drew my attention to the importance of pyrodramas and toga plays and kindly showed me the materials he had collected from the Pain archive. The historians of silent Italian cinema, Vittorio Martinelli and Riccardo Redi, corrected some of my filmographic errors, generously loaned me a large number of visual materials from their private collections, and told me some wonderful anecdotes about silent film production.

Finally, and most importantly, I would like to express my thanks to my nephew Henry, for neatly timing his birth to provide many very happy moments during the last stages of writing this book, and to David Oswell, without whom I would probably have finished this book sooner but have had less fun.

1

Ancient Rome, Cinema, and History

Classics and Cinema

Even before Gore Vidal first visited the surviving ruins of ancient Rome, it was already a place and a time he knew very well. In *Screening History* (1993), the American writer recalls his adolescent encounter with the city in 1939:

> Despite the heat of Rome in August, I was ecstatic. At last I was where I belonged. I haunted the Forum and the Palatine. In addition to all the Roman movies that I had seen, the first grown-up book that I ever read was a Victorian edition of *Stories from Livy*. I was steeped in Rome. I also lived in a city whose marble columns were a self-conscious duplicate of the old capital of the world. Of course Washington then lacked six of the seven hills and a contiguous world empire. Later, we got the empire but not the hills. (58)

For Vidal, his childhood in 1930s Washington opened many doors onto the Roman past—through his schoolbooks, through the public architecture of his home town and, most vividly, through Hollywood's representations of Roman history.[1] (illustration 1.1)

The title of Vidal's book of reminiscences draws specific attention to the great imaginative power of cinema to shape our perceptions of the past, and his account of watching the Depression musical *Roman Scandals* further demonstrates the extent to which cinematic representations of history have also addressed the concerns of the present:

> Although *Roman Scandals* was a comedy, starring the vaudevillian Eddie Cantor, I was told not to see it. I now realize why the movie, which I saw anyway, had been proscribed. The year of release was 1933. The country was

1

1.1 Neoclassical auditorium of the Tivoli cinema in Washington. [Courtesy of BFI
Stills, Posters and Designs.]

in an economic depression. Drought was turning to dust the heart of the
country's farm land, and at the heart of the heart of the dust bowl was my
grandfather's state of Oklahoma.... At the beginning of *Roman Scandals* we
see the jobless in Oklahoma. One of them is Eddie Cantor, who is knocked
on the head and transported to ancient Rome, much as Dorothy was taken by
whirlwind from Kansas to Oz; thus, a grim Oklahoma is metamorphosed
into a comic-strip Rome. (21)

The young Vidal, who was later to contribute to Hollywood's production of
Roman histories, saw *Roman Scandals* in a city that still displayed architectural monuments to the Founding Fathers' deployment of the Roman
republic as an analogy for the civic virtues of the new nation. Yet, in the
course of the Depression film's narrative, a dispossessed citizen of the Oklahoma city West Rome comes to recognize the corruption of present-day
politicians through his bizarre encounter with a tyrannical Roman emperor.
Vidal's grandfather (a senator from Oklahoma) clearly recognized in the
Hollywood musical an unwelcome message of social protest which suggested, however comically, that America was now beginning to imitate the cruelties of the Roman empire in its treatment of the poor and unemployed.[2]

In *Screening History*, Gore Vidal describes his first tour of Rome's ruins as
charged by a childhood already suffused with images of the ancient city.
Similarly, Federico Fellini's film *Roma* (1972) shows the arrival in Rome in

the late 1930s of the pseudo-autobiographical hero and treats his encounter with the capital as infected by a distant childhood acquaintance with a half-fantastic city. In the first part of *Roma* the child, who lives in the provincial Italian city of Rimini, is provided with access to the history of the capital through an array of ludicrous Fascist refractions: a school trip that bathetically reenacts Julius Caesar's crossing of the river Rubicon, a local's cynical comments on the supposedly Fascist significance of a decaying statue of Julius Caesar in the town square, a bombastic performance of the play *Julius Caesar*, a ranting school lecture on glorious moments from Roman history, a disrupted slide show on the splendors of Roman architecture. The climax of the sequence occurs when, in the town's packed cinema, a Roman historical film is screened juxtaposed with newsreel footage of young Italian athletes who are pompously described in the documentary's voice-over as "the sons of the she-wolf."[3]

Within Fellini's *Roma*, it is the screening of the historical film that constitutes the most immediate, personal, and authentic experience of ancient Rome. The film-within-the-film's narration of romantic love fatally destroyed by the opposition of a lustful empress has the greatest impact on the watching child and on his assimilation of the Roman past to the Italian present. For the fascinated boy turns from the cinematic representation of imperial Rome to stare at the dentist's wife in the auditorium, while a voice-over describes her sexual voracity as worse than that of Messalina. The sequence then cuts away from the dentist's wife to a vision of her outside the cinema literally transformed into the insatiable empress dancing in an open convertible as a number of men in ancient Roman attire await their turn to be serviced by her. (illustration 1.2) Thus the representations of imperial depravity in Fellini's invented historical film are made to intersect with and shape the erotic fantasies which the boy's growing sexual awareness calls forth.[4]

Both Vidal's and Fellini's recollections of their childhood experiences of ancient Rome in the early 1930s serve to remind us that, in the twentieth century, cinema has been crucial to the formation and wide dissemination of an historical consciousness of ancient Rome and that cinema has operated in tandem with, and sometimes in opposition to, more direct access to the surviving monuments and literary texts of antiquity to resurrect a vivid past intimately connected with present interests. Knowledges of "Rome" have become effects of its reconstruction in moving images. Is historical film, therefore, a proper object of study for classicists? And should cinema have a place in the investigation of antiquity's reception?

Constantly at play in twentieth-century interpretations of classics and the classical tradition have been notions of "high culture" and "the classic." In the introduction to *The Classical Tradition* (1949)—Gilbert Highet's compre-

1.2 "Messalina" and her lovers, from Fellini's *Roma* (1972). [Courtesy of BFI Stills, Posters and Designs.]

hensive study of the reception of classical literature—the Professor of Latin declared that

> Our modern world is in many ways a continuation of the world of Greece and Rome. Not in all ways—particularly not in medicine, music, industry, and applied science. But in most of our intellectual and spiritual activities we are the grandsons of the Romans, and the great-grandsons of the Greeks. Other influences joined to make us what we are; but the Greco-Roman strain was one of the strongest and the richest. Without it, our civilization would not merely be different. It would be much thinner, more fragmentary, less thoughtful, more materialistic—in fact, whatever wealth it might have accumulated, whatever wars it might have fought, whatever inventions it might have made, it would be less worthy to be called a civilisation, because its spiritual achievements would be less great. (1)

Similarly, according to the notable address delivered by T.S. Eliot to the Virgil Society in 1944, *What is a Classic?*, the *Aeneid* was destined to set the standard for subsequent European literatures and unite them in a common cultural heritage because it is a unique "classic"—that is, for Eliot, a work that evinces the moral and stylistic qualities of universality and timelessness, maturity and amplitude.[5] In such definitions of literary classicism, tradition is viewed as a sacred process of handing down formally complex, morally rich, critically insightful themes and genres to a present viewed as a passive recipient of the texts of the past. The value of studying "antiquity itself" would thus seem to be comfortably secured and the exploration of the modern manifestations of Greco-Roman culture can then operate as a reverential celebration of that culture's vitality and worth.[6]

Cinema, however, has long been kept at a distance from such notions of high culture and the classic. Soon after the development of the new medium, supporters of the older arts such as theatre, opera, painting, and the novel raged against attempts to call it "the tenth Muse"—in, for example, Germany's "Kinodebatte" of the first few decades of this century. For later critical theorists such as Walter Benjamin in his essay on "The work of art in the age of mechanical reproduction," cinema is not only discontinuous with tradition but also potentially inimical to it. The mechanical process of film's reproduction, in Benjamin's view, challenges the "aura" of cultural texts, their sense of authenticity, authority, autonomy, and distance. The technique of reproduction detaches film from the reverential rituals of tradition and can bestow on the modern medium a positive social significance in "the liquidation of the traditional value of the cultural heritage." For Benjamin, perhaps, there should be cinema *instead* of classics.[7]

Benjamin's high hopes for cinema (and popular culture more generally) constitute the deepest fears of many classical scholars. In his 1980 address to the American Philological Association, Bernard Knox—described on the dust-jacket of a recent collection of such addresses, reviews, and essays as "classicist, historian, literary critic, and defender of the humanities"— warned that the humanities were now suffering a significant loss of interest as an academic pursuit. More disturbingly still, according to Knox,

> it is only logical that in such a situation our discipline should take heavy punishment. Our texts *are* the humanities, the original humanities, the humanities in their most concentrated and genuine form. Without the two languages and literatures which are our province the humanities are hardly conceivable.... And it is only to be expected that in this age of cultural dilution, of plastic substitutes, of mindless television shows, not to mention television dinners and instant coffee, the genuine article is no longer valued.[8]

Such appeals to the purity, the authenticity and the primacy of Greco-Roman culture have taken on even more dramatic and strident form since classics and the classic have become key components in the educational agenda mapped out by the American New Right. In his ultra-conservative bestseller, *The Closing of the American Mind* (1987), Allan Bloom maintained that American higher education was impoverishing "the souls of today's students" because the classic texts are no longer reverently read, and popular culture (and, especially, film) has usurped them in influence. Bloom advocated a return to the traditional canons of literature and traditional literary studies, and to the firm values, established truths, and intellectual discipline which they could supposedly inculcate. According to Bloom, moreover, the gratitude of students "at learning of Achilles or the categorical imperative is boundless."[9] For conservative educators like Bloom, the concept of the classics is polemically constructed as a term in a binary opposition where there are classics and the contemptible. He interprets the introduction of popular culture into the academy as symptomatic of profound political disorder, and seeks the policing of culture as a route to conserve social order and authority. Bloom would be likely to see the relationship between classics and cinema in Arnoldian terms—as a struggle between Culture and Anarchy.[10]

Evaluation of the merits of researching and teaching the classical tradition has not been unaffected by such conservative discourses as those which culminated in the publication of Bloom's book. For example, in 1984, in a foreword to Meyer Reinhold's *Classica Americana*, William Calder had already speculated that Reinhold's explorations of the Greek and Roman heritage in eighteenth- and nineteenth-century America may have been motivated by the modest desire "to remind forgetful Americans how much they owed their classical past in a banausic age ignorant of that great legacy."[11] But ten years on, in Bernard Knox's foreword to his own collection *Backing into the Future: the Classical Tradition and its Renewal*, the author could speak in sinister and apocalyptic terms of a plan by multiculturalists, feminists, and the politically correct "to abolish the cultural tradition on which the West's sense of unity and identity is founded," a plan comparable (although, he concedes, not in scale) to the cultural "innovations" of the French Revolutionaries or the Russian Bolsheviks and as likely to lead to historic catastrophe.[12]

The interlinked concepts of "high culture," "the tradition," "the canon" of approved authors, and "the classic," however, have long since been contested both outside and within the discipline of classical studies. Their formation and deployment in literary studies have been seen as "one means whereby local ideological interests are given the status of eternal values, the gap between past and present is elided, and 'literature' is depoliticized by an occlusion of those constraints and cultural processes which determine the nature of its discourses."[13] Cultural theorists, such as Pierre Bourdieu or Stuart Hall, have argued that distinctions between the high and the popular, between "ideal" and "substandard" culture, work to legitimate class distinctions and are principally sustained by an educational system in the continuity of which the elite have a major investment.[14] Specifically concerning classical scholarship and the classical tradition, in *Black Athena: the Afroasiatic Roots of Classical Civilisation* (1987 and 1991), Martin Bernal has drawn attention to the pressing ideological interests (the racism and anti-Semitism) that underlay the fabrication in the nineteenth century, and the subsequent persistence of a Greco-Roman model for Western Europe's cultural origins.[15] Disclosing the contemporary horizon of interest of those who deploy such terms as "the classic" and "the classical tradition" demonstrates that, far from being a sacred inheritance handed down from the past, classicism is "an active, open process intimately connected with the pursuit of particular interests in the present."[16] While T.S. Eliot, for example, appropriated Virgil's *Aeneid* in 1944 as the metaphoric bloodstream that might still pump some life into wounded, war-torn Europe and render it a whole living entity once more,[17] Gilbert Highet in contrast constructed his classical tradition four years after the end of the Second World War to demonstrate the cultural superiority of the victorious countries over a Germany portrayed as feeling "foreign and half-civilized in face of the Greek spirit."[18]

As classics and the classical tradition have been divested of their moral purity, political neutrality, and cultural primacy, so some classicists have been at pains to divest their academic discipline of the title "Classics" and to replace it with less charged descriptions such as "ancient Mediterranean studies" while concerning themselves more and more with disclosing rather than occluding the local ideological interests—the various misogynies, ethnocentricities, elitisms and imperialisms—of both antiquity and its subsequent appropriations. Nowadays when beginners are introduced to the subject in accessible works such as *Classics: A Very Short Introduction* (1995) by Mary Beard and John Henderson, they are informed that the aim of classics is not only to uncover the ancient world but also "to define and debate *our* relationship to that world."[19] For Beard and Henderson, classics concerns not high culture but whole cultures, and not just an elite response but a whole range of responses to them.[20] Classics thus newly conceived welcomes as its objects of study "the imaginative entertainments and instructive re-creations of Greece and Rome" which are to be found on the page, stage, and celluloid of popular cultural production.[21] Similarly, in Martin Winkler's edited collection *Classics and Cinema* (1991), both Mary-Kay Gamel (who analyzes the tragic structures of the film *Chinatown*) and Peter Rose (who explicates the use of films such as *Clash of the Titans* and *Superman* in his teaching of a classical mythology course) argue that a fundamental purpose of their comparative investigations of classics and cinema is to challenge the conventional definitions of classics and classicism that have received so much support since the late 1980s. Confronting the neo-conservative revival of a distinction between high and popular culture, they seek to dissolve that distinction from the supposedly high ground of the classical scholar. In doing so, their essays might be thought responsive to post-modernist criticism, which has declared the collapse of any overarching Arnoldian metanarrative that lays claim to a categorical distinction between high and low in the field of cultural production.[22]

The purpose of my own book is to explore part of the cycle of cinematic reconstructions of Roman history to which Gore Vidal and Federico Fellini have drawn such vivid attention. The ensuing case studies of films about Spartacus, Cleopatra, Nero, and the city of Pompeii demonstrate that such historical films, whether produced by the Italian or the Hollywood film industries, belong within a broadly conceived classical tradition and deserve the attention of classicists because they constitute a pervasive and engaging set of modern knowledges of ancient Rome. Drawing on a whole constellation of nineteenth- and twentieth-century historiographic genres, cinema has long provided its own distinctive historiography of ancient Rome that has vividly resurrected the ancient world and reformulated it in the light of present needs. Cinema's historical narratives of antiquity have worked to interpellate spectators into their reconstructions of ancient Rome and have left their traces even on the subjectivities of those fascinated spectators. In turn, spectators have read their "direct" contacts with the surviving fragments of ancient Rome as texts in dialogue with cinematic reconstructions of antiquity and other contemporary discursive formations of the Greco-Roman past. This book operates, therefore, as a challenge to such recent definitions of classics and classicism as would bolster the discipline with the timeless, universal values of the classic against the seemingly temporal, local, and trivial interests of popular culture. Denaturalizing the distinctions between high and popular culture allows for both a more complex and a richer relationship between ancient and modern cultures, and a process of productive exchange between scholarship on classical culture and cultural theories of the popular.

Cinema and History

Projecting the Past not only contributes to recent debates about definitions of classics and the classical tradition, but also provides a useful point of entry into and interaction with current debates about the nature of history and the relationship between cinema and history.[23] Although films about Nero, for example, center on the same historical figure and are set in the same historical time and place, they evince interesting ruptures and discontinuities in their portrayal of the emperor's persecutions and pyromania. An exploration of the changing mode of their historical reconstructions and the changing cultural force of their narratives within and between the countries of their production engages with a number of pertinent concerns about history in cinema and cinema in history.

Film is a medium that initially located itself as an extension of nineteenth-century representational forms. The new technology of the moving image could be seen as a further development of a nineteenth-century technical progression through engraving, lithography, and photography towards ever more refined "realistic" representations, whether of the present or of the past. Such technological developments further abetted the nineteenth-century historical sensibility that sought to make the past live again in the present. Thus one of the most fascinating attractions which the new medium soon claimed to offer was the possibility of reconstructing the past with a precision and a vivacity superior to that of documentary sources or the nineteenth-century historical fictions of painting, theater, and the novel.[24] In the same year as the release of *The Birth of a Nation* (1915), a monumentally successful epic film that recreated the American Civil War, its director D. W. Griffith wrote in utopian terms of the medium's newly disclosed and unique capacity to narrate history. He declared that cinema was not just a cold instrument for the recording of reality, as in documentary films, but also and above all a powerful mode of historical writing which could better transmit an historical consciousness to the public than months of study. For Griffith, cinema taught history in lightning and would soon usurp the educative value of conventional history books.[25] A year earlier, in Italy, audiences and film reviewers had certainly responded with extraordinary enthusiasm to Giovanni Pastrone's film *Cabiria* (1914), which recreated on screen the ancient conflict between the territorial ambitions of Rome and Carthage:

> An intense emotion grasped the entire audience, the emotion of the incomparable spectacle which, through a set-designer's tenacious effort, revived the people of the third century [B.C.] and flung them into tremendous struggles before the steep walls of a city, into the burning waves of a flaming sea, at the feet of a idol crimson with fire.... On their feet, on all sides of the theatre, the crowd shouted with enthusiasm and joy. A genuine, sincere, unrestrainable frenzy accompanied the majestic film from beginning to end.... *Cabiria* is something that will last. It will last because at that instant the vulgar art of cinema ceases and history succeeds, true history.[26]

For their early promoters and for many of their consumers, historical films were true histories. Cinema could supply a new mode of historiography of lasting value for the immediacy with which it reconstructed the past and for the intimacy with that past which it gave to its enthusiastic spectators. But the constant claims to truth, accuracy, and pedagogic value which have also been made for historical films throughout the twentieth century by their makers and distributors are, in a sense, a masquerade. Whatever the attention paid to accurate reconstruction in an historical film's surface texture—the antiquarian aesthetic, for example, manifest in the set designs, costumes, and props of epics set in the classical world—all such films partake of fiction.[27] Most notably, no historical film (in the terms of Stephen Heath) escapes the obligation of a narration. According to the "classical" narrative strategies of historical epics to which films about ancient Rome largely conform, romance is the point of the historical discourse—very often pagan boy meets Christian girl. History is contained within domestic conflict and provided with the perfection of a story and an end in the rescue or the death of the loving couple.[28]

Although cinema's historical fictions provided a door to the past for the young Gore Vidal, until recently they were scarcely considered by professional historians and other critics as a mechanism for constructing the past that might have a legitimacy of its own. From the beginnings of cinema, many intellectuals had expressed disquiet at the public's apparently debased taste for the representation of historical romance on screen. By the time the neo-realist movement was initiated in the late 1930s, the historical films which had previously dominated Italian film production (and so excited the youthful hero of Fellini's *Roma*) were savagely castigated by Luchino Visconti as a "cinema of corpses":

> They live blissfully unaware that times have changed, in the reflection of things long extinct, in that unreal world of theirs where one could blissfully tread on false floors of coloured chalk and paper, where backdrops wobbled at the rush of air from a suddenly opened door, where tissue paper roses bloomed perpetually, where styles and epochs blended in a generous confusion, where, to drive the point home, bewigged Cleopatras, "Liberty" style and clutching their whips, vamped morose and brawny Mark Anthonies in whalebone corsets.[29]

Such films, according to the historian Guido Fink, produced a double masquerade in which producers adapted and distorted the Roman past to the dictates of a Fascist propaganda, which was itself inspired by the remote and rhetorical heroes of a distorted Rome. For Fink, the subsequent production of Visconti's *Ossessione* (1943) and other neo-realist works constituted a healthy and refreshing reaction against the pompous farce of the

Italian historical films of earlier decades. The new neorealist style of film production represented "a pent-up thirst for truth, a need to discover the real Italy that the cautious and guilty artificiality of Fascist cinema had concealed for so many years."[30]

After the United States came to dominate the international market in historical films in the 1930s and again in the 1950s, Hollywood's film histories were frequently dismissed as garish, vulgar, and sensational spectacles and derided as standardized studio products.[31] Here too criticism of these films intensified as their market value began to decline. In one of the many appraisals of Hollywood's historical "blockbusters" to be published in the film journals of the early 1960s, Penelope Houston and John Gillett wrote in *Sight and Sound* of the blockbusters' stylistic and moral conservatism necessitated by the studios' huge financial investment in such products:

> When in doubt, use a well-tried formula. For producers seeking inspiration in a time of crisis, the familiar Hollywood dictum could mean only one thing. The religious spectacle, whether inspired directly by the Bible or by the highly exploitable conflicts of Romans and Christians, is as old as the cinema itself. Hollywood carried on from where the silent Italians left off, and Cecil B. DeMille converted the formula into his own personal (and profitable) mixture of would-be eroticism and biblical tub-thumping. With wider screens and greater facilities, there seemed no reason why even his grandiose flights of fancy should not be surpassed. And the audience was ready-made, waiting to respond with the proper degree of self-satisfaction to the overwhelming righteousness of it all.[32]

Similarly, in an issue of *Films and Filming* of the same period, Raymond Durgnat denigrated the Hollywood penchant for presenting history in a contemporary and provincial mode:

> It's a pity that by sheer weight of budget the epic has come to be thought of as an American speciality, for the Americans are rather bad at them.... Even the sophisticated Aldrich's *Sodom and Gomorrah* boringly opposes the virtuous, hard-working, patriarchal Hebrews and the rich, corrupt, Lesbian-dominated Sodomians. Stewart Granger tries to get the Israelites to control Sodom by means of their virtual salt-monopoly, and the ethical dilemmas of fighting capitalist greed by capitalist means are honestly stated. Aldrich's film is vitiated however by its stilted style and by the Israel-Sodom antithesis, based as it is on the contrast too often made by old-fashioned American puritans, between rural America (hardworking, frugal, virtuous) and the big city (rich, pleasure-ridden, corrupt).[33]

In more recent years, however, film scholarship has elaborated a variety of productive critical strategies for interpreting the relationship between cinema and history.[34] According to the account of Marc Ferro in *Cinéma et histoire. Le cinéma, agent et source de l'histoire* (1977), cinema has much to offer the historian. Documentary films should be of interest as sources of contemporary history and propaganda films (such as those produced with the assistance or in the interests of the Fascist, Nazi, and Soviet regimes) as agents of history. But historical fiction films are only allocated a limited role by Ferro as secondary source material for an analysis of the present period of their production. Even if it speaks about the past, film is for Ferro always and only a narrative in the present tense. "True" historical reality, then, resides not in the represented past, but in the present so represented. The medieval Russia, for example, of Sergei Eisenstein's *Alexander Nevsky* (1938) and Andrei Tarkovsky's *Andrei Rublev* (1966) becomes a kind of historical veneer which can be chipped away to reveal the contemporary Soviet Union lying beneath its surface.[35] But if, in that paradoxical sense, the historical film is always contemporary, it would scarcely seem to matter which historical period has been chosen for cinematic reconstruction. The cinematic representations of the slave rebellion of Spartacus, for example, would have no common bond at all but be grounded entirely in the specific moment of their production, each operating independently as a pretext for narratives about the present.

For decades, scholars like Ferro privileged the documentary over other modes of filmic discourse as the most direct and objective cinematic instrument for historical analysis. But others have questioned the appropriateness of such a strict separation between history and fiction, or between cinema as a "trace of the real" and a "machine of dreams."[36] As Geoffrey Nowell-Smith has observed, soon after the invention of cinema it inserted itself into "the problematic of the historical record" and itself interrogated the supposed distinctions between fact and fiction, truth and falsehood in history, for its photographic dimension also became the essence of its capacity for illusion.[37] Moreover, since the 1970s, a new self-consciousness about traditional conceptions of history and the rhetorical conventions for its presentation have collapsed the formerly clear boundaries between history and fiction. *All* historical discourses, according to this mode of analysis, are a form of fiction. All history involves storytelling and a plot, troping and figurality. Such "metahistory," as defined by Hayden White, has drawn attention to the overlapping codes and conventions of nineteenth-century historical representation, whether those of "professional" history, museum displays, or historical novels, paintings, plays, and (eventually) films. These interconnected structures of historical narration have, it is argued, made possible the emergence over the last two centuries of an integrated regime of historical representation in which modern societies have made meanings out of the remains of their past and, thereby, addressed their present.[38]

For the film historian Pierre Sorlin, in his influential works *Sociologie du cinéma* (1977) and *The Film in History: Restaging the Past* (1980), history as used in film is a useful device to speak of the present time while also being a discourse about the past. For Sorlin, the historical dimension of an historical film lies not only in its relationship to the period of its production, but also in its utilization of a more or less rigorously constituted past in which its audience is disposed to take an interest. The analysis of historical film then opens up two possible sectors of research for historians: the study of contemporary society through cinematic rereadings of a selectively represented past, and the study of the modern transmission of historical consciousness. Historians should try to understand not whether a particular cinematic account of history is true or disinterested, but what the logic of that account may be, asking why it emphasizes this question, that event, rather than others. The address to the past may embrace an appeal to authority, an escape into nostalgia, or a search for origins; the selection of a particular historical episode or reference period may carry particular political allegiances or have a specific bearing on current social conflicts in a given community. As a powerful new mode of historiography emerging from nineteenth-century representational forms, historical films should be examined not only in terms of their stylistic conventions for representing the past in the present, but also in terms of their economic and technological strategies for the creation of a consciousness of history that far exceed those of historical scholarship in range and impact.[39]

Thus according to the productive approach initiated by Pierre Sorlin, historical film is a discourse about the past as well as the present and, echoing the much earlier rhetoric of the director D. W. Griffith, such film constitutes an imaginative historiography, one distinctive and significant component of a modern culture's historical capital. The cinematic representations of Roman history then are fictions, but fictions thatshare the usage of a well-defined and limited historical period that calls up a constellation of specific meanings for its mass audiences. And the cinematic resurrection of ancient Rome operates not as a mere substitute for a narrative of present times, but as one of the chief transmitters of twentieth-century historical knowledge of the Roman world.

2

Projecting Ancient Rome

Invented Traditions

If historical films set in ancient Rome have now become a legitimate object of study for both classicists and historians, then what work needs to be done to write a history of such films? According to the terms recently set for cinema's own strategies for screening history, these films form part of an integrated regime of historical representation that constitutes the historical capital of twentieth=century cultures, and the reference period selected for projection ceases to be arbitrary and instead generates historical meaning through its relationship with other, extra-cinematic discourses about the past. Knowledge of those intertexts facilitates the exploration of how historical films function within a culture.[1] The reminiscences of cinema-going in the 1930s offered by Gore Vidal and Federico Fellini, their respective recollections of the neoclassical public architecture of Washington or the various Fascist celebrations of ancient Rome, suggest one important set of intertexts for the production and consumption of films about Roman history—namely the deployment of ancient Rome in the formation of the national identities of the United States and Italy.

The two nations which have been most prolific in their manufacture of cinematic histories of ancient Rome also assiduously created a whole array of "invented traditions" to connect themselves with the Roman past. I use "invented traditions" (a term taken from the historian Eric Hobsbawm) to refer to those discursive practices that, from the mid-eighteenth century, attempted to establish for a modern community a continuity with a suitable historical past. The purpose of these traditions was to cement group cohesion and legitimate action through the use of history, and the communities whose institutions, policies, and social relations were being established, symbolized, or legitimated historically were more often than not the newly formed nation-states. The awareness of an historical continuity, the creation of a cultural patrimony, served to enhance a sense of communal identity, legitimating the new nation and bolstering its sovereignty in the eyes 0f its own and other peoples. By tracing its origins back into the past, a nation could validate its claims to power, property, and international prestige. And, if rooted in the remotest antiquity, a nation could make claims to the earliest precedent and the greatest dignity.[2]

The United States had constant recourse to an invented tradition of *romanitas* in the early years of the nation's foundation. American national identity had to be forged out of a mass of heterogeneous immigrants who were encouraged to accept and participate in a whole host of rituals and historical discourses which commemorated the history of the new nation and rooted it in a more remote past. Classical antiquity readily supplied America with a usable past—instant, communal history and cultural legitimacy in the eyes of Europe. America was thus created according to the model of an ideally conceived Roman republic. Roman republican ideals of liberty, civic virtue, and mixed government were densely evoked as precedent for and validation of the new republic during the struggle for independence and the subsequent constitutional debates of 1787–1788. In August 1777, for example, when replying to the peace offer made by the British general John Burgoyne, George Washington claimed: "The associated armies in America act from the noblest motives, liberty. The same principles actuated the arms of Rome in the days of her glory; and the same object was the reward of Roman valour." In the early national period, George Washington in particular became a focal point of efforts to Romanize American history. In pictures and statues and victory arches, he was to be seen draped in a Roman toga or attired in military costume. [illustration 2.1] In the literature of the period, the "father of his country" was hailed as another heroic symbol of the republican virtues of patriotism, self-sacrifice, frugality, and military acumen along the lines of the Roman leaders Cincinnatus, Cato, or Fabius.[3]

America's rhetoric of *romanitas* became more complex and ambiguous as its expansion southward and westward appeared to endanger its republican institutions and its Christian ethics. The international expositions and fairs held throughout the United States from the late nineteenth century until the end of the First World War celebrated the success of America's recent quest for empire through their use of pseudo-Roman imperial architecture, as did similarly designed state capitols, court houses, museums, universities, libraries, and railroad stations. Imperial Rome, however, had supplied the Founding Fathers with a striking anti-model for the social organization and government of the new nation. During the Revolutionary period, British politicians had been regularly clothed in the vices and villainy of the Roman emperors, and British colonial policy had been compared to the tyranny

2.1 Statue of George Washington in Roman military attire, from original by Antonio Canova, commissioned in 1815. [North Carolina Division of Archives and History, Raleigh.]

which Rome had supposedly exercised over her provinces. As America's own empire grew from the mid-nineteenth century, so such earlier critiques of imperialism were turned against America itself. By the beginning of the twentieth century, critics were warning apocalyptically that, having forsaken Christianity and fallen into decadence, the nation was heading toward Armageddon. According to Henry Adams, the great-grandson of the Founding Father John Adams, when he looked out of his hotel window at New York in 1905 he "felt himself in Rome, under Diocletian, witnessing the anarchy, with no Constantine the Great in sight."[4]

Scholars, politicians, and intellectuals, ever since, have looked to the decline of the Roman empire to provide support for their dire predictions of America's coming fall. Perpetuated in the public architecture of the United States, allusions to Rome could thus assume a contradictory quality. Nonetheless, parallels between ancient Rome and modern America continued to surface and circulated widely in the popular representational forms of the nineteenth and twentieth centuries, in classical-subject paintings and pyrodramas, toga plays and historical novels.[5] Most notably, General Lew Wallace's religious novel *Ben-Hur: A Tale of the Christ* constructs a stirring narrative in which the fictive Judaean's resistance to Roman rule and his conversion to Christianity effectively cast America as a new Holy Land capable of driving out its imperial rulers and establishing peace through the embrace of Christ. The novel was first published in 1880 and stayed on the bestseller lists for some fifty years. It was spectacularly staged from 1899, was adapted for the screen in 1907, 1925, and again in 1959, and even gave its hero's name to a town in Texas.[6]

American formulations of its relationship to ancient Rome, however, have always been less intimate and ultimately less pressing than the Italian conception of *romanità*. A certain confusion reigned over the relevance of both republican and imperial Rome to America because America's place within history, unlike that of European nations, was not clearly demarcated. Material remains of the classical past did not litter America's landscape as they did Italy's.[7] The surviving monuments and iconography of ancient Rome were frequently deployed in Italy during the course of the nineteenth century as political symbols in a struggle for power between the Papacy and the *risorgimento* revolutionaries. The Colosseum was pitted against the Roman forum, the Christian cross against the republican *fasces*. While the Church exploited archaeology as proof of the ultimate triumph of the Christian martyrs over the cruel persecutions of imperial Rome, the emerging nationalist movement sought out and paraded a precedent for a unified, secular Italy that was rooted in an earlier republican tradition of civic rather than religious virtue, of triumvirs and consuls, not tyrants. Thus when

Giuseppe Garibaldi was elected to the Constituent Assembly of 1849, he declared (if somewhat prematurely): "I believe profoundly that, now the papal system of government is at an end, what we need in Rome is a republic. . . . Can it be that the descendants of the ancient Romans are not fit to constitute a Republic? As some people in this body evidently take offence at this word, I reiterate 'Long live the republic!'"[8]

After the unification of Italy in 1861, the problem of assimilating its disparate peoples into a single nation was summarized by Massimo d'Azeglio thus: "We have made Italy: now we must make Italians."[9] Needing to justify itself historically, and in the face of continued opposition from the Vatican, the new secular body politic was able to find a major, and apparently self-evident, justification in the ancient civic virtues and military glories of the Roman republic and empire. The invented tradition of *romanità* gave to the heterogeneous Italians a piece of common national history, and, in an epidemic of literary production from unification into the first decade of the twentieth century, historical fictions such as Pietro Cossa's Roman tragedies or Raffaello Giovagnoli's Roman novels attempted to supply a unifying popular culture in which the grand figures of Roman history "get off their pedestals of togaed rhetoric" and speak simply and with a quotidian *verismo* of sacrifices for or betrayals of their country.[10]

Until the 1910s, however, narratives of imperial Rome were often vulnerable to appropriation by religious opponents of Italy's liberal government as gruesome analogies for the state repression of Catholic organizations and as ominous warnings of the Church's certain victory in the continuing struggle to reclaim her temporal power. But by the time the fiftieth year of Italian unity was grandly celebrated in 1911, both state and Church were finding common cause in imperial Rome as historical legitimation for Italy's colonial aspirations in the Mediterranean. In a speech to open an archaeological exhibition held at the Baths of Diocletian during the Great Exhibition of 1911, the Christian archaeologist Rodolfo Lanciani expressed clearly the pressing imperial agenda that now lay behind such Italian displays of its Roman past. According to Lanciani, the *mostra archeologica* ought to form the basis of a future museum of the Roman empire "where Italian youth may seek inspiration for all those virtues which rendered Rome, morally as well as materially, the mistress of the world." On the eve of Italy's war against Turkey to wrest the colonies Tripolitania and Cyrenaica from the Ottoman empire, and despite the reservations of some critics, imperial Rome was everywhere invoked as the model of and reason for a new Italian empire. And, after victory in Africa, the discourse of historical continuity between ancient and modern imperialism continued to circulate widely, as a postcard reproduced in the English magazine *The Sphere* towards the end

2.2 "Italy brandishes the sword of ancient Rome," postcard from 1910s celebrating Italian victory in North Africa. [From private collection of Peter Bondanella.]

of 1911 testifies. An Italian sailor triumphantly grasps the sword of empire from the skeleton of a Roman soldier partially buried in the African sands. The caption beneath declares "Italy brandishes the sword of ancient Rome."[11] [illustration 2.2]

Historians of silent Italian cinema, such as Gian Piero Brunetta, have long argued that the war in Africa gave a decisive push toward the meeting of Italian cinematic production and the imperial ambitions of the nation-state. The many grand historical films set in ancient Rome which were produced in the period leading up to the First World War (and which obtained enormous critical acclaim and box-office success both in Italy and abroad) held a crucial role in the formation, interrogation, and dissemination of the rhetoric of *romanità*. Such films were both *about* ancient Rome and *for* modern Italy.[12]

The recently established institutions of cinema changed the relationship between historical narration and its audiences. The practice of cinema-going brought huge numbers of Italian spectators out of their homes into a shared public space and thus rendered their experience of historical reconstruction a more collective event than the private reading of a novel. The technologies of cinema spectacle could also accommodate on screen huge masses of people before whom, or even for whom, the protagonists of the narrative acted. Through these crowds of extras, mass audiences were able to visualize on screen their own collectivity and gain a stake in historical action. Historical films, therefore, became ideal vehicles for addressing the nation's sense of its own identity.[13] In the years preceding the First World War, there was a substantial increase of capital investment in the production of Italian feature-length historical films. Bound to the dictates of high finance and to the bourgeois values of its financial backers, Italian historical films began to prosper as an instrument of cultural hegemony. In the logic of their producers, they came to be regarded as a new form of popular university, capable of shaping the historical consciousness of their mass, largely illiterate audience and transmitting to them the symbols of Italy's recently constituted national identity. Historical films set in ancient Rome became a privileged means for the production and consumption of an imperial *romanità*. The projection on screen of the imperial eagles and the *fasces*, Roman military rituals and parades supplied a concentrated repertoire of glorious precedents for present combative action.[14] Thus, soon after victory in Africa, the celebratory film *Cabiria* (1914) represented a unified Roman community under the leadership of the morally upright general Scipio triumphing over a decadent and disorganized Carthage.[15]

Similarly, despite the relative political independence of the Italian film industry during the early years of the Fascist regime, at the time of the

African campaigns of 1935–1936 the Fascist government helped procure considerable capital investment for the production of the spectacular historical film *Scipione l'Africano* (1937), in which the hero is seen to lead a unified, rural, and warlike Rome to victory in Africa. The cinematic construction of the Roman general's character rehearsed a model for the perfect Fascist citizen, and his designed analogy with Mussolini was both exploited by the *duce* himself and recognized by the film's contemporary audience. Even before the March on Rome in October 1922, Mussolini had begun to appropriate the miltant rhetoric of *romanità* to establish historical legitimacy and popular support for Fascism. In a speech reproduced in his newspaper *Il popolo d'Italia* for 21 April 1922, he declared:

> We dream of a Roman Italy, that is to say wise, strong, disciplined, and imperial. Much of that which was the immortal spirit of Rome is reborn in Fascism: the Fasces are Roman; our organization of combat is Roman, our pride and our courage are Roman: *civis romanus sum*. Now, it is necessary that the history of tomorrow, the history we fervently wish to create, not represent a contrast or a parody of the history of yesterday. . . . Italy has been Roman for the first time in fifteen centuries in the War and in the Victory: now Italy must be Roman in peacetime: and this renewed and revived *romanità* bears these names: Discipline and Work.[16]

In the 1930s, Roman iconography, architecture and sculpture, political rhetoric, and military ritual were systematically exploited to justify historically the Fascist aspiration to a colonial empire in the Mediterranean.[17] And, under the impetus of events in Africa, with the conquest of Ethiopia and the ensuing proclamation of Empire on 9 May 1936, the production of the historical film *Scipione l'Africano* became a work of the regime, on which the Ministries of Popular Culture, Finance, Home Affairs, and War collaborated (the last supplying infantry and cavalry troops as extras for the battle sequences).[18]

Soon after shooting the film, the cinematographer Luigi Freddi (who had been appointed four years previously to run a new film directorate within the Ministry of Popular Culture) avowed that the cinematic representation of Scipio's conquest of Africa had been expressly undertaken to service Italy's renewed imperial project. Writing in *Il popolo d'Italia* for 6 April 1937, he announced that

> *Scipione* was conceived on the eve of the African undertaking and was begun soon after the victory. It was desired because no theme for translation into spectacle seemed more suited than this to symbolize the intimate union

between the past grandeur of Rome and the bold accomplishment of our epoch. And it seemed also that no filmic representation was capable of showing and framing, in the august tradition of the race, before ourselves and the world, the African undertaking of today as a logical corollary of a glorious past and an ardent present's indisputable reason for living. Perhaps never, in the history of cinema, has a film initiative been so full of deep spiritual significance derived from active consideration of history.[19]

The film was presented at the Venice Film Festival of November 1937, where it won the Mussolini Cup. Its subsequent distribution was supported by an extensive publicity campaign in the Italian press and by admiring reviews. Its political effectiveness then appeared to be confirmed by interviews with schoolchildren, whose essays on their viewing of the film were printed in a special edition of the cinema journal *Bianco e Nero* for August 1939. According to the introduction furnished by Giuseppe Bottai, the Minister for National Education: "For the children, Scipio is not the Roman hero, it is Mussolini. Through a subconscious power of transposition, the actions of Scipio become the actions of Mussolini. The analogy becomes identity."[20]

The evident meeting between liberal Italy's geopolitical ambitions and the narrative structures of *Cabiria* (1914), the seemingly perfect propagandist match between the Fascist regime's combative discourse of *romanità* and the production, distribution, and consumption of *Scipione l'Africano* (1937), may suggest that films concerning Roman history can be read as effective instruments of ideological control which, through spectacular and engaging historical reconstructions, manipulate their audiences to assent to a celebratory model of national identity. Yet the independently produced *Cabiria* was a huge commercial success in Italy, the (uniquely) state-supported *Scipione* a failure. Furthermore, many successful Italian films of the 1910s and 1920s resurrected ancient Rome's imperial cruelties and Christian martyrdoms rather than its republican triumphs, while Hollywood histories of Rome have appropriated Fascist constructions of *romanità* to turn them back against the regime which produced them, and have constantly exploited the ambiguities and contradictions inherent in the American national discourse of *romanitas* to address iniquities within the United States itself. Screening ancient Rome could supply equivocal history lessons for both Italians and Americans.

In the *New York Times* of 22 November 1959, the film critic Bosley Crowther heaped the highest praise on MGM's latest adaptation of the famous novel *Ben Hur* for the film's perceived pertinence and timeliness:

Obviously, this story, with its personal conflicts based on religious and political differences, is more concrete to present generations, which have seen
tyrants and persecutors at work than it could have been to most of the people
who read it in the nineteenth century. And it is this paramount realization of
the old story's present significance that properly has been foremost in the rea-
sonings of Mr. Wyler and the man (or men) who prepared the script. It is
indeed this realization that has justified a remake at this time.

   Now, in the hero's conversations with Messala, one can hear echoes of the
horrible clash of interests in Nazi Germany. In the burgeoning of hatred in
Ben-Hur one can sense the fierce passion for revenge that must have moved
countless people in Poland and Hungary. And in the humble example of
Jesus, most tastefully enacted in this film, one can feel genuine spiritual
movement toward the ideal of the brotherhood of man.

As Michael Wood has observed in *America in the Movies* (1975), Hollywood
epics of the Cold War era frequently cast British theater actors as villainous
Egyptian pharaohs or Roman patricians, and American film stars as their
virtuous Jewish or Christian opponents. Thus films like *Ben-Hur* replay in
an ancient setting the glorious struggle of "the colonies against the mean
mother country."[21] In New Testament epics, the United States takes on the
sanctity of the Holy Land and receives the endorsement of God for all its
past and present fights for freedom against tyrannical regimes (imperial
Britain, Fascist Italy, Nazi Germany, or the Communist Soviet Union). In
such narratives, a hyperbolically tyrannical Rome stands for the decadent
European Other forever destined to be defeated by the vigorous Christian
principles of democratic America.[22] Critics have also argued, however, that
such film narratives sometimes exhibit an additional and contradictory
analogy between the repressions of the Roman empire and those exercised
within the United States. When in *The Robe* (1953), for example, the
emperor Caligula demands that a Roman soldier infiltrate Christian subversives and name names, Bruce Babington and Peter Evans hear clear
echoes of the directives of the House Un-American Activities Committee,
which required those called before it to disclose the names of colleagues
with Communist Party connections. *The Robe*, momentarily, offers a political critique of the surveillance, investigation, and police-state manoeuvres at
work during the course of America's "Red Scare."[23]

   If film scholarship has problematized the function of historical film as a
national discourse, it often seems to utilize a form of discursive slippage
between film and society which requires interrogation. Ever since the psychoanalytic readings of German cinema offered by Siegfried Kracauer in

his seminal book *From Caligari to Hitler: A Psychological History of German Film* (1947), where Kracauer posited a relationship between Weimar films and Fascism, many film critics have justified reading the films of a particular nation as a manifestation of that nation's psycho-social disposition, as an expression of that society's subconscious fears and desires. Against the trends of auteur theory, films are regarded as the outcome not of an individual creativity, but of a team or social group. Since film needs a public, it addresses itself and appeals to a heterogeneous mass audience whose desires it must satisy. If filmmakers and their financial backers then seek to correspond to the beliefs and values of their audiences, films can be considered as reflections of the mentality of a nation. By means of this convenient critical shift from film to society, the historical film in particular can be viewed as a central component of the historical text that a society writes about itself, as a modern form of historiography that, if properly investigated, can disclose how a society conceives and exploits its past to construct its own present and future identities. The inadequacies of Kracauer's approach, however, are well documented. Such accounts of the relation between film and society tend to place most emphasis on the social and ideological contexts of film production and to overlook the specificities of the institution of cinema. But only a partial examination of the relation between film and society (or cinema and history) can be achieved if any sociological or psychoanalytic examination of film texts is separated from the study of the technical and economic conditions of their production, the formation and development of their representational conventions, and the process of constructing and consuming their aesthetic pleasures.[24]

The Pleasures of the Look

The cinematic reconstructions of Roman history produced by the Italian and Hollywood film industries have always exceeded in function any imperative to make proprietarial claim on classical virtues and victories (or to question those claims). In the 1910s, for example, they were also utilized to legitimate cinema as a new art form and win international cultural prestige for their country of origin, in the 1930s to showcase commodities, and in the 1950s to combat television's assault on film industry profits. In all these respects and more, the projection of ancient Rome on screen has often worked to place its spectators on the side of decadence and tyranny.

In the first decades of the twentieth century, a new generation of Italian entrepreneurs began to invest heavily in the production of films (as they had in the manufacture of automobiles and aeroplanes) in order to raise Italy to the ranks of the great industrial powers and to affirm for it a position of commercial prestige on foreign markets. As a result of capital investment, industrial competition, and the economic and aesthetic need to increase the artistic status and range of motion pictures, Italian films rapidly increased in length; developed their own formal strategies of editing and camera movement, staging, set design and special effects; dealt with more ambitious themes; and often filled the screen with huge numbers of extras and expensively produced spectacles to rival and outdo theatrical shows and the narrative scale of the novel. Feature-length film narratives set in antiquity, such as *Quo Vadis?* (1913) and *Cabiria* (1914), formed part of a strategy to win over the bourgeoisie to the new cinematic art-form by bestowing on the modern medium a grandiose register and an educative justification. Such films borrowed from the whole spectrum of nineteenth-century modes of historical representation (literary, dramatic, and pictorial) in pursuit of authenticity and authority for cinema as a mode of high culture, and to guarantee mass, international audiences through the reconstruction in moving images of familiar and accessible events of Roman history.[25]

In their search for intertexts that would be familiar to bourgeois spectators, however, Italian filmmakers did not confine themselves to the domestic narratives of ancient Rome available in the novels of Rafaello Giovagnoli or the tragedies of Pietro Cossa, but repeatedly adapted to screen the historical fictions of religious persecution which had permeated the popular literary imagination of nineteenth-century Europe, such as Lord Bulwer Lytton's *The Last Days of Pompeii* (1834), Cardinal Wiseman's *Fabiola* (1854), or Henryk Sienkiewicz's *Quo Vadis?* (1895), although such fictions were now at odds with the secular *romanità* being promulgated by the liberal government. The commercial and critical success of such film adaptations, therefore, cannot be explained wholly in terms of nationalistic drives. Films like *Quo Vadis?* principally won domestic and international acclaim because they were capable of demonstrating the imaginative power of the cinematic mechanism at a time of virulent attack on the new medium. Putting into the present an exhibitionist spectacle of pomp and magnificence, of grand crowds and monumental architecture, of orgies, seductions, and sadistic martyrdoms, these extraordinarily costly historical reconstructions excited the voyeuristic look of their spectators and provoked the pleasure of gazing on the vividly realized vices and exoticisms of Rome's imperial villains.[26] Even the magnificently depicted scenes in *Cabiria* of child sacrifice in the gigantic Carthaginian temple of Moloch have been described as a double conquest—over the watching Romans within the film's narrative and over the film's external spectators. According to film critic Paolo Cherchi Usai:

Heroes and enemies— . . . they may hesitate between the duty to defend their country and the temptation to yield to the impulses of luxury—but they are slaves to what they see: the power of the eye, in *Cabiria*, aspires to finality.

The crucial theme of the film is, in this respect, the tragedy of the senses. The most fleeting of all, the look, makes palpable what cinema cannot offer to the touch: the perception of the dimensions of the royal palace's architecture, the movement of the armies beneath the gaze of the cinecamera-Moloch, the sway of the figures knelt before the altar of the eternal fire. Demoniacal music accompanies the bloody scenes, the aroma of incense carries onto the film the odours of the temple. . . . For the first time cinema pretends to a total, definitive, conquest of the sensible world.[27]

Early Italian cinematic histories of Rome such as *Quo Vadis?* and *Cabiria* had been released in the United States to critical acclaim, obtained substantial box-office success, and achieved a significant influence over American film production in the years preceding the First World War. After the war, however, Hollywood studios began to standardize both the production and the consumption of their feature-length films according to the formalized codes of a new cinematic representational system now known customarily as "the classical Hollywood style," while nonetheless differentiating their products in accompanying publicity as both original and unique. The classical Hollywood style for representing history departed substantially from the mechanisms for the visualization of the collective that had driven the historical narratives of Italian cinema in the 1910s. Whereas in the earlier aesthetics of Italian silent cinema its protagonists had merged visually in space with the community and its heroes had acted in a socially structured landscape, the protagonists of the classical Hollywood narrative were more frequently isolated from the collective through the use of medium, close, and point-of-view shots and through their positioning in the center of the film frame. Emphasis was now placed on individuals whose psychological motivations were seen to cause historical action. Detached from their surroundings, associated with the personae of the stars who played them, no longer located in a strongly specified historical moment or a socially structured community, they were transformed into characters endowed with traits and in search of private fulfillment. The development, in the late 1920s, of the technologies of synchronized sound also led to a preference for presentist or contemporary film narratives. The protagonists of American sound films in the late 1920s and early 1930s, whether they were housewives, gangsters, newspaper tycoons, Roman emperors, or Ptolemaic queens, spoke in a dialogue that was grounded in the idioms of contemporary America.[28]

Hollywood's classical film style, the development of film technology, and the economic imperatives of the American film industry, all contributed to the privileging of both the individual and the present in the film narratives of the 1920s and 1930s. In a consumer-oriented economy, Hollywood films became showcases for the display of commodities; and the film studios, on the release of their products, encouraged the organization of merchandising tie-ins with other consumer industries. Through their displays of fashions, furnishings, accessories, and cosmetics, the interconnected institutions of cinema and the department store could train the view and orient the material aspirations of their consuming subjects.[29] Pressure was accordingly brought to bear on the studios by their marketing and sales management to produce films with contemporary themes, such as the popular social comedies directed by Cecil B. DeMille in the 1920s. Even films of Roman history, such as DeMille's *Cleopatra* (1934), were subjected to such marketing strategies and commodified—for the Egyptian queen was sold to female spectators in the form of "Cleopatra" gowns, perfumes, hairstyles, soaps, and cigarettes.[30]

The commodification of the past and the solicitation of a consumer gaze frequently generated a conflict between the diegesis and the visual style of films set in antiquity. Thus *Roman Scandals* (1933), the musical comedy which Gore Vidal was forbidden to see, troped imperial Rome in two distinct and antithetical ways. The film's narrative drive abandons any satisfying equation between American society and the civic virtues of republican Rome to present instead an hyperbolic articulation of the Depression's socio-economic problems, where bankers become emperors and the poor dispossessed slaves. In a pointed, populist message, imperial Rome stands in for the corruption and injustice of 1930s America.[31] Yet embedded in this narrative of social protest is a musical sequence that is quite at odds with it. Directed by Busby Berkeley, the elaborate production number is set in the women's baths of the imperial court at Rome, where the hero Eddie (in order to keep up his disguise) is compelled to sing advice to the female slaves on how to "Keep Young and Beautiful." Through the similarity of the women's appearance, and through Berkeley's repetitive choreography and rigid editing, the dancing girls are dismembered into body parts— thighs, nails, lips, hair, and eyes—all of which require attentive cosmetic care, according to the song's lyrics, "if you want to be loved." For the consuming female spectators at this point, imperial Rome no longer stands for corruption and tyranny but for luxury, eroticism, and a glamor available for purchase at their local department store.[32]

Even the godly historical epics produced in the Cold War era, such as *Quo Vadis* (1951), *The Robe* (1953), *Demetrius and the Gladiators* (1954), and

Ben-Hur (1959), commodified their religious narratives. A substantial part
of the enormous profit made by the MGM studio out of their second screen
adaptation of General Lew Wallace's nineteenth-century novel, for example, came from the sale of associated "Ben-Hur" merchandise such as toy
swords, helmets and armor, model chariots, wallpaper, jewelry, sandals, and
even raincoats and umbrellas.[33] Part of the motivation for the production of
such historical epics and their deliberate link with the pleasures of shopping
lay in Hollywood's economic need to recoup the severe loss
of earnings it had experienced in the early 1950s as a result of the competition of television for cinema's audiences. Hollywood's fight against television was conducted as "a duel of screens," in terms of the size of the
budget and the size of the image.[34] The industry invested heavily in the
technological novelties of Technicolor, widescreen, and stereophonic sound,
which it considered necessary to recapture the market, and privileged for
big-budget production genres such as the musical, the adventure film, the
Western, and the historical epic as those whose narratives were most capable of accommodating and naturalizing the new emphasis on stylization
and ostentatious spectacle.[35]

Grand enough to fill the screen, lavish historical films about the rise of
Christianity played a decisive role in Hollywood's battle to reconquer a
mass audience during the 1950s. Such epics, as the film theorist Stephen
Neale has observed in his discussion of genre, readily supplied many oppor-
tunities for cinematic exhibitionism and spectatorial scopophilia.[36] Exotic
locations, extravagant sets, colorful decor and costumes, spectacular action
(chariot races, gladiatorial combats, Christian martyrdoms, military parades
and battles), overwhelming visual effects, and conspicuous costs were all
available to the astonished gaze of both the films' internal and external spectators.[37] The films' narratives were also thought capable of matching their
spectacle in scale and appeal, offering subjects that were prestigious yet
familiar, seemly uncontroversial, educational, spiritually uplifting, and of
immense relevance to conservative America's self-portrayal during the Cold
War era as the defender of the Faith against the godlessness of Communism.[38] Thus *The Robe* (1953), the first film to be launched in a
widescreen format, was based on a vastly popular religious novel published
in 1942 by the Congregational minister Lloyd C. Douglas. His account of
the conversion of a Roman soldier to Christianity (after witnessing the
Crucifixion and coming into contact with Christ's discarded robe) had been
immediately bought up by the film producer Frank Ross for its strong market potential. According to an article in *The Tidings* of 27 January 1950,
Ross had anticipated that a wartime adaptation to screen of a conflict
between Roman decadence and Christian purity would present a parallel

with the persecutions currently being instigated by Hitler and Mussolini. Still unmade as a film in 1950, the critic of *The Tidings* suggested an even more pressing parallel now available to the novel's supposedly reluctant adaptors:

> It is easy to appreciate that Mr. Ross and his collaborators were brought to a complete stop when the lights later changed to red and one whom they had regarded as an ally of Democracy became the greatest modern despot of them all.
>
> If, however, there was anything to the idea of extending the Douglas novel into modern parallels, it would seem that the Hollywood dramatists now had more to go on than ever before. For at last the great struggle between Christ and anti-Christ had been joined, not merely upon political levels but upon the fundamental level of religion also.

When, however, the widescreen version of *The Robe* was finally released by 20th Century-Fox in 1953, in its production, distribution, and reception as much (if not more) attention was paid to its technical virtuosity as to its political parallels with the present. [illustration 2.3] The intense spectacle of CinemaScope threatened to eclipse the film's pious religious narrative in celebration of Hollywood's newly enlarged film frame. In particular, the opening sequence of *The Robe* has been described by Bruce Babington and Peter Evans in *Biblical Epics: Sacred Narrative in the Hollywood Cinema* (1993) as an ultra-dramatic rendering of this moment of technological history in which dark red curtains open in a slow movement to reveal an ever-increasing panoramic spectacle of ancient Rome to the astonished viewer.[39] The self-reflexive invitation of *The Robe* to enter into a newly extended screen space was met with extraordinary enthusiasm at the time of the film's release. A review in *Time* magazine for 28 September 1953, for example, stated admiringly that

> *The Robe* would have been a good movie in two-dimensional black and white. In CinemaScope, which uses a wide-angle lens to throw its picture on a curved screen nearly three times the normal width, it all but overpowers the eye with spectacular movie murals of slave markets, imperial cities, grandiose palaces and panoramic landscapes that are neither distorted nor require the use of polarized glasses. In CinemaScope closeups, the actors are so big that an average adult could stand erect in Victor Mature's ear, and its four-directional sound track often rises to a crescendo loud enough to make moviegoers feel as though they were locked in a bell tower during the Angelus. Obviously, Hollywood has finally found something louder, more

2.3 Poster advertising the widescreen technology of *The Robe* (1953). [Postcard from private collection of Maria Wyke.]

colorful and breathtakingly bigger than anything likely to be seen on a home
TV screen for years to come.

The Roman historical epics of the 1950s provided a site for the display of
the new technologies developed by the Hollywood film industry to rival and
outdo television in the pleasure of the look, but what excited that look and
drew spectators back into cinemas was as much the widescreen wickedness
of the Romans as the piety of their Christian victims. As Michael Wood has
argued, despite casting Christians as the diegetic heroes, such Cold War
films visually celebrated their Roman oppressors:

> All these stories invite our sympathy for the oppressed, of course—all the
> more so because we know that by generously backing these losers we shall
> find we have backed winners in the end. But then the movies, themselves, as
> costly studio productions, plainly take the other side. They root for George
> III against the founding fathers, they are all for tyranny and Rome, more
> imperialist than the emperor. The great scenes in these films, the reasons for
> our being in the cinema at all—the orgies, the triumphs, the gladiatorial
> games—all belong to the oppressors. The palaces, the costumes, the pomp . . .
> are all theirs. It is the Romans who provide the circuses, who give us a Rome
> to be gaudily burned. It is Nero and the Pharaohs who throw the parties with
> all the dancing girls.[40]

The pleasures of looking were accentuated by CinemaScope, while the
money and labor invested in the manufacture of those pleasures were self-
consciously paraded within the widescreen epics and in the extra-cinematic
discourses generated around the films' production and exhibition. Unprecedented press, radio, and television coverage, for example, constantly
attended the making of *The Robe* and its extravagant worldwide premieres.
Its initial screening at the Roxy in New York, on 16 September 1953, was
held in a carnival atmosphere, while king-sized searchlights played over the
arrival of huge numbers of invited guests and the vast crowds assembled to
catch a glimpse of them.[41] Both on and off screen, Hollywood celebrated its
capacities to duplicate the splendors of the past. Thus, again in the words of
Michael Wood, Hollywood's histories of Rome became "a huge, many-
faceted metaphor for Hollywood itself."[42] The reconstruction on screen and
exhibition of ancient Rome came to stand for Hollywood's own fantastic
excess—its technological and aesthetic innovations, its grandeur and glamour, its ostentation, and the lavishness of its expenditure and consumption.
And spectators of Hollywood's widescreen epics were invited to position

themselves not only as pure Christians but also as Romans luxuriating in a surrender to the splendors of film spectacle itself.[43]

The Case Studies

The projection of ancient Rome on screen has functioned not only as a mechanism for the display or interrogation of national identities but also, and often in contradiction, as a mechanism for the display of cinema itself—its technical capacities and its cultural value. One way, therefore, to interrogate films about ancient Rome is to examine their intersection with the national, political, economic, and cultural identities of the communities in which they are produced while, at the same time, exploring the ways such films reformulate those identities in specifically cinematic terms, building up their own historiographic conventions of style, address, and aesthetic pleasure.[44]

Broad surveys of the huge numbers of cinematic representations of ancient Rome made in the United States, Italy, France, Great Britain, and elsewhere, are already conveniently available in such works as Jon Solomon's *The Ancient World in the Cinema* (1978) or Derek Elley's *The Epic Film: Myth and History* (1984). *Projecting the Past* will proceed, instead, by exploring in depth four case studies—specific segments of Roman history that have been repeatedly resurrected on screen by both the Italian and the Hollywood film industries from the 1910s up to the early 1960s. This strategy accounts for the absence of attention to films centered around the fictive hero Ben-Hur which are all exclusively products of the United States, or films centered around the African victories of the Roman general Scipio, which are characteristic of the Italian film industry. There is, nonetheless, a certain arbitrary quality to my choice as case studies of the rebellion of Spartacus, the affairs of Cleopatra, the persecutions of Nero, and the destruction of Pompeii. The assassination of Julius Caesar or the intrigues of the empress Messalina, for example, have also been frequent objects of both Italian and American cinematic recreations, and I propose to explore their use in future publications.

There are also inevitable evidentiary limits to my analyses. For example, more Italian films set in ancient Rome have survived from the silent era than American ones, and the former are accordingly better documented, while prints, production records, or press reviews for Hollywood historical films of the sound era are often more readily accessible than for Italian historical films of the same period. Furthermore, there are many textual variations to the individual films here investigated. Prints have been mutilated, shortened, or sometimes reedited for distribution at different times or to different markets.[45] *Projecting the Past*, therefore, makes no claims to comprehensiveness either in the choice of case studies or in the selection of films for detailed analysis within each case study. Instead, this book constitutes an assembly of disparate histories of the social, ideological, formal, technological, and economic determinants of a limited number of films set in ancient Rome, which histories are then juggled to form a variety of configurations and hierarchies. No attempt is made to recuperate such heterogeneity into a project that might narrate the "total history" of ancient Rome on screen.[46]

According to the historian David Lowenthal:

> The past remains integral to us all, individually and collectively. We must concede the ancients their place. . . . But their place is not simply back there, in a separate and foreign country; it is assimilated in ourselves, and resurrected into an ever-changing present.[47]

The aim of this book is to explore, through the consideration of some notable cinematic representations of ancient Rome, the place of antiquity in twentieth-century mass culture. It will become clear from the subsequent case studies that, within the institutions of cinema, ancient Rome performs its own specific operations and that those operations are not uniform. The Roman films so frequently manufactured in the United States and Italy demonstrate a considerable variety and discontinuity in their narrations of Roman history, in the rapport they establish between the Roman past and the present moment of its cinematic reconstruction, in the cultural competences on which the films draw, and in the aesthetic pleasures of historical reconstruction which they offer their disparate audiences. Ancient Rome has been constantly reinvented to suit new technologies for its cinematic narration and new historical contexts for the interpretation of the Roman past in the present. *Projecting the Past* thus aims to disclose the rich variety of functions Roman historical films have had in twentieth-century culture and the diversity of readings of ancient Rome they have offered their millions of spectators.

3

Spartacus: Testing the Strength of the Body Politic

A Hero of Liberty

In 1914, George Kleine distributed throughout the United States an Italian film that portrayed the gladiator Spartacus leading a rebellion against the armies of Rome. The promotional material produced to market *Spartaco* boasted of the ethical and aesthetic value of the historical film. Above a letter of endorsement from a teacher at Ohio University, who described his pupils' rapturous reception of the film, Kleine's publicity declares:

> The eyes of the greatest men in history have been fixed on the splendid character of this hero of liberty who was the first to dare cry out against the tyrannical force of Rome, the Mistress of the World. Pictures and statues represent the valiant gladiator in the historical moments of his adventurous life, always in the struggle against the power of tyrants and in favor of the weak and oppressed. Such a source has inspired the finest works of art; the French theatre employed the genius of two writers in two powerful tragedies in which the gigantic hero is represented in his dream of love and freedom. Taking our inspiration from the sublime verses of Bernard Joseph Sauria [sic] and of M. H. Marget, we have constructed the plot of this kinematographic tragedy which abounds in profoundly emotional situations, and which is splendidly loyal to the reconstruction of Roman grandeur. We are sure that we have composed a true work of art and we do not hesitate to affirm that "SPARTACUS" is one of the most splendid jewels of the screen.

In the ancient tradition that concerns the slave insurrection led by the Thracian gladiator Spartacus, however, little trace survives of the rebels' aims and ambitions. The sources for the slave revolt that lasted over two years from 73 B.C. to 71 B.C. and appeared at one point even to threaten the safety of the city of Rome are relatively late and do not give voice to the servile perspective.[1] The summary of the rebellion which appears (some one hundred years after the event) in Plutarch's *Parallel Lives* is largely incidental to a biography of the Roman victor Marcus Licinius Crassus and is incorporated into a narrative that, through the representation of the Roman general's career, seeks to demonstrate to Plutarch's readers the dangers of political ambition. Reference to the revolt in the survey of Roman history provided by Florus in the second century A.D. is even briefer and more partisan, designed to illustrate the ignominy that for Romans was attendant on a war against gladiators:

> One can tolerate, indeed, even the disgrace of a war against slaves; for although, by force of circumstances, they are liable to any kind of treatment, yet they form as it were a class (though an inferior class) of human beings and can be admitted to the blessings of liberty which we enjoy. But I know not what name to give to the war which was stirred up at the instigation of Spartacus; for the common soldiers being slaves and their leaders being gladiators—the former men of the humblest, the latter men of the worse, class—added insult to the injury which they inflicted upon Rome.[2]

For the ancient epitomist Florus, the insurrection led by Spartacus is not a glorious "struggle against the power of tyrants" but draws Rome into a disgraceful "war against slaves"; liberty is a blessed condition to be bestowed by the Roman elite not seized upon by its inferiors; and Spartacus himself is not a "splendid character" but a Thracian mercenary, a deserter, a highwayman, and finally, and worst of all, a vengeful gladiator.

Little material is available from antiquity on the slave war led by Spartacus because the Roman elite, as the producers or consumers of ancient historiography, did not find slave rebellion a worthy subject for historical discourse. Furthermore, although many late nineteenth- and early twentieth-century historians of the rebellion found in Spartacus a champion of the oppressed in Roman society, a revolutionary hero of the class struggle, several more recent analyses of the ancient evidence have concluded that Spartacus was not a revolutionary, that he did not proffer systematic opposition to the power and the rule of Rome nor plan to remodel Roman society, but probably had as his limited design the restoration of the largely foreign slaves to their respective homelands.[3] The contrast between the fragmentary ancient sources on Spartacus and the narrative image of the Italian film with which Kleine sought to attract his American audience could not be sharper.

The tradition on which George Kleine drew to launch an Italian film about Spartacus on the American market stems from the mid-eighteenth century, when Spartacus began to be elevated in Western European literature, historiography, political rhetoric, and visual art into an idealized champion of both the oppressed and the enslaved.[4] From this period, representations of the ancient slave rebellion and the gladiator Spartacus were profoundly driven by the political concerns of the present. If, according to Walter Benjamin, all history is informed by "the presence of the now," it was the appropriation of Roman republican history by the French Revolution which Benjamin cites as a prime example of history's presentist rhetorical strategies. As Benjamin observes, "the French Revolution viewed itself as Rome incarnate," and Paris became steeped in the political rhetoric and iconography of republican Rome.[5] The eagles which had adorned the standards of the Roman legions were introduced as the regimental insignia of the French army and the Roman *fasces*—symbol of the authority of the republican magistrates—were painted on the walls of the revolutionary government's seat of power when the National Assembly moved to the Tuilleries in 1793. The revolutionary cult of republican antiquity found popular expression in the renaming of streets, towns, and individuals, and in the diffuse display of the "liberty cap"—modeled on that worn in ancient Rome by liberated slaves.[6]

The French theater of the late eighteenth century, to which George Kleine's promotional material draws attention as a source for the Italian cinematic representation of Spartacus, was radicalized by the French Revolution. Plays concerning figures from the period of the Roman republic were performed and consumed as commentaries on current political events. Thus, when Voltaire's tragedy *Brutus* was revived in 1790, the audience at its first performance hailed Mirabeau, one of the early moderate constitutionalists of the revolution, as the "Brutus of France."[7] Similarly, Bernard Joseph Saurin's tragedy *Spartacus,* to which the American film distributor refers, although first performed in 1760, was revived in the libertarian atmosphere of Paris in 1792. When Kleine treats the cinematic Spartacus as politically exemplary for opposition to tyranny and support of the oppressed, he echoes the sentiments of the French dramatist Saurin. In an early nineteenth-century edition of his plays, Saurin justifies giving a voice to the Thracian gladiator on the grounds that until now historians and poets have done much harm to the human race by representing too often the lives of conquerors and the ambitious. He continues:

How many young princes, seduced by the glamour of a false heroism, have caused desolation and havoc in order to march in the footsteps of Alexander

or Caesar? . . . [Instead, historians and poets] should make them know true
, glory and make them nobly ambitious for the good of men.[8]

The profoundly presentist interest in the history of the slave rebellion led
by Spartacus received further impetus from the turn of the nineteenth century, at a time when the slave rebellion led by Toussaint l'Ouverture in the
French colony of St. Domingue was the first to match in scale the ancient
revolt, and when slavery and its possible abolition became a burning political and social issue in Britain, America, and France.[9] Between 1807 and
1820, the slave trade was prohibited by the governments of first Denmark,
then Britain, America, France, Spain, and Portugal, while slavery was formally abolished by the British government in 1833, the French in 1848, and
the American in 1865. Even historical scholarship on ancient slavery was, in
this period, inextricably enmeshed in contemporary debates and policy deci-
sions about abolition. Most notably, when Henri Wallon published his
three-volume work, *Histoire de l'esclavage dans l'antiquité*, in the Paris of
1847, his study of ancient slavery was preceded by an analysis of modern
slavery in the French colonies. The second edition of the history, published
in 1879, concluded the introduction with the text of the final act of abolition
of 1848, which Wallon in the interim had himself helped to compose.[10] It
was during this period of intense and ultimately successful campaigning for
slave emancipation that, in 1830, a statue of Spartacus was positioned in the
Tuilleries, and, in 1831, Edwin Forrest first played the role of Spartacus in
the American melodrama *The Gladiator*.

Garibaldian Romanticism

Despite Kleine's attempt to construct from the theater of revolutionary
France a narrative image for the American distribution of "the jewel of the
screen," at least two of the surviving Italian film versions of the slave rebellion, *Spartaco* or *Il gladiatore della Tracia* (Giovanni Enrico Vidali, Pasquali,
1913) and *Spartaco* (Riccardo Freda, Consorzio Spartacus, 1952) are equally,
if not more, indebted to a more immediate and enduring appropriation of
Spartacus for the articulation of Italian political struggles. In 1874, Raffaello
Giovagnoli published his historical novel *Spartaco*. Like Lytton's *The Last
Days of Pompeii* (1834), Wiseman's *Fabiola* (1854), Wallace's *Ben-Hur* (1880),
and Sienkiewicz's *Quo Vadis?* (1895), the novel was widely disseminated
throughout the late nineteenth and early twentieth centuries and contributed to a novelistic typology and repertory of dramatic situations on
which the historical films of the early 1900s would draw for the emplotment
of their cinematic narratives of antiquity.[11]

Like those other historical novels, Giovagnoli's *Spartaco* is written in the tradition of Walter Scott. It authenticates its fictive history of slave rebellion by incorporating substantial quotations from the ancient sources within the body of the text and by interspersing the narrative with a liberal deployment of Latin tags and antiquarian footnotes that explain Roman customs and cite further ancient sources to support the author's explanations.[12] The novel also humanizes the history of the rebellion by embodying in a personal confrontation between Julius Caesar and Spartacus the opposing principles of despotism and liberty, and by partially domesticating events within a melodramatic narration of romance and vendetta. Spartacus falls in love with a patrician matron, Valeria, whom he must tragically abandon when the opportune moment arises to pursue his holy cause of liberty for the oppressed. He cannot accept the Romans' offer of marriage to Valeria nor her own later pleas to surrender to Crassus and live with her in a Tuscan hideaway when the terms would necessitate the betrayal of his followers. In the latter part of the novel, Spartacus' military campaign against the Roman commanders is constantly thwarted by the vengeful machinations of a Greek courtesan, Eutibide, whose passionate advances he had earlier declined. The novel closes with Valeria weeping over the ashes of her lover in the company of her daughter by Spartacus. Secretly, the Roman noblewoman has had his body removed from the battlefield where, finally and courageously, he had fallen.

Giovagnoli's *Spartaco* is like other source novels for the cinematic representation of ancient Rome in its style and romantic emplotment but, unlike most of those other novels, it does not have its origins in a nineteenth-century opposition to contemporary religious scepticism. Not only is the novel unconcerned with the triumph of early Christianity over a decadent Roman empire but its tone is also decidedly anti-clerical. For example, when describing the priest of a temple dedicated to Hercules, Giovagnoli observes in passing that

> the priest of those days, like the priest today, like the priest of all ages, of all religions, of all peoples, minister of hypocrisy and superstition, used to judge the religious fervour of the idiotic, brutish and gullible masses, by the quantity and quality of the gifts brought to the temple, gifts which, in the name of the supposed God, fattened the insatiable belly of the ministers of the cult. (672)[13]

The narrative strategies of *Spartaco* locate it squarely within the anti-clerical and nationalistic agenda of many works of fiction produced in Italy around the time of unification. For example, when, in the novel, Spartacus encounters Julius Caesar just before the initiation of the gladiators' revolt and discloses his objectives in an impassioned speech, his political rhetoric parallels both that of the French revolutionaries and of the leaders of the *risorgimento*:

> "I hope," replied the gladiator, with eyes flashing and in an outburst of uncontrollable passion, "to smash this corrupt Roman world, and from its ruins to see rise up the independence of the people. . . . I seek liberty, I desire liberty, I hope for and invoke liberty, liberty for individuals as for the nation, for the great as for the small, for the powerful as the wretched, and, with liberty, peace, prosperity, justice and all that greater happiness that the immortal gods have granted man to be able to enjoy on this earth." (271)[14]

Not only were national independence, liberty, and equality key political concepts for the *risorgimento* propagandists, but those concepts were also frequently incorporated into a classicism borrowed back from the French revolutionaries.[15]

Already, towards the end of the eighteenth century, the Italian dramatist Vittorio Alfieri had composed a tragedy on the second Brutus, assassin of Julius Caesar, which he dedicated to "the future people of a free Italy" and which was designed to stir in his fellow Italians the same hatred for tyranny and love of liberty and republican government that was embodied in his play's hero.[16] Throughout the early nineteenth century, the Italian nationalists sought political authority in Italy's republican past. From the "Roman Republic" of 1798–1799, to that of 1849, classicizing imagery was everywhere adopted into the oratory, edicts, coins, seals, standards, and public ceremonial organized by the Italian revolutionaries.[17] By the middle of the nineteenth century, Giuseppe Mazzini was declaring that "there must not be on this earth either masters or slaves but only brothers," and at the center of attempts to achieve a republican liberty and equality for Italians by force of arms was the charismatic figure of Garibaldi.[18]

Giovagnoli's novel *Spartaco* was clearly conceived and circulated as a tribute to the achievements of the *risorgimento* and, in particular, to the military heroism of Garibaldi. Garibaldi, the militant advocate of Italian unity and independence from the rule of the papacy, both practiced and advocated the composition of novels that would record for Italy the brave men who gave up their lives on the battlefield for her and the turpitudes and betrayals of her past leaders and priests. Many Italian novels took up the call to produce this *romanticismo garibaldino* (Garibaldian romanticism) and were quickly pressed into the service of the *risorgimento*.[19] Giovagnoli himself had fought in the war of independence under the standards of Garibaldi, during which he was promoted to captain and cited for bravery. After unification, he then composed his narrative of the revolt of Spartacus not only in conformity with the requirements of a "Garibaldian" nationalistic agenda but also as a homage to the achievements of Garibaldi himself.[20]

The didactic function of the historical novel *Spartaco* is made evident in the encounter between Julius Caesar and Spartacus, when Spartacus indignantly replies to Caesar's accusation that the revolt cannot succeed:

> I shall meet a glorious death for a just cause, and the blood we shed will fertilize the plant of liberty. It will brand a fresh mark of disgrace on the brow of our oppressors. It will arouse avengers without number by means of the most beautiful inheritance it is possible to leave to our descendants: an example! (273)

Similarly, at the novel's close, Spartacus' stirring words to his fellow rebels as they prepare for their final battle against the Romans authorize an interpretation of the gladiator's actions as a role model for the political struggles of the Italians to come:

> Our cause is holy and just and will not die with us. The road to victory must flow with blood, and it is with self-denial and sacrifice that great designs succeed. A courageous and honourable death is worth more than a disgraceful and shameful life. Falling in battle, we will leave to our descendants, dyed in our blood, the legacy of vengeance and victory, the banner of liberty and equality. Brothers! do not retreat one step. Conquer or die. (715)

Who, then, are the "avengers without number" who have brought "the plant of liberty" to full blossom? Who has taken up Spartacus' holy cause and, carrying the rebels' banner of liberty and equality, finally completed the bloody route to victory? That Giovagnoli means his readers to think of the *risorgimento* revolutionaries and their military leader, Garibaldi, is made clear both by an explicit comparison between Spartacus and Garibaldi as champions of liberty in the body of the text (447), and by the inclusion of a letter of endorsement from Garibaldi himself that, in the editions of the novel, precedes the historical narration. Describing himself as almost a *libertus*, a man freed from slavery, Garibaldi thanks Giovagnoli for a description of Spartacus' victories that, very often, moved him to tears. He concludes his letter by asking:

> Can our citizens strengthen themselves with the memory of such great heroes—who all sleep on land composed of our own same clay—land which no longer will have gladiators—but neither masters? (6)[21]

Placed as an introduction to the subsequent narration of the slave revolt, Garibaldi's letter effectively prepares the novel's readers to acknowledge that Spartacus' example of heroism in the cause of liberty has generated "avengers without number" in the very recent past. Under the leadership of Garibaldi, those avengers have at last created a united Italy without slaves or masters.

Embodying Italian Nationalism

The nationalistic pretensions and anti-clerical thrust of Raffaello Giovagnoli's historical novel *Spartaco* was ideally suited to the climate of Italian cinematic production in the 1910s. The 1900s saw the Italian production houses making tentative experiments in the cinematic reconstruction of Roman history, such as *Gli ultimi giorni di Pompei* (1908) and *Nerone* (1909) of the Ambrosio production house, Itala's *Giulio Cesare* (1909), and Latium's *Spartaco* (1909).[22] By the time Giovanni Enrico Vidali's *Spartaco* or *Il gladiatore della Tracia* was released by the Pasquali film company in 1913, the Italian film industry was in a state of extraordinary expansion, fueled by its own nationalistic agenda and the huge commercial success of the historical film *Quo Vadis?* (1913). The constant flood of historical films onto the national and international markets had coincided with the entry of Italian aristocrats into the financial backing of the Italian studios. Film production was viewed as an instrument for the enhancement of the new nation's prestige both at home and abroad, and historical reconstructions of Italy's glorious past seemed highly appropriate vehicles for the acquisition of that prestige both for the Italian nation and its film companies. Extravagant cinematic reconstructions of Italy's past allowed for ambitious and visually spectacular themes, the exploitation of complex literary narratives, and the display of the production houses' own technical virtuosity in, for example, the construction of huge, often sumptuous set designs and exotic costumes, and the movement of vast crowds of extras in a newly developed cinematographic space that vastly exceeded the bounds of the proscenium stage.[23]

Furthermore, films set in Italy's Roman past were perceived and deployed as instruments particularly suited to the moral, civic, and patriotic improvement of their mass audiences. The Italian state born from unification in 1861 continued to view itself as the legitimate heir of its Roman past. Only two years before the release of *Spartaco*, Italy had celebrated the fiftieth anniversary of unification, still nourished by the myth of continuity with ancient Rome, and the nation's imperialistic ambitions which had recently been fired by the Italo-Turkish war of 1911–1912 were being legitimated by recourse to a vision of historical continuity with an ancient Rome that had once been mistress of the Mediterranean.[24] Rome could therefore supply the

Italian film companies with a repertoire of illustrious precursors through whom audiences could read their present as the crowning epoch of a long, glorious and communal history.[25]

After the huge national and international success of the film *Quo Vadis?* in 1913, the Italian production houses were all stirred to respond to the domestic and foreign demand for historical films and sought to produce works that would possess the same nationalistic drive and technical skill.[26] In the same year as the release of *Spartaco*, its director Giovanni Enrico Vidali rushed out a version of *Gli ultimi giorni di Pompei* (otherwise known as *Ione*) for the Pasquali company to circulate in competition with another version from the Ambrosio production house.[27] Although Vidali then incorporated into *Spartaco* a sequence of lion-fighting in an arena to fulfill audiences' expectations raised by the arena scenes in both *Quo Vadis?* and *Gli ultimi giorni di Pompei*, the selection of his literary source material from the theater of revolutionary France and the Garibaldian novelistic tradition of 1870s' Italy may have been, at least for Italian audiences, a uniquely suitable choice. For, unlike Sienkiewicz's *Quo Vadis?* and Lytton's *The Last Days of Pompeii*, Giovagnoli's novel *Spartaco* had been written by an Italian who was, moreover, a hero of the *risorgimento*. The novel *Spartaco* had received an enthusiastic endorsement from Garibaldi, and its protagonist, although ostensibly a Thracian gladiator, had already been configured as a secular Italian hero uniting disparate peoples with his calls for *luce e libertà* (light and liberty), *costanza e vittoria* (perseverance and victory).

Around the time of the release of *Spartaco* in 1913, the association of the Thracian gladiator with Italian nationalism had become almost inescapable. In 1907, for example, Raffaello Giovagnoli assisted in the publication of a pamphlet to celebrate the centenary of Garibaldi's birth in which he described the Italian general as having been endowed with all the military gifts and stratagems of Spartacus.[28] Many editions of Giovagnoli's novel continued to be printed both before and after the release of the film, prefaced always by Garibaldi's letter of praise and often containing illustrations which abetted the association of Spartacus with the *risorgimento*. Thus, three years after the distribution of the cinematic representation of the slave rebellion, a seventh edition of the novel was published that, when illustrating scenes of the slave victories, displayed on top of the slaves' military standards the "liberty cap" beloved of French revolutionaries and Italian nationalists.[29] [illustration 3.1]

The anti-clerical thrust of the novel *Spartaco*, or at least its setting in a pre-Christian Rome, was also more suited to the glorification of the secular Italian state of the 1910s than the depictions of Christianity triumphant that figure in Sienkiewicz's *Quo Vadis?* and Lytton's *The Last Days of Pompeii*. In

3.1 Spartacus leads his victorious troops in battle, illustration from a 1916 edition of Giovagnoli's novel *Spartaco*. [Seventh edition published in Milan by Paolo Carrera.]

1913, although Catholic support had been obtained for the election of Conservative or Moderate candidates to the Italian parliament, only a tacit truce rather than a general reconciliation operated between Church and state.[30] Cinematic representations of the early Church's triumph over Rome would therefore be fraught with potential difficulties. Guazzoni's film adaptation of the novel *Quo Vadis?* for Cines—a production house funded through Catholic banks—had achieved the status of a national cultural artefact largely through its technical accomplishment and despite its potentially ambiguous depiction of the rescue of Christianity from the persecutions of the Roman imperial state.[31] The subsequent Italian film adaptations of *The Last Days of Pompeii* released in 1913 both conveniently expunged any reference to Christianity from their representations of a city purged of Orientalism.[32] The cinematic depiction of Spartacus was at least free of such representational problems.

Following on a cinematic convention launched so successfully by the already canonic *Quo Vadis?*, *Spartaco* (1913) valorizes the populist figure of the strongman.[33] In *Quo Vadis?* the popular dimension of Italian nationalism was expressed briefly through the exhibition of strength demonstrated by the humble Christian Ursus. His fight with a bull in the arena helps incite the assembled Roman populace to revolt against the tyranny of the emperor Nero.[34] *Spartaco* extends the populist spectacle of muscular strength, which was displayed in the earlier film, by now placing the strongman centrally within the film's verbal and visual narration. The film opens, for example, with "the return of the conquering hero Crassus from the conquest of Thrace." From long shots of the general's triumphal procession through Rome, during which *fasces* and standard bearers, soldiers and senators march past a triumphal arch, the camera moves to a medium shot in order to focus on the naked, muscled right arm of Spartacus in chains; "but yesterday a warrior of Thrace—young, joyous, triumphant—today a shackled slave of Rome." As the parade passes across the screen, only Spartacus gazes out at the camera and thus establishes a look of engagement with the cinema spectators of the 1910s. As *Spartaco* proceeds, the spectator's look is constantly brought back to the muscular physique with which the hero breaks his chains of bondage. When Spartacus is forced to defend himself against the assaults of other gladiators, the film's play of light and darkness sculpts his tensed and semi-naked torso on the screen. And, towards the close of the film, when Spartacus bends back the iron bars that imprison him in the cells of the arena, the hero even stops momentarily to gaze on the taut bicep with which he effects his escape.[35]

This cinematic presentation of an ancient hero fighting against his Roman masters conveniently conjoined in the physique of the actor Mario

Guaita Ausonia a classical ideal of the muscular male athlete with a more recent, populist grammar of the body derived from circus shows—the breaking of chains, the bending of iron bars.[36] Before his appearance in *Spartaco*, Guaita was a "king of force." In Italian variety theaters, he performed a series of living reproductions of famous paintings and statues, while providing himself with the grand title of "gladiator of the early nineteen hundreds."[37] Reviews of the film constantly focused on the singular appropriateness of casting Guaita as Spartacus. *La vita cinematografica* for February 1914, for example, declared that

> Mario Guaita Ausonia has directly personified Spartacus. The sculptural beauty of his figure, the handsomeness and the combined agility and vigour of his perfect body, his lively and penetrating glance, his faultless acting, have made of this man . . . an artist, worthy of every consideration, a more than perfect protagonist.[38]

And George Kleine's American publicity for the film described Guaita as

> a celebrated Italian wrestler and fine actor, whose physique and finely chiseled face make him an extraordinary prototype [sic] of the ancient gladiator.

As the rhetorical strategies of Giovagnoli's novel overlaid the rebellion of Spartacus with the subsequent victories of Garibaldi, so the iconography of the strongman in the film *Spartaco* overlays the body of the ancient gladiator with that of a modern "king of force" and renders the classical body more readily available as a site for the display of the strength of the modern Italian body politic.[39]

In a memorably spectacular sequence of *Spartaco*, shot on location in a recognizable and expansive Italian landscape, the gladiators are seen gathered on a hilltop where they are trapped by the Roman soldiers visible in the far distant valley. The ingenious escape of the gladiators from the Roman blockade—described in several of the ancient sources—is here initiated by Spartacus, whose back and arm muscles are once again seen to tense when he tests the strength of the vines which will bear the weight of his men as they clamber down a steep incline of Vesuvius. The intertitle at this point then boasts hyperbolically that "History records no more gloriously daring act than the escape of the gladiators from the heights of Vesuvius." The subsequent extreme long shot contained within an equally hyperbolic framing iris displays large numbers of men lowering themselves down the mountainside.[40] [illustration 3.2] Like *Quo Vadis?* before it, *Spartaco* utilizes the spectacular display of vast crowds of extras (before whom and for whom

3.2 Gladiators climb down the slopes of Vesuvius, from Vidali's *Spartaco* (1913). [From postcard in private collection of Vittorio Martinelli.]

the strongman acts) to provide the mass audiences in the Italian cinemas of 1913 with an opportunity to visualize their own collective engagement with their national history. But the latter film draws the cinema audience more closely into the depiction of grand historical events by having its strongman also act with the crowds who appear on screen. Thus the film *Spartaco* utilizes the musculature of the screened male body to construct a popular historical and national consciousness.

This cinematic narrative of the revolt of Spartacus might be thought to bear the risk of offering its mass audience a radical critique of the Italy of the 1910s, for the representation of Spartacus' resistance to the cruelty and corruption of the Roman general Crassus (with which the film is initiated) could be read as an attack on the political authority of the present Italian state and as a call to further political struggle. That risk, however, is moderated and controlled by the narrative progression of the second half of the film, where Spartacus departs from the militant and rebellious characterization bestowed on him in Giovagnoli's novel and is refigured to match the nationalistic needs of the present moment. Here Crassus is defeated in battle by Spartacus, who then shows the Roman general mercy and expresses only a moderate desire for "the common right of all men—to live in peace and freedom." Crassus makes Spartacus the commander in chief of the Roman army and the freed gladiator, like a triumphant Garibaldi, marches to Rome in the midst of popular acclaim.[41] The latter part of the film sets Spartacus' feats not against the might of the Roman state but against the jealous gladiator Noricus—a figure borrowed from Saurin's tragedy. Noricus conspires to kill Crassus and have Spartacus thrown to the lions as the supposed culprit.[42] The closing moments of the film show Spartacus heroically escaping the lions only to throw the villain Noricus to them. Against all the historical records, and against the tragic conclusion of Giovagnoli's novel, Vidali's film ends with a triumphant and successful Spartacus, a Roman now, and one able to unite the country's discordant factions. Spartacus then rejoins his beloved Narona who, as daughter of Crassus, acts as a female embodiment of the power and authority of the city of Rome fought for and finally gained by the brave gladiator.[43]

Whereas Giovagnoli's novel concluded with a Spartacus still in need of a militant Garibaldi to bring his holy cause to completion, Vidali's film *Spartaco* closes with a protagonist who has already become the victorious creator of a unified Italian state.[44] The nineteenth-century novel's Spartacus/ Garibaldi parallel suggests a need for continued vigilance in support of a yet young and fragile Italy. As befits the nationalistic sentiments of a nation some fifty years after unification, the film's Spartacus/Garibaldi parallel suggests only the self-satisfaction of a nation strong and secure. The *Spartaco* of 1913, which was a triumphal success both in Italy and abroad, looks back to and exalts the creation of the modern Italian state rather than looking forward to a need for continuing political struggle. Victory and unity, the film informs its Italian spectators, have already been accomplished.

Resistance and Collaboration in Modern Italy

The next Italian cinematic reconstruction of the slave rebellion of Spartacus, *Spartaco* (Riccardo Freda, Consorzio Spartacus) was released in 1952. In the first half of that same year, a weekly magazine of the Italian Communist Party (PCI) published a serialization of Giovagnoli's novel in 27 installments.[45] The investment of the magazine *Vie Nuove* in the fictive narration of Spartacus' uprising belongs to a Marxist tradition of both admiration for Spartacus and academic analysis of the history of ancient slavery. That tradition has sustained interest both in the Thracian gladiator and Giovagnoli's novelistic representation of him throughout a large part of the twentieth century. In a letter to Engels of 27 February 1861, which was subsequently much published and quoted, Marx expressed his admiration for Spartacus as a grand general who had nothing to do with Garibaldi but who was rather a "genuine exponent of the ancient proletariat." Transformed by Marx into a leader of the proletariat struggling against exploitation, Spartacus came to be read as acutely relevant to the consolidation of the modern class struggle.[46]

Spartacus soon became incorporated into a Marxist historiography of ancient slavery such as that published by the Italian academic Ettore Ciccotti in 1899, *Il tramonto della schiavitù nel mondo antico,* in which ancient slavery was interpreted as a mode of economic production and ancient struggles against it as a part of a larger, continuing historical process.[47] In the early decades of the twentieth century, Spartacus was appropriated by the German socialists Karl Liebknecht and Rosa Luxemburg, who signed their pacifistic appeal during the First World War with the name "Spartacus" and later called their revolutionary movement the *Spartakusbund* (the Spartacus league).[48] The Russian Revolution, and the subsequent publication in the 1930s of Lenin's and Stalin's observations on the subject of Spartacus' revolt, stimulated a constant stream of Marxist historical writings on ancient slavery in the Soviet Union, and further enhanced Spartacus' symbolic status as a hero of the class struggle for several more decades.[49]

In the Italy of the post-war period, the posthumous publication of the prison writings of the Marxist intellectual Antonio Gramsci led to a renewed interest in Giovagnoli's novel *Spartaco* as a work which could have a radical, educative value for the masses. In the notebooks he had written while imprisoned at the orders of Mussolini, Gramsci was drawn to comment on the cultural value of Giovagnoli's *Spartaco* after observing a news item in the *Corriere della Sera* of 8 January 1932. The paper had published a copy of Garibaldi's letter endorsing the novel, since the original letter was now to be donated by Mussolini to the Museum of the Risorgimento. Drawing a connection between the particular "poetics" of popular literature that Garibaldi's letter appeared to advocate and the structures of Giovagnoli's novel, Gramsci argued for the modernization of the nineteenth-century novel's baroque narrative style to render it more contemporary. Gramsci favored such treatment of the novel because he regarded it as having a *culturale-populare* value, that is to say *Spartaco* could provide the masses with ready access to a highly significant, and politically charged, historical event.[50] It was therefore as a result of Gramsci's posthumous impetus—his prison notebooks were published in six volumes from 1948 to 1951—that the PCI magazine *Vie Nuove* serialized Giovagnoli's novel during the first half of 1952.[51] In the years after the release of Freda's film *Spartaco* (1952), a Marxist, didactic reading of Giovagnoli's novel continued to find acknowledgment. In 1955 an edition of the novel appeared in Italy prefaced by a detailed account of its association with Garibaldi, its contemporary utility as noted by Gramsci, and its current wide circulation in the Soviet Union.[52] And, as late as 1963, a Soviet handbook for secondary school teachers was issued on how to teach "the role of the masses in ancient history." The author suggested that instruction should be based on two pictures by contemporary Soviet artists and on two novels—that of a modern Soviet writer and that of Giovagnoli.[53]

During the year 1952, Riccardo Freda's film *Spartaco* circulated in Italy only a matter of months after the serialization of Giovagnoli's novel in *Vie Nuove*. It does not appear, however, that the Italian film director was working to the same educational, Gramscian agenda as the Italian Communist Party's weekly magazine. Nor does the reappearance of a cinematic Spartacus in post-war Italy align Freda's film with the celebratory, Garibaldian poetics of Vidali's silent version of 1913.

Towards the end of the 1940s, when the Italian film industry was deprived of state subsidies and found itself unable to compete with the huge influx and popularity of the Hollywood studios' products, the industry's possible salvation was perceived by some producers and directors to reside in the revival of the genre of historical films which had achieved such extraordinary commercial success and international artistic acclaim in the 1910s. Faith in the viability of the genre, and specifically in remakes of earlier silent films, appeared to be rewarded by the box-office success of Alessandro Blasetti's post-war *Fabiola*, which drew on the previous prestige of Enrico Guazzoni's silent *Fabiola* of 1918 and became the top grossing Italian film of the year 1948–1949. The following year saw the release of another version of *Gli ultimi giorni di Pompei* directed by Paolo Moffa with Marcel L'Herbier, to be followed in 1951 by Carmine Gallone's *Messalina*—the empress having already supplied the title for two earlier silent films by Mario Caserini (1910) and Enrico Guazzoni (1923), respectively. The return to the historical genre, and the spectacular display of the Roman past, received further impetus from the international success that attended the release in 1951 of MGM's remake *Quo Vadis*, made (like Blasetti's *Fabiola*) at the recently reopened Cinecittà studios at Rome. Many remakes of past historical films followed, including Riccardo Freda's *Spartaco* (1952). This time, however, the introduction of ancient Rome onto Italian cinema screens did not occur in coordination with a strident, nationalistic interest in the visual reconstruction of Italy's continuity with its Roman past. On the contrary, *romanità* and its cinematic display was, in the immediate post-war period, inextricably bound up with memories of its exploitation by the Fascist regime and, therefore, with recollections of Italy's inglorious role in the Second World War.[54]

For this reason, the historical films in distribution in Italy during the

years from 1948 to 1954 have been interpreted by some film critics as examples of mere commercial opportunism. The film industry's primary imperative at this time was to restore faith in the Italian national product, to sell its
films, and to secure foreign markets by, for example, the manufacture of
international coproductions that would appeal to the widest possible audience.[55] If many such films were set in the Roman past, their historical component functioned to recall to spectators the glorious traditions not of the
Italian nation in general but of its own film industry. Remakes of historical
films which had made that industry famous in the early decades of the century allowed the Italian production houses to attract customers for their
products through the glamor and prestige those new products might accrue
simply by association with the industry's past splendors. New versions of
silent films allowed Italian cinema to recall its glorious heritage and to put
on display its current technological virtuosity—its renewed capacity to
recreate on a vast and spectacular scale the costumes, decor, cities, crowds,
and sweeping historical events of antiquity.[56] And the setting in the Roman
past could justify the intrusion of sadistic and erotic scenes—the by-now
conventional tortures and bloody battles, the exotic dances, orgies, and
seductive patrician women—which might better evade the stringent requirements of post-war film censorship.[57] But, according to film critics such
as Jacques Siclier, if these historical films also reproduced the analogical
structures of their predecessors, it was only another piece of commercial
opportunism, the better to gain an audience through the pleasures of the
reconstructed past's apparent immediacy and relevance.[58]

In that commercial context, a remake of *Spartaco* would seem an appropriate choice. It could look back to the great success of the earlier Italian
version of Roman history, pick up on the continuing popularity of
Giovagnoli's novel, easily insert a lion fight in an arena to appropriate for
itself the attractions of MGM's recent *Quo Vadis*, and fill the screen with
scenes of violent battle and erotic seduction—the latter legitimated by the
presence in Giovagnoli's novel of both a pure beloved and a sensuous, sexually avaricious villainness. But the extensive refiguring of Spartacus that
takes place in Freda's *Spartaco* to suit contemporary concerns provides a
richer terrain for analysis than the label "opportunism" might imply.

For twenty years, the Fascist regime had found in the culture of ancient
Rome a rich source for the mass dissemination of propaganda to legitimate
its rule. The Roman *fasces* and the supposed "Roman" salute had given to
Fascism an identity as the inheritor of Roman civic virtues and imperial
policy. Roman symbols and rhetoric, architecture, sculpture, and public ceremonial became part of an efficient semiotic language with which to arouse

popular support for the domestic and foreign policies of the regime. Mussolini himself was presented as the modern embodiment of a diverse array of Roman leaders. The *duce* was associated with Julius Caesar for having crossed his Rubicon when marching on Rome in 1922. He was identified closely with Scipio Africanus for having conquered Ethiopia in 1935. And he was linked with the first emperor Augustus for having transformed liberal Italy into an imperial monarchy.[59] Cinema too was to play its part in placing *romanità* at the service of the regime. In *Il Mattino* of 2 June 1936, the director Alessandro Blasetti had argued that

> the historical film can recall moments that are perfectly analogous to those which we now live, or, at least, that would have so clear a relation to them as to abolish the intervening centuries an instant after we recalled that they have passed, and from these analogies and from these relations can flow warnings, incitements, cognitions that serve to reinforce the popular consciousness of today.[60]

In the following year, the historical film *Scipione l'Africano* presented so close an analogy between the victorious Roman general and Mussolini that the writer Luigi Malerba recalled

> Well, yes, the Duce's image had become fixed in my memory against my will, precise and cinematographic, sepia-toned like a figure of *Scipio Africanus*. A mute image, as if cut out of a silent movie.[61]

In the immediate post-war period, such a close identification between cinematic antiquity and the legitimacy of the Fascist regime had to be exorcized from the memories of the Italian spectators who watched historical films. Hence the first post-war Italian film to be set in ancient Rome, *Fabiola*, paid tribute not to the civic virtues and military achievements of the Roman state but to the suffering and endurance of its victims. Blasetti, now putting his advocacy of historical analogy to a quite different use, assimilated the early Christians of *Fabiola* to the peoples and organizations which had been persecuted by the Nazis and Fascists during the Second World War.[62] Even the name of the company set up by API Film of Rome and Rialto Film of Paris to service the coproduction of Freda's *Spartaco* suggests that this film too was attempting to dissociate itself and its Italian spectators from the Fascist rhetoric of *romanità*. It was the production company "consorzio Scipione," assisted by organs of the Fascist state, that had configured the Roman general Scipio as a prototype of Mussolini. Now the production company "consorzio Spartacus" was to configure the Thracian gladiator as a prototype of Italy's wartime resistance heroes.

Spartaco begins in a city of Thrace which has been reduced to burning rubble by the imperial ambitions of Rome.[63] An opening, expository title states

> In the year 74 B.C., Rome was expanding her domination over the Mediterranean world. Thrace, though conquered, refused to accept defeat.

The ensuing sequence, in which the Roman army overruns the war-torn city and proceeds to insult and to murder its citizens, recalls much more recent scenes when northern Italian villages and towns had been devastated by the Allied carpet bombing of 1942–1943 and then occupied by German troops to a line south of Rome. The wartime devastation of northern Italy and the atrocities inflicted on its inhabitants by the Nazis had already been famously depicted in such neo-realist films as Roberto Rossellini's *Roma città aperta,* released in 1945.[64] In the historical film, Spartacus first appears as a Thracian mercenary in the Roman army committed to Rome's authority, but he is then immediately transformed into a rebel who refuses to support the army's unjust treatment of the city's conquered inhabitants. Thus the film's spectators are given the opportunity to identify with a hero who has been, in some sense, a Roman but who is prepared to discard that Romanness when confronted by the cruel exercise of its authority. Similarly, the film's first vision of the city of Rome is of a military procession comprising both soldiers and prisoners which moves between majestic buildings towards the Colosseum, to the acclaim of a large crowd of Roman spectators. The anachronistic presence of the Colosseum in *Spartaco* is highly significant. Few Italian spectators could fail to recall that, from 1932, vast military parades had been staged by Mussolini along the *via dell'impero* (the Road of Empire) which had been especially designed to connect the Colosseum, as symbol of imperial Rome, with the headquarters of the Fascist government in the Palazzo Venezia.[65] In the processional sequence of *Spartaco*, however, Italian cinema audiences could witness the replay of such a Fascist parade now set to mournful music, and confront their wartime selves embodied in the crowds who face the camera and cheer the procession which passes before them. The experience offered, however, is a comforting one, as the film audience is being asked to identify not with the acquiescent crowds but with the resisting Spartacus who breaks away from the parade and attempts to escape the pursuing Roman troops. Resisting the cruelties of an occupying Roman army, escaping through the streets of

3.3 Crassus' daughter looks at Spartacus in chains, from Freda's *Spartaco* (1952). [Courtesy of BFI Stills, Posters and Designs.]

Rome, or successfully attacking a Roman encampment after an ingenious descent down the vines of Mount Vesuvius, Spartacus is refigured in Freda's post-war film in the mould of an Italian partisan fighting in the resistance movement that developed in northern Italy after it fell under Nazi rule in September 1943.[66]

In Vidali's *Spartaco* of 1913, the body of the strongman Mario Guaita was repeatedly displayed with muscles tensed in the successful service of a Garibaldian struggle for liberty and unity. The muscular screen body confidently celebrated the perceived vigor and cohesion of the Italian body politic in the early years of the twentieth century. In Freda's *Spartaco* of 1952, however, the body of the actor Massimo Girotti appears at one point in the pose of a crucified Christ, outstretched arms in chains, naked torso lashed by a Roman whip. [illustration 3.3] The framing of Spartacus in a Christ-like pose when tortured in the prison-cells of a gladiatorial school invokes the shocking sequence in Rossellini's *Roma città aperta,* where the Communist partisan leader Manfredi suffers and dies under interrogation at Gestapo headquarters.[67] In the spate of Italian films about the resistance which were released in the period 1944–1946 and distributed to considerable acclaim throughout Europe and the United States, such scenes of male martyrdom encouraged spectators to feel that Italy had more than paid for its support of Mussolini's regime with the courage its partisans had demonstrated in resisting the German occupation.[68] Freda's *Spartaco* thus gives an historical authority to and exemplifies the sufferings and the bravery of wartime Italy through its representation of the physical torments endured by the film's hero at the hands of the cruel and sadistic Romans. The cinematic transformation of Spartacus from militant to martyred body belongs within a broader history of post-war alterations to the Italian national self projected in historical films.[69] After the muscular body of a Spartacus or a Maciste in the silent era and the statuesque body of Scipio in the heyday of the Fascist regime, the immediate post-war period saw Italian cinema screens filled with the wounded and suffering bodies of martyrs sacrificed to the despotism and ambition of Rome. Such a transformation from the militant to the martyred male body had already been rehearsed in the star image of the well-known actor who played Spartacus in 1952. Ten years earlier, Girotti had been cast in Roberto Rossellini's *Un pilota ritorna*—a propaganda film financed by the Fascist government—as an Italian airman who heroically escapes from a prisoner of war camp in Greece. By 1949 the actor was now starring as the persecuted and brutally murdered Saint Sebastian in Alessandro Blasetti's post-war apology *Fabiola*.[70] The Italian national self incarnated by Girotti in his subsequent role of Spartacus, however, is not wholly redeemed through a martyr's display of acts of bravery and physical suffering.

In sharp contrast to the moral commitment, triumphal progress, and unwavering success of Spartacus in Vidali's silent rendition of the slave rebellion, a central section of Freda's film shows the hero temporarily entrapped and unmanned by the seductive charms of Sabina, the evil and vindictive daughter of the Roman general Crassus. Faith in the leadership of Spartacus, both his own and that of his comrades in arms, is never fully restored, and the hero falls in battle convinced that he has betrayed his followers and assisted in their defeat. The pessimism of the film's narrative drive is mitigated only by the wholly fictional figure of Spartacus' Thracian lover and fellow victim Amitis, onto whom the film audience is allowed to displace their hopes for the future when, at night, in a field of corpses, she reassures the dying gladiator of the victory to come:

SPARTACUS: I betrayed you all. . . . I made promises I didn't keep. I led you to disaster not to victory.
AMITIS: It wasn't your fault.
SPARTACUS: This is the end of our road. All is lost.

AMITIS: Even if this battle is lost, the fight will go on until victory is ours. Be at peace. Your example will be followed. The flame you've lit is still burning. It will burn until the world is free.
[*Spartacus offers Amitis his sword.*]
SPARTACUS: Take this. Today it has failed. But you're right, some day it will be victorious.

This final scene of *Spartaco* ends with the camera moving forward to a close-up of Amitis's upturned face that cuts the prostrate Spartacus out of the film frame and relegates him to a space somewhere off screen.

The focus in the second half of Freda's film on the temptations, the self-doubt, and the failings of Spartacus, his marginalization in the fight for freedom and his final replacement on screen by the fictional Amitis, further demonstrate the considerable departure of the post-war cinematic historiography of the slave rebellion from the triumphant, Garibaldian romanticism that had been projected in the silent era. Nor does the largely pessimistic narrative drive of Freda's film align it with contemporary Gramscian readings of the gladiator's cultural significance for post-war reconstruction Italy. At the beginning of the year in which the film *Spartaco* was released, in the pages of the Italian Communist Party's weekly magazine *Vie Nuove*, the serialization of Giovagnoli's nineteenth-century novel was justified on the grounds that Spartacus' insurrection had prepared the way for the eventual collapse of the Roman ruling classes and that his name had become ever since a symbol for and inspiration to popular revolt.[71] Such contemporary veneration of Spartacus by Italian Communists facilitated the deployment of the gladiator in Freda's film as a figure for the PCI itself, and its troubled relations to power in the climate of the Cold War.

It has long been recognized that Alessandro Blasetti's earlier cinematic reconstruction of Christian martyrdom in *Fabiola* (1949) operates with a multiple historical focus. Through the narration of ancient religious persecution, the historical film addressess not only the wartime violence inflicted on victims of and rebels against the Nazi occupation of Italy but also the post war intolerance exhibited towards Italian communism.[72] Such a complex traffic in historical analogies was propelled by the popular identification of the Italian resistance with the Communist Party. Since the Communists had maintained constant underground activity during Mussolini's regime and since almost half of the armed resistance to the German occupation had been organized in Communist "Garibaldi" brigades, immediately after the war the PCI was able to base its moral and political prestige (and its participation in government) on its commonly acknowledged history of ceaseless and devoted struggle against Fascism and Nazism.[73] But when in 1947 the Cold War set in, the heroes of the resistance were expelled from the coalition government of Alcide De Gasperi and demonized in a sustained and ferocious propaganda campaign that led to a landslide victory for the Christian Democrats in the elections of April 1948, to be followed swiftly by the attempted assassination of the PCI leader Palmiro Togliatti.[74] Released in the year after the elections, *Fabiola* paraded in historical guise a humanitarian denunciation of such recent outrages.

In Freda's *Spartaco*, the historical narration most closely addresses (and, perhaps, attempts to justify) the recent marginalization of the PCI in Italy's political life where it represents operational differences between the commanders of the slave army. Towards the close of the film, Spartacus is characterized as a moderate and conciliatory leader prepared to accept Crassus' offer of liberty and peace for his followers, only to have his negotiations rudely terminated by the military aggression of Octavius who has, in Spartacus' absence, initiated a foolish and ultimately fatal assault on the Roman army.[75] Such rifts between the slave leaders resemble those lately reported between the leaders of the post-war PCI. While Palmiro Togliatti, for example, advocated a policy of noninsurrection and coalition in the government of Italy, Pietro Secchia criticized such apparent compromise and called upon the party to recuperate a more oppositional profile.[76] In Freda's film, political division is met by historically inevitable defeat, and Amitis, who in the course of the film has been swayed against the conciliatory Spartacus by the false, combative rhetoric of Octavius [illustration 3.4], is left to acknowledge the wisdom of her betrayed leader but the need now to carry on the fight for freedom without him. If the shifting historical analogies set in play by the narrative of Freda's *Spartaco* call upon spectators to associate the slave rebellion with both the heroism of the wartime Italian resistance and the political failure of the post-war PCI, it is hardly surprising that after initial enthusiastic reports in *Vie Nuove* on the coming production of the film, its release was then met by complete silence.

A Gladiator for the Colonies

Freda's *Spartaco* carried no appeal for the Italian Communist Party magazine *Vie Nuove*, but the film fared little better when it was reviewed in the foreign press more than a year later. Although critics admired its spectacular action sequences, photography, and score, *Spartaco* was dismissed for its relatively unknown cast, its lack of dramatic compulsion, and the emptiness of its historical reconstruction.[77] When the Italian recreation of the ancient slave rebellion was distributed in the United States in 1954, it was projected almost begrudgingly in a severely truncated print and under a title—*Sins of Rome*—which even left its specific historical focus unidentified.[78] Yet some

3.4 Amitis turns against the conciliatory Spartacus, from Freda's *Spartaco* (1952). [Courtesy of BFI Stills, Posters and Designs.]

six years later, in 1960, the biggest draw at the American box-office was *Spartacus* (Stanley Kubrick, Bryna Production for Universal-International). Pressbooks and souvenir programs ignored the rich Italian tradition for the representation of Spartacus and instead appealed for authority to a more familiar, native tradition initiated in the early nineteenth century (the literature proclaimed) by Dr. Robert Montgomery Bird's American play *The Gladiator*. In the United States, the cultural force of Spartacus lay not in the rhetoric of national unity or wartime resistance, but in that of anti-imperialism and democracy, abolition, and racial equality.

In the late eighteenth century, the Founding Fathers had trawled antiquity for historical precedents to legitimate the emerging American nation. The Roman republic was viewed by them as the greatest and most serviceable exemplar of liberty and republicanism, and the heroes of the independence movement were dressed in the civic virtues of a Cincinnatus, a Cicero, or a Cato. In dynamic tension with the model of the virtuous Roman republic operated the anti-model of the corrupted Roman empire. Turning the British rhetoric of imperial *romanitas* back on itself, the war of independence was often re-enacted in American novels, drama, poetry, and paintings of the early nineteenth century as an historic struggle for liberty against Roman tyranny, as the struggle of a subjugated people against their

3.5 Edwin Forrest as Spartacus, in Bird's play *The Gladiator,* first performed in 1831. [Billy Rose Theatre Collection, New York Public Library for the Performing Arts, Astor, Lenox and Tilden Foundations.]

imperial oppressors.[79] First performed in 1831, Bird's patriotic melodrama *The Gladiator* staged the ancient slave rebellion in accordance with the broader political rhetoric of this New World *romanitas.* The uncompromising, charismatic hero (embodied in the theatrical star Edwin Forrest) displayed his muscles, fought, suffered, and died in laudable revolt against an aristocratic despotism that had ravaged his distant country and victimized his people. [illustration 3.5] *The Gladiator* was a tremendous success and held the American stage for over seventy years.[80]

Bird's first staging of the ancient slave rebellion, however, occurred in the same year as William Lloyd Garrison launched a campaign for slave emancipation. Just as, from the mid-nineteenth century, America's territorial expansion was to challenge the Founding Fathers' unsullied version of New World *romanitas* (with America itself now appearing to have slipped from virtuous republic to tyrannical empire), so from the 1830s attacks on the institution of slavery often implicitly or explicitly compared early nineteenth-century America to a (now) insidious Roman state, both equally doomed to decline for their corruption, luxury, and dependence on a slave economy. Thus in 1834, some three years after performances of Bird's *The Gladiator* began, George Bancroft published a long essay analyzing the decline of "the Roman people" together with the first volume of his *History of the United States* while, some forty years later, William Dean Howells was even to find a resemblance between the antique portrait busts of Roman senators and those of American senators from the southern states, declaring that they possessed the common physiognomy of slaveholders.[81] Among the contemporary American audiences of Bird's *The Gladiator*, therefore, many interpreted the historical play as a loosely veiled address to the pressing contradiction between their ideals of liberty and their own institution of slavery. Reviewers such as Walt Whitman regarded the play's first act in particular, in which slaves are brutally sold, flogged, and torn from their families, as full of Abolitionism. The playwright himself, conscious of the contemporary resonance of his historical melodrama, suggested that "if *The Gladiator* were produced in a slave state, the managers, players, and perhaps myself in the bargain, would be rewarded with the Penitentiary!" Despite Bird's acknowledgment of the polemical potential of his play, however, he did not regard Spartacus' rebellion as a welcome paradigm for current uprisings by Negro slaves. When several hundred slaves in the state of Virginia were reported to have rebelled under the leadership of Nat Turner, Bird wrote that

> If they had had a Spartacus among them to organize the half million of Virginia, the hundreds of thousands of the [other] states, and lead them on in the Crusade of Massacre, what a blessed example might they not give to the world of the excellence of slavery!

Similarly, audiences in the South, perceiving that *The Gladiator* did not treat of an enslavement based on race, could choose to read its representation of terrible servitude as a vivid metaphor for the burdens presently endured by America's poor whites, and the heroic revolt of Spartacus as comparable to the populist Democratic campaigns of the recently inaugurated President Andrew Jackson.[82]

Long after the emancipation of America's slaves had been effected, narratives of Spartacus' rebellion against a corrupt Roman state continued to be produced and consumed with an eye to their relevance for the internal economic, political, and social structures of the United States. In a brief preface to Howard Fast's novel *Spartacus* (1951)—the most immediate source for the Hollywood representation of the Thracian gladiator—the author dedicated the work to his two children, and made clear that his account of "brave men and women who lived long ago" had been written in order to inspire them and other readers to struggle against oppression and wrong and to fulfill the dream of Spartacus "in our own time."[83] Nine years later, in souvenir programs and publicity releases detailing the production of the film *Spartacus* (1960), Fast was permitted to reiterate his view that the novel (and, by implication, the film) bore a pointed message for modern times:

> Here is the story of Spartacus, who led the great slave revolt against Rome. I wrote this novel because I considered it an important story for the times in which we live. Not in the mechanical sense of historical parallels, but because there is hope and strength to be taken from such a story about the age-old fight for freedom—and because Spartacus lived not for one time of man, but for all times of man. I wrote it to give hope and courage to those who read it, and in the process of writing it, I gained hope and courage myself.

Although in neither case did Fast refer explicitly to a fight for freedom within the United States, the narrative devices of his historical novel and the conditions of its production underscore its address to Cold War America.[84]

According to his revisionist autobiography *Being Red* (1990), Howard Fast first became interested in Spartacus while incarcerated in an American prison for his allegiance to the Communist Party.[85] The launching of the Cold War by President Harry Truman in 1947 had been immediately followed by a systematic assault on domestic Communism, including the investigation of Communist influence in Hollywood by the House Un-American Activities Committee (HUAC). Fast became one of the infamous Ten, the "unfriendly" witnesses who refused to answer the committee's question "are you or have you ever been a member of the Communist Party?" Cited for contempt of Congress and suspended from employment in Hollywood, he was eventually sent to prison in 1950, to be released in 1951 just as HUAC had reestablished its investigation into Hollywood "subversives" and was blacklisting hundreds of writers, directors, and actors.[86] In the face of this consolidation of the Red Scare, when American popular fiction largely stressed the themes of individual acquisition, business success, conformity, military authority, and anti-Communism, when the private investigator "Mike Hammer" was reveling in the murder of Commies in the pages of Mickey Spillane's bestseller *One Lonely Night* (1951), Howard Fast attempted to popularize a Marxist hero of the class struggle aided by an account of ancient slavery which he had once received as a gift after a Party training school.[87]

In this respect, Fast's novelistic account of the slave revolt is more in keeping with the Gramscian injunction to circulate works with a radical, educative value for the masses than Freda's film version released in the following year, for in the novel Spartacus' rebellion is designed to signal indirectly the profound value of Communist activism. Thus, in historical guise, Fast's *Spartacus* graphically enacts for Americans (according to the social historian William Vance) the "liberation of the masses of laboring men and women, the productive members of society, from their 'enslavement' by the parasitic possessors of wealth and property."[88] At one pivotal moment in the novel, for example, a Roman recalls the stern message Spartacus sent to the Senate after his memorable victory at Vesuvius over their cohorts:

> What a foul crew you are and what a filthy mess you have made of life! You have made a mockery of all men dream of, of the work of a man's hands and the sweat of a man's brow. Your own citizens live on the dole and spend their days in the circus and the arena. You have made a travesty of human life and robbed it of all its worth. (171)

This speech rises to a stirring climax as Fast's Spartacus borrows from Marx's famous phraseology and, converting the metaphorical back into the more distressing literal, calls upon "the slaves of the world" to "rise up and cast off your chains!" (171)

While the representation of the slave rebellion as a conflict between labor and capital might not appear to engage Fast's *Spartacus* with a "fight for freedom" of specific reference to the United States, the elaboration of a significant plot line for a wholly fictitious character named Draba clearly marks the novel's radical commitment to American civil rights issues. In the gladiatorial school at Capua, Spartacus is compelled to fight to the death against Draba, a black man, for the amusement of a party of Roman nobles. Rather than kill Spartacus, Draba leaps up to attack the spectators in their box. The Romans construe this as an act of madness since, according to the novelist's account, they are incapable of making the journey to the black man's beginnings, and only if they had made that journey would they have known that the black man did not go mad at all. Not even in mind could they have seen the house he had by the riverside and the children his wife bore him and the land he tilled and the fruit of the land, before the soldiers came and with them the slave dealers to harvest that crop of human life so magically transmuted into gold. (104–5)

Aided by persistent references throughout Fast's novel to the "plantations" from which Spartacus frees the slaves, the historical narrative recalls the discourse of emancipation in which the American Spartacus had been articulated from the time of Bird's productions of *The Gladiator*. It also thereby establishes an heroic parallel for the contemporary engagement of American Communists in the political struggle for racial equality, since Party members had found a major site of resistance to the culture of the Cold War in the struggle against racial discrimination.[89]

Similarly, Fast lays down traces in the novel of both the American Left's commitment to women's rights (in intermittent references to a past and future golden age when women are equal to men), and its commitment to Zionism (in the fictional character of David, a Jewish gladiator who, towards the end of the novel, recalls how he had fought for freedom once before in Galilee). One civil rights movement, however, is not accorded the same respect. In the same year as the publication of Fast's *Spartacus*, the Mattachine Society was established in Los Angeles in order to protest against the persecution of homosexual behavior, yet homosexuality is deployed throughout the novel as a narrative device to mark the political perversity of the Roman elite. At a time when blacklistees were frequently accused of failing to match up to an idealized McCarthyite hyper-masculinity, when those suspected of political subversion were labeled "lavender lads," Fast turns such charges instead against the novel's representatives of state authority and lends credibility and historical legitimacy to his homophobic tropes by locating the acts of sexual "depravity" in a Roman setting.[90]

In *Spartacus*, Fast attempted to validate and popularize the political activism of the American left by displacing it circumspectly into a remote, but heroic and familiar, past where oppression and its resistance could take an especially violent and Manichean form. Attention to the book's radical narrative drive was further enhanced by public knowledge of both its origins in Fast's own victimization by HUAC and the difficulties that subsequently beset the book's publication. Deprived of the support of any American publishing house, Fast persisted in producing the book himself and was later to claim that reading it became "an act of defiance by people who loathed the climate of the time."[91] Even in 1960, political and commercial risks attended the employment of so apparently subversive a source for the making of a Hollywood film. Kirk Douglas proceeded to exacerbate those risks by appointing Dalton Trumbo to adapt the historical novel for the screen. Trumbo too had been a member of the convicted and notorious Hollywood Ten and, in common with other blacklistees, his real name had not appeared in screen credits since 1947. When, at the premiere of *Spartacus* thirteen years later, the names of both Howard Fast and Dalton Trumbo were finally listed again in screen credits, the press avidly scrutinized the film in case it might be furthering "the cause of the Kremlin."[92]

The Cause of the Kremlin

Spartacus (1960) inscribes itself into Hollywood's earlier tradition of epics set in antiquity by, for example, conjoining in one scene two actors who had both previously played Nero on American screens—Charles Laughton in *The Sign of the Cross* (1932) and Peter Ustinov in *Quo Vadis* (1951).[93] Yet the film also diverges significantly from the reverential historical epics that had typified the previous decade—films like *Quo Vadis* (1951), *The Robe* (1953), *The Silver Chalice* (1954), *The Ten Commandments* (1956), and, most recently, *Ben-Hur* (1959). These religious films were privileged and, for the most part, enormously successful products of the Hollywood film industry. They were also steeped in the rhetoric of the Cold War. In a pre-credit prologue to *The Ten Commandments*, DeMille himself had appeared on screen to identify his film narrative centred on Moses as "the story of the birth of freedom," a freedom obedient to the laws of God rather than the whims of a dictator. The widescreen gaze of God is constructed in alignment with contemporary American political interests and in opposition to the perceived godlessness of the Antichrist, Communism.[94] Similarly, a long pre-credit sequence in *Ben-Hur* had displayed a painterly depiction of the nativity in anticipation of the narration of conflict between ancient Judaea and Rome, thereby establishing Christ as the historical agent who ultimately motivates resistance to a pagan, totalitarian rule.[95] In the noticeable absence of such opening religiosity, however, the titles of *Spartacus* roll over isolated images of Roman portrait busts cracking under the internal pressure of a more abstract, political force (the institution of slavery), and the film closes with its revolutionary hero crucified not for his religious faith but for his political challenge to corrupt government. The production company's publicity explicitly differentiated *Spartacus* from the earlier, conservative examples of the genre by labeling the film "the thinking man's epic," thereby hinting at its more enlightened political perspective, while in press interviews the director Stanley Kubrick even made the then highly provocative claim that he had been more influenced by Soviet historical films like *Alexander Nevsky* (1938) than Hollywood's *Ben-Hur* or the oeuvre of DeMille.[96]

Such dissidence had already surfaced in the Kubrick/Douglas partnership which produced *Paths of Glory* (1957). There a radical assault on the militarism of 1950s America had been doubly displaced into an account of a mutiny in the French army during the First World War.[97] *Spartacus* demonstrated its radicalism more overtly through the credited employment of the blacklistees Fast and Trumbo, and through its emplotment of a rebellion long since assimilated to a revolutionary Marxist agenda. The film's box-office success was a measure of the degree to which the culture of the Cold War had been eroded by 1960. By then Truman had spoke out publicly against the blacklist, Khrushchev had toured the United States, and the election of President Kennedy was initiating a climate in which the representation of social and political problems might no longer be construed wholly as an act of treason.[98] Nonetheless, the production history of *Spartacus* exposes the problems of political focus that still beset Hollywood filmmaking at the beginning of the 1960s.

In the early 1950s, 20th Century-Fox had required numerous rewrites of the screenplay for the film *Viva Zapata!* (1952) in order to ensure the conversion of the contentious Mexican revolutionary hero into a more congenial liberal and supporter of American-style democracy. It was commercially expedient for the studio to "keep the red-baiters in check."[99] In the repressive atmosphere of the 1950s, there was no economic incentive even for leftist films to bear clear political messages, and they were often subject to the conflicting ideological pulls of their writers, directors, producers, and exhibitors.[100] According to the detailed account of the production of *Spartacus* by the film historian Duncan Cooper, an enormous gap began to open up between Fast's novelistic vision of Spartacus and that being prepared for projection. The screenwriter Trumbo constantly reproached the director Kubrick and the executive producer and star Douglas for what he took to be their "unremitting attack on the political meaning and the intellectual content" of every proposed scene in the historical film. In Trumbo's view, the omission from the film of any sequence displaying a significant victory for the slave army emasculated the heroic gladiator, while the decision to close the film with his crucifixion—against all the historical evidence and against the narrative closure of both book and screenplay—created an "irritating allusion" to Christ (which appeared to remodel the political militant as spiritual martyr).[101] But far greater risks and constraints were attached to film production than book publication, even in the period of transition away from the culture of the Cold War. In the 1950s, the Hollywood "blockbuster" in particular was a producer's picture. As an immense financial ven-

ture and huge industrial undertaking, the widescreen historical epic needed
to address a very broad constituency at a time when cinema was fighting to
survive the competing attractions of television.[102] Confronted by the market
interests of the studios, the scrutiny of the Production Code Administration
and the vociferous threat of boycotts by pressure groups such as the
American Legion of Decency, even "the thinking man's epic" had to have
attempted limits imposed upon its political provocation. Thus Douglas, who
made *Spartacus* for his own independent production company Bryna while
receiving financial backing for the twelve million–dollar project from the
major Hollywood studio Universal-International, circulated an uncontentious, seemingly patriotic narrative image for his film as "an American statement by an American film company about the cause of freedom and the
dignity of man."[103]

The big budget, Super Technirama, Technicolor *Spartacus* of 1960 only
partially preserves or adapts for screen the defense of American political
activism and the investigation of labor which had been encoded in Fast's
self-published novel concerning the ancient slave rebellion. It is possible, for
example, to read the representations of slave labor and incarceration in the
first part of the film as a visual translation to screen of the Marxist concern
with the conflict between labor and capital manifested in Fast's novel. The
mines and the gladiatorial school vividly display a grim, brutal and inhuman world of enforced production which provides both wealth and entertainment for the unperturbed elite of the Roman state.[104] Similarly, in the
second part of the film, frequent cross-cutting (aided by sharply contrasting
musical motifs) juxtaposes and contrasts the rebel and the Roman armies,
where the rebel camp is presented as a kind of utopian, proto-Communist
society peopled by whole families who share their work and meagre possessions along with a common aspiration to equality and liberation from slave-
labor, while the Roman troops are marked by their sinister, machinelike
maneuvers, their lack of individuality, and their complete obedience to a
rigid hierarchy controlled by rich, ambitious politicians.[105] [illustration 3.6]
The Hollywood historiography of Spartacus, moreover, raises issues of
labor both on and off screen. Extra-cinematic discussions of the making of
the film drew attention to claims that it had instituted good labor practice.
Variety for 18 January 1961 noted that, in the American labor press,
Spartacus was being touted as the most expensive film ever made in
Hollywood under union conditions of employment, and that (unlike the
earlier "runaway" production of *Ben-Hur* in Italy) almost all its sequences
had been shot in California. Recognition that *Spartacus* had been given a
special screening for labor leaders in New York and that union leaders were
sending out "please support" pleas to their members encouraged audiences

3.6 Regimented Roman soldiers on the march, from Kubrick's *Spartacus* (1960). [Courtesy of BFI Stills, Posters and Designs.]

to read the historical film itself as one which confronted the difficult conditions endured by at least one sector of the American labor force.[106]

Although *Spartacus* reveals surviving traces of the general Marxist commitment to class struggle encoded in Fast's novel, it manifests a more immediate, liberal concern with the American Communist Party itself and the

recent hounding by HUAC of Party members, like Fast and Trumbo themselves. Just as Freda's *Spartaco* had refigured the Thracian gladiator to
explore the marginalization of the PCI in post-war Italy, so Kubrick's
Spartacus refigures the ancient hero to expose the vicious assaults on domestic Communism that had been such a feature of American culture in the
Cold War era. In the late 1940s and early 1950s, witnesses who appeared
before a congressional investigating committee were expected to inform on
their friends and associates as a test of their patriotism and as the price of
full citizenship. Howard Fast and Dalton Trumbo had both been vilified in
the press when, in 1947, they chose not to be "friendly" witnesses before
HUAC.[107] Yet, towards the close of *Spartacus*, after the rebel army has been
defeated and the surviving slaves taken prisoner, a Roman soldier an-
nounces that their lives are to be spared on condition that they identify the
body or the living person of Spartacus in their midst. Rather than do so, the
slaves rise up in turn to declare "I'm Spartacus." As the camera focuses first
on Crassus perplexed by such behavior and then on Spartacus moved to
tears, as the musical theme rises to a stirring crescendo, the sequence insists
not on the virtue of incriminating, but rather on the heroism of shielding,
the subversive within.[108] Similarly, soon after the scene in which the solidar-
ity of the rebels has been championed, *Spartacus* denounces the brutality of
their persecutors. In a darkened and near-empty Senate-house, bereft of all
semblance of the democratic process, Crassus threatens the demagogue
Gracchus with the fate of the crucified slaves:

> As those slaves have died, so will your rabble, if they falter one instant in loy-
> alty to the new order of affairs. The enemies of the state are known. Arrests
> are in progress. The prisons begin to fill. In every city and province, lists of
> the disloyal have been compiled. Tomorrow they will learn the costs of their
> terrible folly, their treason.

The familiar Cold War rhetoric of vigilant patriotism takes on an extremely
sinister turn when relocated in the setting of the proscriptions of the late
Republic. The historical dressing helps justify the breaking of the blacklist
which brought out large numbers of pickets to the film's premiere. In Los
Angeles, for example,

> Uncle Sam, an intense gentleman in striped trousers and frayed satin tails,
> showed up, too. He joined a picket line of pickets which formed at the
> theater to protest the work of "Unfriendly Ten" writers Howard Fast and
> Dalton Trumbo on the "Spartacus" script. The pickets who carried such

signs as "Stamp out Red Writers" said they represented the "Democrats United for America, Inc."[109]

Such a troubled context for viewing *Spartacus*, in turn, lent an immediate, contemporary relevance to the film's Senate house sequence.

The Hollywood film also sustains the novel's commitment to American civil rights by preserving on screen a significant role for the fictitious character of Draba, the African gladiator who is ruthlessly cut down for refusing to kill Spartacus in the Capuan arena. The film's narrative drive offers two immediate motivations for Spartacus' vividly portrayed breakout from the gladiatorial school—the purchase and removal of his beloved Varinia and the noble sacrifice of Draba, whose body the Romans leave hanging as a lesson against (and, it turns out, in) insurgence.[110] [illustration 3.7] Thus in the Italian popular tradition for Spartacus, in Giovagnoli's novel and in the films of Vidali and Freda, ancient slavery functions as a metaphoric narrative device to intensify concerns with Italian nationalism and the body politic, while in the American popular tradition, from the time of Bird's *Gladiator*, slavery partially operates as the originary economic institution that has laid the foundation of American racial oppression. During the course of the 1950s, the Eisenhower administration constantly evaded the question of civil rights. Black activists instead achieved victories in the courts (such as the racial desegregation bill of 1954), through individual acts of civil disobedience (such as Rosa Parks's famous refusal to submit to the segregation laws operating on Alabama's buses), and through the formation of campaigning organizations such as the Southern Christian Leadership Conference established in 1957 under the presidency of Martin Luther King.[111] In locating the inspiration for revolt largely in the brave defiance of a black gladiator, *Spartacus* acknowledges the central role of black activism in the emerging protest movements which, in 1960, confronted Kennedy's new administration.

The narrative function of the African gladiator played by Woody Strode was already marked out for audiences of the period by Strode's earlier portrayal of a persecuted black soldier in *Sergeant Rutledge* (1960).[112] But, in the course of *Spartacus*, black suffering interlocks with and is soon superceded by Jewish suffering, a slippage aided by the tradition common to African Americans and Jews of narratives concerning diaspora and slavery, such as the shared use of the Exodus story, which celebrates the liberation of the Israelites from Egyptian enslavement.[113] In the same year as Otto Preminger's *Exodus* (1960) put the Zionist case for a Jewish homeland in a provocatively contemporary setting, the *Spartacus* associated in particular with its executive producer and star Kirk Douglas constructs a more discrete histor-

3.7 Gladiators see the punishment of Draba, from Kubrick's *Spartacus* (1960).
[Courtesy of BFI Stills, Posters and Designs.]

ical parable in which a Moses-like hero courageously attempts to lead his
surrogate Israelites to the Promised Land.[114] This reading of the film and
its characterization of the Thracian gladiator has retrospectively gained
authoritative support from Douglas's autobiography, which was published
in 1988. There Douglas constructs for himself the persona of "the ragman's
son," and discloses that his original name was Issur Danielovitch, that he
was the son of an illiterate Russian-Jewish immigrant to the United States,

and that he identified with the oppressed slaves of ancient Rome because he too came from a race of slaves.[115] According to Duncan Cooper, it was Douglas' Zionist convictions that above all caused an ideological rift between the narrative drive of Fast's novel and that of the Hollywood film, for the Zionist Spartacus appears on screen as a leader of a mass migration of slaves back to their homelands rather than as a revolutionary aiming to overthrow the oppressive Roman state, and his revolt appears driven more by religious piety than by class struggle.[116]

As in Fast's novel, gender and sexuality also function within the film *Spartacus* as a persistent and powerful cultural metaphor for oppression. On screen, as in the novel, Roman homosexuality marks the political and moral decadence of the regime. By comparison, however, its representation is distinctly muted—displaced, in the case of Crassus' attempted seduction of Antoninus, into an oblique conversation about oysters and snails. The Production Code forbade overt references to homosexuality, and even this scene was eventually cut by Universal under pressure from the American Legion of Decency.[117] Such specifically cinematic operations of gender and sexuality in *Spartacus* have been the subject of some recent critical attention within wider debates about the construction of masculinity and the display of the male body in Hollywood cinema.[118] Although Spartacus's fictitious beloved Varinia first appears in the film unconventionally experienced in sexual matters and equal to the hero in her desire for liberty, she soon falls back into the more familiar patterns for encoding gender in Hollywood cinema, whereby she is presented as the pleasurable object of a desiring male gaze, as a helpmeet to Spartacus rather than an agent of historical narration.[119] The more troublesome display of the male body, however, plays an integral part in the narrative trajectory of the film, which traces the hero's attempt to liberate himself from the humiliating condition of being looked at—a mere spectacle for the gratification of his Roman masters.[120] As in Freda's *Spartaco*, the hero never achieves the complete restoration of a "proper" masculinity and, in an image wholly out of keeping with the McCarthyite hyper-masculinity frequently projected in the Cold War era, ends the film with his crucified body posed as a spectacle of suffering martyrdom.[121] *Spartacus* even problematizes the epic genre's customary invitation to audience pleasure in the display of male bodies. During the Capuan arena sequence, when Spartacus and Draba fight for the perverse pleasure of the onlooking Romans, the cinema spectator's visual pleasure in looking at their bodies is frequently frustrated and then violently terminated. When Draba throws his trident at the watching audience, the weapon flies straight at the camera, suggesting that to take pleasure in looking upon such a scene is to become no better than a Roman.[122]

Certainly at the time of the original release of *Spartacus*, it was the contributing personnel explicitly linked to the film rather more than its content that caused an outcry. Both the right-wing columnist Hedda Hopper and the American Legion of Decency attempted to instigate mass boycotts of the film under slogans such as "Red Writers are back!" but the protests proved ineffective when the newly elected President John F. Kennedy openly crossed a picket line to attend a public screening of the film in Washington.[123] If, however, *Spartacus* went on to be an international box-office success, it was due, in no small measure, to the ways in which the film also laid itself open to reappropriation by the American Right as a Cold War sermon in historical guise no different from the earlier, religious blockbusters from which Byrna had attempted to differentiate its product.

Liberal readings of *Spartacus* require its spectators to assimilate the oppressive Roman state and its corrupt leaders to an American society still in need of radical transformation. But much of the film's accessibility resides in its deployment of conventions for narrating Roman history familiar from the earlier Hollywood historiography of Rome. Following the aural paradigm set by Cecil B. DeMille's historical epics, the heroic Spartacus and his fictitious companion Antoninus speak in the American cadences of the actors Kirk Douglas and Tony Curtis, while the sadistic villain Crassus, played by Laurence Olivier, speaks in the oratorical diction of the English stage.[124] Through the continuation of this earlier analogical device, *Spartacus* provides its audiences with the more comfortable opportunity to equate the repressive Roman state with foreign empires and the rebellious slaves with a principled America in perpetual, heroic struggle against tyranny.[125] Similarly, the Judeo-Christian religiosity of the Cold War epics momentarily resurfaces at the beginning and the end of *Spartacus*. In the post-credits voiceover, which introduces the Hollywood history of the slave rebellion, we are told that it is Christianity (rather than class struggle) which "was destined to overthrow the pagan tyranny of Rome and bring about a new society," while at the film's close the crucified Spartacus is posed above his newborn son and its mother in a manner that simultaneously invokes, through composition and lighting, the iconography of the Nativity and the Passion.[126] Although this closing Christian tableau may have been employed to suggest a more positive outcome, and even a divine sanction, for radical social action, it enabled conservative reviewers of the film, in the rhetoric of the Cold War, to extricate Spartacus from his godless, ghastly Communist tradition and to convert him into a blameless spiritual reformer. Thus a review of *Spartacus* in *Time* of 24 October 1960 righteously declared

> Despite his personal predilection for the 20th century's most crushing political orthodoxy, Trumbo has imparted to *Spartacus* a passion for freedom and the men who live and die for it—a passion that transcends all politics and

persons in the fearful, final image of the dying gladiator, the revolutionary on
the cross.

Studio press releases, souvenir programs, study guides, and press interviews did not attempt to pinpoint a specific ideological message for the film
but stated noncommittally that its hero's "passion for human rights and dignity is an inspiration to this very day," and spoke of its plot line as a powerful demonstration of "man's eternal desire for freedom."[127] But the fight for
"freedom against tyranny" was precisely the terminology President Truman
had used to launch the Cold War in 1947, and it belonged to the rhetoric in
which the historical blockbusters of the 1950s had been steeped. Picking up,
therefore, on the film's narrative image as a depiction of the eternal fight for
freedom, many writers in the popular press instated *Spartacus* as an historical film that did not further the cause of the Kremlin so much as hinder it:

> Although it deals with a revolt by slaves against the pagan Roman Empire,
> the desire for freedom from oppression that motivates Spartacus has its mod-
> ern counterpart today in areas of the world that struggle under Communist
> tyranny, and it stands as a sharp reminder for all mankind that there can be
> no truly peaceful sleep whilst would-be conquering legions stand poised to
> suppress.[128]

In the right-wing press, Spartacus became refigured as a Cold War warrior
fighting against the autocracy, atheism, and state control of the Soviet
Union, and his aspirations were assimilated to the alternative, divinely
blessed values of democratic America.[129]

4

Cleopatra:
Spectacles of Seduction
and Conquest

Competing Images

Under the headline "'Cleopatra' never had it so good," a journalist from the *New York Times* recounted a visit he had paid to the Cinecittà studios in Rome in January 1962. He had been sent to investigate rumors that the Twentieth-Century Fox studio was continuing to encounter difficulties in the production of its film *Cleopatra*. Instead, the writer claimed to have found an optimism which stemmed from "the feeling that a film of import is taking shape." On set, the director, Joseph L. Mankiewicz, described the importance and focal point of his new film as residing not so much in its impressive sets or in its imposing cast list as in its characterization of Cleopatra. She is to be depicted as "a vivid and many-sided personality, whom Mankiewicz calls 'a terribly exciting woman who nearly made it'" and her political climbing and intrigue is to be brought out in the "meat" of the film—the scenes of intimacy between Cleopatra, Julius Caesar, and Mark Antony, which Mankiewicz was then shooting.[1]

Some fifty years earlier, however, in November 1913, the newspaper *Giornale d'Italia* carried a significantly different account of the production of a silent film about Cleopatra, in which her "many-sided personality" scarcely figured. According to the Italian director Enrico Guazzoni, he chose to make *Marcantonio e Cleopatra* because

> no theme could better attract and move an artist than that which, through the figures of Mark Antony and Cleopatra, had so much weight over the des-tinies of the ancient world. It provided above all the opportunity to parade before the eyes of the spectator the most distinctive places of ancient Rome and ancient Egypt, which everyone has imprinted in their minds at their

school-desks, but has never seen, nor would have any way of really seeing, not even if they spent the treasures of Croesus. Next it offered the possibility of reconstructing landings and battles which have remained among the most memorable of those times, and which will be seen reproduced on the cinema screen not without trembling emotion. And, finally, the loves of Mark Antony and Cleopatra, besides being of themselves one of the most passionate subjects of history, lent themselves magnificently to the reconstruction of the life led at the sumptuous court of the Ptolemies, with scenes of intimacy full of fascination for their magnificence.[2]

For Guazzoni, what mattered was not so much the seductions instigated by a politically motivated and passionate queen, but the spectacle of Egypt—its magnificence and its conquest by Rome. In that respect, Guazzoni chose to promote an image for his film which showed a greater debt to the ancient, Roman sources on Cleopatra than that proposed by the later Hollywood publicity.

In different periods, cultures, and media, representations of the Ptolemaic queen Cleopatra VII and her relations to Rome have ceaselessly shifted in structure and meaning. Depictions of Cleopatra's encounters with Julius Caesar and Mark Antony, her departure from the battle of Actium, her suicide and the subsequent triumph of Octavian, have taken on many, diverse forms by virtue of, for example, specific technologies for the representation of the queen and distinct cultural conditions for viewing gender, race, empire, and female power. At the time of the battle of Actium itself, in 31 B.C., Cleopatra had already become two competing sets of images designed to validate either her rule or her overthrow. To her Egyptian subjects, in honorific titles, inscriptions, coins, temple reliefs, religious ceremonial, public spectacle, and oracular writings, Cleopatra VII was a loving daughter of her country and its previous kings, a protective and fertile mother-figure, a goddess, a liberator, and a messiah. The Ptolemaic queen came to symbolize resistance to the aggression of the West. She embodied a vengeful Asia who would conquer Rome and, with that victory, unify East and West. She was to establish a glorious world kingdom and initiate a golden age of peace. To Cleopatra's Roman enemies, however, in the propaganda disseminated by Octavian before the battle of Actium, in the ritual of the subsequent triumph, in contemporary Roman poetry, and in later historiography, the Egyptian queen was a barbaric debauchee, a whore, and a drunkard, the mistress of eunuchs. She was the eastern enemy of Rome and the embodiment of an effeminate Asia. She was represented as having seduced one Roman into her eastern ways only to be deservedly overcome by another. In Roman narratives, Octavian became the defender of Rome against the assaults of Egypt. He was the conqueror of Asia, and the founder of a new kingdom of peace and of Roman imperial rule.[3]

In the vicious propaganda campaign waged by Octavian before the battle of Actium, Cleopatra was constructed as an enticing but monstrous character who had lured Antony away from his proper Roman duties and thus endangered the welfare of the whole Roman state. That representation of the Egyptian queen and her Roman lover was then sustained and elaborated in the later histories of Plutarch and Cassius Dio. Plutarch's *Life of Antony* is a case study in the moral disintegration of its hero, whose love for Cleopatra is described as his life's "final and crowning evil."[4] The civil war between Octavian and Antony was restructured as a patriotic campaign to protect Italy from engulfment by an eastern queen who had already seduced, orientalized, and unmanned Mark Antony. Cleopatra became the embodiment of the quintessential adversary. In the twin discourses of ancient racism and sexism, she was marked as doubly Other—both Egyptian and Woman—and, therefore, doubly deserving of defeat by an Octavian who represented the restoration of the authority of Rome, the West, and the Male Principle. The narrative of Octavian's victory over the tyranny of Cleopatra, of Rome's triumph over Egypt, became a founding myth of western culture.[5] It is that myth of western victory over a feminized East which lies at the core of Enrico Guazzoni's silent film *Marcantonio e Cleopatra* (1913).

Shakespeare and Early Cinema

From antiquity, manifold representations of Cleopatra and her seductions have pervaded western culture in, for example, paintings, poetry, plays, operas, biographies, and historical novels, from tapestries to snuff boxes, from theatrical tragedies to music-hall sketches, from fancy-dress balls to cabaret acts.[6] But the title of Enrico Guazzoni's film, and its association with the Roman production house Cines, suggests at first that the primary source material for *Marcantonio e Cleopatra* was Shakespeare's canonical Roman play *Antony and Cleopatra*. In the early years of the film industry preceding the First World War, in the face of considerable hostility to the new medium, both European and American filmmakers transformed Shakespeare's plays into moving pictures as a means of demonstrating the significant contribution film could make to culture. The plays of Shakespeare were perceived as free source material of wide cultural circulation, familiar from numerous editions, school versions, theatrical productions, and even ephemera such as advertising. Both thrilling and culturally respectable, Shakespeare was powerfully attractive as source material for film production. Adaptations of his plays could be marketed not only as entertaining, but also as uplifting and educational. Such film adaptations selected the

most familiar phrases, scenes, and images from individual plays, constructed their mise-en-scène to accord with the Shakespearean iconography
established by play productions, and trumpeted their capacity to substitute
for Shakespearean dialogue the representation on screen of off-stage
action—the transformation of verse into spectacle.[7] George Méliès neatly
capped this defence of cinema in his last "Shakespeare" film of 1907, *Le
Rêve de Shakespeare* or *La Mort de Jules César* (commonly entitled in English,
Shakespeare Writing Julius Caesar).[8] There Shakespeare is himself the protagonist, unable to complete his script for Julius Caesar's murder until he is
inspired by a dreamlike apparition of the conspiracy and assassination.
Positioned like an early cinema spectator who watches the visual reconstruction of Roman history, the Shakespeare of Méliès is conveniently
inspired to the production of high culture by the magic of moving images.

In November 1908, a month before the launch of its controversial *Julius
Caesar*, the American Vitagraph Company released *Antony and Cleopatra*.
The film was structured, packaged, and consumed as an adaptation of
Shakespeare's play. The director, Charles Kent, had for some thirty years
previously played Shakespearean roles on the American stage. The action,
according to the research of the film historian Robert Hamilton Ball, con-
sisted of about a quarter of the play condensed on screen into thirteen
scenes. A favorable review (which Ball quotes from *Motion Picture World* of
7 November 1908) reads the Vitagraph film unequivocally as an attempt to
transform Shakespeare into moving images:

> If Shakespeare could only realize the fate of the works he left behind, the
> modern use of them would cause his prophetic soul to weep. Just think of it!
> Antony and Cleopatra given in its entirety, with the vocal parts and other
> details of the regular production cut out, in less than twenty minutes! What a
> vast difference between the older presentation and that represented by the
> modernized form of amusement. But with all the condensation, the magnifi-
> cence was retained, and I heard several in the audience say the film had cre-
> ated in them an appetite for more of the same kind. The Vitagraph company
> can take pride in the production.[9]

Like the Vitagraph Company, which continued its cycle of Shakespearean
one-reelers with, for example, *King Lear* (1909) and *Twelfth Night* (1910),
the Roman production house Cines had regularly released Shakespearean
adaptations before the launch of the feature-length film *Marcantonio e
Cleopatra* (1913). As the most prestigious film company of the time in Italy,
Cines rivaled Pathé and Gaumont for distribution of its films in the European film market and for their exportation to the United States. It exploited
the international cultural value, therefore, of a whole string of Shakespear-

ean productions such as *Romeo and Juliet* (1908), *Hamlet* (1908), *Othello* (1909), *Macbeth* (1909), *A Winter's Tale* (1910), *All's Well That Ends Well* (1912), and *A Comedy of Errors* (1912).[10] Consequently, by 1913, Cines had established a whole program of Shakespearean films to which *Marcantonio e Cleopatra* might have been a predicted addition.

According to Ball, some of the publicity for the American and the British launch of *Marcantonio e Cleopatra* packaged the film as Shakespearean,[11] yet when, for the Italian launch, Enrico Guazzoni described the merits of his production in the *Giornale d'Italia* (quoted above), the director demonstrated a greater interest in battles than passion, and in ancient places rather than tragic plot. According to Guazzoni (in the Italian press at any rate), the fidelity that needed to be secured was to ancient architecture and art rather than English literature:

> Every part of this reconstruction has been studied with the greatest scruple, on sites, in museums, in libraries. This research completed, a legion of artists and laborers from Cines patiently set to work reconstructing whole sections of cities, palaces, monuments, court-yards, halls, fountains, ponds, furniture, weapons and clothing, so that everything would be in keeping with the most absolute historical truth.[12]

Furthermore, the film text itself proves to be less grounded in the Shakespearean Cleopatra than in her refiguring within nineteenth-century, Orientalist discourses of empire.

Published around the beginning of the seventeenth century, Shakespeare's *Antony and Cleopatra* operates in a direct line of descent from Plutarch's *Life of Antony* (via Sir Thomas North's English rendition of the earlier French translation of Plutarch by Jacques Amyot). The play opens with a description of Antony as "The triple pillar of the world transformed / Into a strumpet's fool." Octavian's Rome, which Antony deserts, is depicted as a soldierly, asexual, masculine world. Cleopatra's Egypt, whose embrace Antony accepts, is depicted as a disorderly, passionate, and feminine world. But critics have observed how Shakespeare's representation of these contrasting domains is less censorious than that of Plutarch. Although the overall drive of the play may be towards a demonstration of the folly of passion, nevertheless, in the course of that demonstration, Octavia is colorless, Octavian ruthless, Antony great-hearted, and Cleopatra both captivating and majestic. Love is gifted with moments of sublimity, as Cleopatra recalls:

> Eternity was in our lips and eyes,
> Bliss in our brows' bent; none our parts so poor
> But was a race of heaven. [I.3][13]

Not only does the narrative of the film *Marcantonio e Cleopatra* bear little correspondence to the tragic plot of Shakespeare's play, but it also attempts to close down the kind of ambivalences that the drama manifests. Guazzoni's Cleopatra is visualized at the beginning of the film as a sinister enchantress (lit from below by the flames of a cauldron, she seeks out a love potion from an old witch around whom a snake slithers). At the close of the film, like the nineteenth-century killer-Cleopatras of Pietro Cossa, Victorien Sardou, or Rider Haggard, she has become a murderous sorceress (returning to the witch to obtain poisons which she proceeds to test out on her slaves).[14] The Roman Octavia, the touchstone of wifely virtue, is indignantly rebuffed by the mistress Cleopatra in a direct confrontation on Egyptian soil.[15] The romantic plot is shifted away from the figure of Cleopatra onto one of her innocent slave girls, who rescues Antony from a conspiracy of Egyptian courtiers only to be whipped and thrown to the crocodiles by a savagely jealous queen. Finally, the narrative closure of *Marcantonio e Cleopatra* exceeds the limits of Shakespeare's play. While *Antony and Cleopatra* concludes with Caesar (Octavian) pitying the dead lovers and giving orders for his army to attend their funeral in Alexandria, the film continues on to Rome where the Italian audiences of 1913 could witness the Roman leader parading on horseback in triumph, accompanied by fasces and standard bearers, trophies of shields and spears, and a procession of the vanquished. The final shot is of Octavian high up beneath a statue of winged victory, standing and saluting the cheering crowds. On this concluding image is imposed the Latin words "AVE ROMA IMMORTALIS" (Hail, Rome the Eternal City).[16]

The Italian Imperial Project

Guazzoni's *Marcantonio e Cleopatra* evidently shifts away from the strategy of Shakespearean adaptation and attempts to contain Cleopatra within a narrative of Roman conquest. The film's historiographic mode is connected to a wider set of discourses which had taken on a great intensity in Italy in the period leading up to the First World War—namely discourses of empire. From the time of unification, Italy had been constructed as legitimate heir to ancient Rome. *Romanità* was called upon both to supply the new state with a national identity and to affirm the importance of that state in Europe.[17] In September 1911, Italy declared war on Turkey and invaded the Ottoman provinces of Tripolitania and Cyrenaica (that is, modern Libya). A year later, when Turkey surrendered Libya, Italy at last could boast possession of a colony in north Africa. Before, during, and after the annexation of Libya, Rome and its ancient empire were appropriated by Italian imperialists as a validation of Italy's territorial expansion into Africa.

Thus Giovanni Pascoli, when advancing toward Ain Zara in Libya on 26 November 1911, was said to have proclaimed:

> O Tripoli, O Beronike, O Leptis Magna . . . you see again, after so many centuries, Doric columns and Roman legions! Look above you: even the eagles are there![18]

The discourse of historical continuity between the Roman conquests in Africa and the victory of the modern Italian state circulated widely, and the Italian film industry, with its already thriving reconstructions of Roman history, played a significant role in further disseminating this conception of a modern Italian empire arising out of the rediscovered traces of ancient Rome,[19] and the cinematic narration of Cleopatra's defeat became a uniquely appropriate vehicle for both the legitimation and the celebration of Italy as once again mistress of the Mediterranean.

Already in antiquity, the narration of Antony's supposed subjection to Cleopatra had been teleologically structured to lead to the just triumph of Rome over Egypt. But the cinematic representation of that triumph could also draw on the much more recent refiguring of Cleopatra and her kingdom within a nineteenth-century "colonialist imaginary."[20] As the western nations looked to occupy the fragmenting Ottoman empire, there was a significant series of adjustments to the Cleopatra narrative and an adscription to it of fresh currency. In her survey of western traditions for representing the Ptolemaic queen, Lucy Hughes-Hallett delineates the numerous ways in which Cleopatra was refigured in the nineteenth-century European imagination as an Orient inviting penetration.[21] A bronze medallion struck in 1826 to commemorate the completed publication of Baron Denon's influential *Description de l'Égypte* displays on the obverse the Napoleonic invasion of Egypt which had taken place in 1789. The Napoleonic campaign constituted a defining moment in the development of the discourse of Orientalism—the western mechanism (as Edward Said characterizes it) for dominating, restructuring, and having authority over the East.[22] On the medallion, France is seen to take possession of an Ottoman province in the guise of a Roman general unveiling a bare-breasted Egyptian queen. She lies reclining passively on a crocodile, before a cluttered scene of pyramids, palm trees, and temple reliefs, gazing up at the conquering Roman—a Cleopatra on display before Julius Caesar, Mark Antony, or, most suitably, Octavian.[23] [illustration 4.1] Appropriated for orientalism, Cleopatra authorizes the articulation of the Orient as Woman, as separate from and subservient to the Occident. Feminized, the Orient can take on, under a gendered western gaze, a feminine allure and penetrability. The colonialist project is provided with an

4.1   France unveils Egypt, bronze medallion of 1826. [Courtesy of Peter A. Clayton.]

ancient and successful precedent, and geographical conquest of a land is nat-
uralized as sexual possession of a woman's body.[24]

Late nineteenth-century orientalism generated "a systematic accumulation of human beings and territories" not just through their domination by
western armies and administrations, but also through their visual reproduction within western culture.[25] From paintings and drawings to magic-
lantern shows, dioramas, and panoramas, from photography on into the
new medium of cinema itself, there was an explosion of images of the
Orient. The spectacle of Egypt, particularly in France and Great Britain,
became an extension of the colonialist project of mapping and photograph-
ing and classifying the country in order to claim ownership of it. Thus, in
the 1840s, Britain opened up an overland trade route to India which crossed
Egyptian soil. Shortly after, British audiences were treated to the spectacle
of a panoramic trip up the river Nile provided for them in the comfort of
the Egyptian Hall in London. Alexandria, Cairo, and Suez all appeared as
moving images.[26] The mechanisms of nineteenth-century Orientalism
transformed Cleopatra into a spectacle to be desired and possessed by
watching Europe. In Jean-Léon Gérôme's *Cleopatra before Caesar* (1866), a
crouching attendant unwraps a bare-breasted Cleopatra from her carpet for
display before the discerning eyes of both Caesar and the painting's viewer.
[illustration 4.2] In Lawrence Alma-Tadema's *Antony and Cleopatra* (1883),
the queen appears in the foreground languidly awaiting possession by an
approaching Antony. In both paintings, as on the earlier medallion, the
visual accumulation of exotic clutter around the body of Cleopatra—the
dark-complexioned attendants, the leopard skins and silks, the animal-

4.2 Gérôme's painting of *Cleopatra before Caesar* (1866). [Courtesy of the Mansell Collection.]

headed idols, the Pharaonic architecture and hieroglyphs—also operates as
a western claim to ownership (through visual reproduction) of a mysterious
and ancient Egypt.[27]

The new medium of film emerged during the height of Europe's imperial project between the late nineteenth-century and the beginning of the
First World War.[28] The colonizing power of cinema, and the Cleopatra narrative in particular, does not appear to have escaped the Cines production
house or the director Enrico Guazzoni. Cines was controlled by the Banco
di Roma, which held a number of investments in North Africa. During the
Libyan campaign of 1911–1912, the Italian production house released documentaries on Egypt along with footage of the Libyan war zone. The following year, its historical film *Marcantonio e Cleopatra* opened with actual shots
of Pharaonic monuments borrowed from Cines documentaries such as
Paesaggi egiziani and *Regno dei Faraoni*. The camera pans around the
avenue of ram-headed lions (or *criosphinxes*) at Karnak, and roams over a
series of temple ruins, statues, and a pyramid, before initiating the historical
narrative proper with the disembarkation of Antony's Roman troops on
Egyptian shores.[29] The film literally cannot escape a colonialist intertext.
The documentary footage helps to authenticate the ensuing historical
reconstruction but, positioned within a narrative of Roman conquest, the
footage is itself authenticated as a display of Italian territorial possession.
The historical film, and the narrative image of it promulgated in the Italian
press by Guazzoni, also discloses what has been called colonialist cinema's
"visual infatuation with Egypt's material abundance."[30] The director
parades, and draws attention to the parade of, "the most distinctive places of
ancient Rome and ancient Egypt." The painstaking labor involved in reconstructing "the sumptuous court of the Ptolemies" is emphasized both in the
press and in the film's mise-en-scène, which is cluttered with reproductions
of Egyptian architecture and artefacts. This reproduction of the Egyptian
past suppresses the colonial conditions of the Libyan present, and the narration of Octavian's victory in Egypt invites the Italian spectator of 1913 on a
visit to an Orient that has long since been won.

In *Marcantonio e Cleopatra*, the narrative of Cleopatra's seduction of
Antony is embedded within a spectacle of politically resonant landscapes,
monuments, *and* troop movements. Parades of Roman troops appear on
numerous occasions and for long sequences of the film. The skill and care
with which Enrico Guazzoni attended to the scenography of warfare—the
location shooting, artificial lighting, camera movement, and crowd control—were highly praised in reviews of the film, both in Italy and abroad.
In *The Moving Picture World* of 10 January 1914, for example, James
McQuade wrote:

Superb scenes are the fall of Alexandria before Octavius; his triumphal entry afterwards at Rome; the landing of the Roman troops in Egypt by moonlight; the long and silent march to Alexandria. . . . What terrific scenes are shown on the lofty flight of steps leading up to the royal palace entrance, and on the Nile within the city! The carnage has all the show of blood and death. The Cines supernumeraries—and there are 3500 of them in the scene showing the fall of Alexandria—are really a marvellous force. Seldom, if ever, do they fail to do the right thing, in the right way, at the right time; and this, it must be remembered, is largely due to able direction. . . . Those beautiful moonlight effects, taken in the eye of the sun, in the afternoon of a cloudy day, with a veiled lens, are so convincing and artistic that one must cry "bravo!". I refer to the scenes showing the landing of the Roman troops in Egypt and to the showing of the beginning of their march to Alexandria. One of these scenes is finely tinted, and gives the effect of an exquisite and gigantic land and sea view in water colors.[31]

The central segments of *Marcantonio e Cleopatra*, however, offer its audiences a lesson in how to read such beautifully crafted troop movements morally.

The moral disintegration of Antony, and his oriental entrapment, is marked externally by Amleto Novelli's costume changes in the course of the film, from commanding Roman soldier in military uniform, to romantic Roman civilian in a toga, to subservient "Egyptian" in Pharaonic headdress and robe. Cross-cutting neatly juxtaposes Antony's life of leisure and subservience at the savage, feminine Ptolemaic court with Octavian's life of authority at the just, masculine Senate House at Rome and Octavian's life of activity commanding the Roman troops on their way to war and victory. The message that Roman civilization is about to triumph over Egyptian barbarity is clearly signaled by the anachronistic presence on screen of a quotation from Virgil's *Aeneid*, seen engraved around the Senate wall high above the heads of the senators as they vote for war in Africa. In Virgil's famous definition of Rome's imperial mission, Aeneas is told

> but yours will be the rulership of nations,
> remember, Roman, these will be your arts:
> to teach the ways of peace to those you conquer,
> to spare defeated peoples, tame the proud.
> [*Aeneid* 6.851–3.][32]

The Roman conception of its civilizing mission was used as a constant cover in all the history of Italian expansionism, even at the official level of Italy's ultimatum to Turkey in September 1911, when Italy was presented as providing Tripolitania and Cyrenaica with the *civiltà* which Turkey had denied them.[33] Significantly, in the Senate House sequence of *Marcantonio e Cleopatra*, only part of the last line of the Virgilian mission appears visible in the film frame (E SUBIECTIS ET DEBELLA). The injunction "to spare" is missing.

The closure of *Marcantonio e Cleopatra*, in order to keep the moral high ground for ancient Rome (and thus, by extension, for modern Italy), works to diminish any pathos or majesty which might accrue to the suicide of Cleopatra and the defeat of Egypt. In the final moments of Shakespeare's play, Charmian famously comments that her mistress' suicide was "Well done, and fitting for a princess," and Caesar, when he catches sight of her body, says of Cleopatra

> Bravest at the last,
> She levelled at our purposes and, being royal,
> Took her own way. [V.2]

As if in defiance of the Shakespearean tradition, the intertitle in *Marcantonio e Cleopatra* which follows on Octavian's discovery of Cleopatra's body declares "truly an inglorious ending for the last of the Ptolemies, the setting of Egypt's star salutes the dawn of Roman rule."[34] The final shot of *Marcantonio e Cleopatra*, in which Octavian's triumphant parade through Rome dissolves into a salutation to the "immortal" city, provides a further key to the political resonance of this film for the Italy of the 1910s. It also suggests why Italian audiences in 1913 might have viewed the troop movements of the film with a "trembling emotion" that was not generated purely by the aesthetic perfection of the military reconstructions. If Rome is eternal, then (in the historical film's terms) what endures for ever is a glorious military victory over the Orient. The cinematic language of justification for Octavian's conquest of Egypt, the necessity of saving Rome from oriental emasculation and depravity, can easily translate into a justification for and celebration of the more recent conquest of Libya. Italy's current imperial project here, as elsewhere, is sustained by an appeal to Roman origins and historical continuity: modern Italy is doing nothing less than carrying on Rome's civilizing mission.

The Oriental Seductions of Cinema

Marcantonio e Cleopatra was a huge commercial success, both in Italy and abroad. From the end of 1913 and during the course of 1914, it was distributed throughout Europe, the United States, Latin America, Russia, Asia,

Africa, and Australia, often accompanied by grand premieres, huge quantities of publicity, and enthusiastic accolades.[35] While reviewers at the time of the film's release dwelt largely on the fine cinematography and careful historical reconstructions of *Marcantonio e Cleopatra*, a year or so later the film critic Vachel Lindsay drew attention to the imperialist ambition that underlies Guazzoni's display of ancient sites, oriental magnificence, and battles on African soil. According to Lindsay, Guazzoni's historical film "is equivalent to waving the Italian above the Egyptian flag, quite slowly for two hours."[36] It would be a mistake, however, to read *Marcantonio e Cleopatra* as unequivocally and unifocally imperialist in design. Italian reviewers and Enrico Guazzoni himself, when commenting on the film in the Italian press, focused explicitly on the film's artistic merits rather than its political ambitions. The film was largely discussed as an attempt to improve upon the cinematographic virtuosity of Guazzoni's earlier success in historical reconstruction, *Quo Vadis?* (1913).

Before the emergence of cinema, its ancestral forms (panoramas, dioramas, magic-lantern shows, and photography) were frequently utilized for the visual reproduction of Egypt within western culture. The material culture of Egypt, meanwhile, gained the status of a silent and mysterious spectacle as ancient tombs were excavated, interpreted, and exhibited throughout the nineteenth century and into the twentieth. From the advent of cinema, its form and content were linked with the discursive constructs of Egyptology. The blackened enclosure of the silent cinema auditorium was assimilated to the dark depth of the Egyptian necropolis, and that assimilation was reinforced through the use of a pseudo-Egyptian architectural style in the construction of some of the new moving-picture palaces. Like a western traveler to the monuments of ancient Egypt, the cinema spectator entered a silent world which spoke through pictorial images akin to hieroglyphs, and saw a kind of immortality preserved on screen akin to the secrets of mummification. The constructs of Egyptology explained, legitimated, and conceptualized the new medium, lending cinema mystery, grandeur, history, and an artistic aura.[37] Reconstructions of ancient Egypt on screen, therefore, could acquire a self-reflexive status as celebrations of cinema's quasi-archaeological powers. With regard to *Marcantonio e Cleopatra*, the skillful reconstructions of ancient Egypt, and discussion of them in the press, drew attention to and celebrated the operations of Italian cinema, and arguably positioned the film's spectators not just as conquering Romans but also as Romans surrendering to the oriental splendors of film spectacle itself.

The film's representation of Cleopatra, moreover, does not consistently promote a narrative drive towards the just triumph of Octavian. At one point, for example, Cleopatra visualizes the coming Roman victory and reels back in horror as she watches togaed crowds jeering a procession which includes herself and her bound Egyptian subjects. It is this vision of public humiliation that compels her to suicide. Thus, juxtaposed with the final scene of Octavian's victory parade at Rome, film spectators are offered, for at least a brief moment, Cleopatra's tragic point of view. Beyond the film text, the Italian actress who played the Egyptian queen (Gianna Terribili Gonzales) sometimes promoted *Marcantonio e Cleopatra* through personal appearances at screenings or in magazine interviews, since erotic display of the female body was not an insignificant attraction of the film.[38] [illustration 4.3] Her use as a promotional vehicle further restructured the cinematic Cleopatra into a pleasurably seductive but sadly tragic figure with whom the actress could then claim much sympathy. Both the Egypt reconstructed by Guazzoni, and the Cleopatra performed and disseminated by Terribili Gonzales, exceed the requirements of representational conquest.

In the particular case of Cleopatra, Roman history provided the film industry with a narrative of great cultural prestige, with a seemingly momentous justification for cinematic eroticism and the spectacle of the female body, and with a biography that could be appropriated to shape and enhance the public personae of some of cinema's earliest female stars. In 1914, in the same year that Gianna Terribili Gonzales expressed a passing sympathy with the figure of Cleopatra, the Fox film studio inititated a far more elaborate and sustained association with the queen and her kingdom for the actress Theodosia Goodman. Her public image was designed to introduce American audiences to a cinematic character which had been successfully launched a few years earlier by the Danish film industry, namely the dangerous yet alluring "vamp"—the modern woman of the 1910s who ruthlessly seduces men, draining them, in the process, of their will and their blood.[39] The vamp persona created for the actress (now renamed Theda Bara) was heavily invested in orientalist structures of meaning.

Nineteenth-century Orientalism was a discourse of desire as well as empire. It troped the relationship between West and East as one of sexual dominance, and represented the western soldier, explorer, or scholar as penetrating either inviting virginal landscape or resisting, libidinal Nature. The Orient, therefore, suggested sexual promise or threat.[40] Offering a ready-made gendered narrative of oriental temptation, seduction, and conquest, the Cleopatras of the nineteenth-century were often figured as capable of affording transcendent, terrifying sexual pleasures to their lovers. In an act of identification rather than possession, many would-be femmes fatales chose to enhance their own attractions by adopting some of those which had accrued to Cleopatra. Thus Sarah Bernhardt, who performed the role of Cleopatra in productions of Victorien Sardou's play, claimed that the snakes she used on stage in the death scene were live and kept in her house

4.3 Poster advertising Gianna Terribili Gonzales in *Marcantonio e Cleopatra* (1913).
[From private collection of Vittorio Martinelli.]

adorned with jewels. She walked, it was said, a crocodile on a leash. In the
1910s, as the star system emerged and was exploited to market films, cinema
appropriated and then elaborated the personae of nineteenth-century theatrical stars such as Bernhardt for a new kind of "diva."[41]

4.4 Poster advertising Theda Bara in *Cleopatra* (1917). [Photograph from private collection of Maria Wyke.]

From 1914, Theda Bara began to play film roles as a woman who uses a man sexually and then abandons him for her next victim. At the same time, the Fox studio wrapped Bara up in Orientalist publicity. Her name was hailed as an anagram of Arab death. Although the actress was the daughter of a Jewish tailor from Cincinnati, publicity releases from Fox claimed that she was born in Egypt and, as an infant, sucked the venom of serpents. While the actress lived with her parents, the Fox publicists generated a star image for Bara as a heartbreaker, a "torpedo of domesticity," whose dark and voluptuous beauty would bring "suffering and ruin to thousands of sturdy laborers and their families." She was photographed surrounded by skulls and snakes to advertise the film *A Fool There Was* (1914), and in a *Photoplay* article of September 1915 she was described as a "daughter of the sphinx." The culmination and apparent legitimation of this procedure, whereby a Hollywood studio articulated the vamp's aggressive eroticism in Orientalist terms, came with the release of *Cleopatra* in 1917. Directed by J. Gordon Edwards, the historical film was a vehicle for the display of Theda Bara's sensual exoticism. [illustration 4.4] The Fox publicity bureau (ostensibly reproducing the words of a fan) now identified Cleopatra as "the most famous vamp in history" and Theda Bara as her "reincarnation." On advertising posters, Bara's face was superimposed over that of a sphinx.[42]

Orientalism gave the Hollywood film industry an array of defensive mechanisms with which to assuage concerns about the modern woman of the 1910s: she is an age-old riddle, the "eternal feminine," as indecipherable as the sphinx.[43] The Cleopatra narrative, in particular, provided both an exotic setting within which to locate a tantalizing spectacle of transgressive female sexuality, and an inescapable closure which appeared safely to contain that sexuality. With this shift of emphasis from imperialism towards gender and sexuality, the Hollywood representation of Cleopatra became an account of a woman as much as a war, and its visual pleasures became the spectacle of erotic seductions as much as military maneuvers. Centering its narrative around the Egyptian queen, the Fox studio trebled the number of her seductions. Audiences of *Cleopatra* (1917) could witness not only the queen's sumptuous strategies for enticing Antony on board her barge at Cydnus, but also the unveiling of her physical charms before Julius Caesar in the palace at Alexandria, as well as her captivation of the Egyptian Pharon (a character inherited from an earlier *Cleopatra* released in 1913 by the Helen Gardner Picture Players). A review in *Motion Picture News* of 3 November 1917 imagines the thought-processes of a man on leaving the cinema where he has just seen Theda Bara's Cleopatra in action:

His mind will drift back to the first half of the picture when Miss Bara wore a different costume in every episode. Different pieces of costume rather; or better still different varieties of beads. His temperature will ascend with a jump when he recalls the easy way in which the siren captivated Caesar and Pharon and Antony. If he knows the picture business he may wonder about Pennsylvania and Chicago and other places with censor boards that have no appreciation for the female form in a state that so nearly approaches nudeness that only a few strings of beads stand in the way. He might suddenly realize that his mother back in Hohokus would shut her eyes once or twice for fear the beads might break or slip, but then—mother never did understand Egyptian history after all.

The Hollywood Cleopatras of subsequent eras did not continue to be shaped along the contours of an exotic and destructive vamp. With, for example, the further development of the Hollywood star system and the classical Hollywood style of film production, with the advent of the new technology of sound, with the rise of consumerism, and the increased entry of women into the public domain, the Hollywood Cleopatra came to be structured along the lines of a figure who lived inside rather than outside the borders of the United States. She was now glamorous rather than outlandish, to be watched, desired, consumed, and even identified with, rather than overwhelmingly defeated. And the excess and seductiveness of her spectacle-making now operated more readily as a self-reflexive metaphor for the excess and seductiveness of America's Orient within, that is, Hollywood itself.

The Mysteries of the New Woman

From the late 1910s and throughout the 1920s, Orientalism suffused the contemporary sexual comedies directed by Cecil B. DeMille. *Don't Change Your Husband* (1919) dealt with a bored wife who temporarily abandons the dissatisfactions of her marriage for the luxurious world of a gigolo. The artwork employed to promote the film included the image of a sphinx and a pyramid, and the title "The Eternal Feminine," in order to advertise a concern with the question of what the "New Woman" wanted. The perceived problem of female self-gratification was associated with the mystery and the antiquity of Egypt.[44]

"New Woman" was a term that circulated in America from the 1890s. Its coinage signaled a recognition of and debate about an evident shift away from the Victorian conception of a woman's sphere of operation as tied to the home and the family. From the 1890s on into the 1930s, there occurred a growth of labor mobility in the United States, a significant increase in the proportion of women in paid labor, and a dramatic rise in wealth and in the purchase of consumer goods such as cars, leisure activities, cosmetics, and home furnishings. DeMille's sexual comedies of the silent era projected on screen the radical changes in family and sexual life that accompanied these developments, such as an increase in pre- and extra-marital sex, and in rates of divorce. By the 1920s, when American women had achieved general suffrage and were campaigning for legalized birth control and for an equal rights amendment to the constitution, DeMille was pioneering a fresh marital ethics for Hollywood cinema. DeMille's New Woman, on gaining access to the new middle-class life style of conspicuous consumption and secular hedonism, is, by the close of each film, safely restored to marriage as a fashion plate and passionate sexual playmate.[45] In several of these films, historical flashbacks, such as a Babylonian fantasy in *Male and Female* (1919) or a Roman orgy in *Manslaughter* (1922), provide both wish-fulfillment and warning. Scenes set in the ancient world give an opportunity for more ostentatious display than the contemporary ones into which they are inserted. Historical flashbacks also provide a suitably salutary lesson for the present, since the films imply that it is the sexual and material excess exhibited in these sequences which once led to the downfall of civilizations.[46]

When DeMille's *Cleopatra* was released in 1934, journalists frequently commented on the modernity and humor of its dialogue, as if the director had produced yet another sexual comedy about a modern woman, but this time set entirely in antiquity. A review in the *New York Times* of 17 August 1934 observed that

> When a gathering of Roman women are talking about Caesar, it is done in the modern fashion, with one of the fair ones remarking that "the wife always is the last to hear" of her husband's love affairs.

In the censorious judgment of *Variety* for 21 August 1934, the same Roman social gathering was played, ill-advisedly, "like a modern bridge night," and Claudette Colbert, in the role of Cleopatra, conducted herself like "a cross between a lady of the evening and a rough soubrette in a country melodrama." It was not only the colloquial dialogue of *Cleopatra* that appeared to elide any significant distinction between the social habits of the past and those of the American present. The film was a product of Paramount, a studio whose house style derived from its success in producing and distributing DeMille's contemporary romantic comedies throughout the 1920s. During the 1930s, Paramount became celebrated for its production of an array of elegant comedies, characterized by witty scripts and an opulent mise-en-scène.[47]

Director and dialogue, studio and casting all helped to mark *Cleopatra* (1934) as a comedy of modern manners in fancy dress. The casting policy for the film, especially regarding the opening half where Warren William is seen playing Julius Caesar, connects the scenes in ancient Rome with contemporary life in New York. For the star images of both William and Colbert, by which audiences would have been attracted into the cinema to see *Cleopatra*, included their previous appearances on screen as members of urban America's smart set. William was already famous for taking on roles as a refined New Yorker, and Claudette Colbert had just played a sophisticated modern wife in the Academy Award–winning *It Happened One Night* (1934).[48]

Some of the promotional material which followed the release of *Cleopatra* even drew explicit attention to DeMille's cinematic modernization of the ancient Romans and Egyptians, and attempted to solicit from its young addressees a suitably prestigious justification for that process. Paramount set up a contest for college students and high-school seniors offering prizes, or "Cleopatra scholarships," of five hundred dollars each for the three essays which best responded to a range of questions the studio posed concerning the film director's treatment of history. Question 44 of the *Study Guide and Manual* (which Paramount published to launch the contest) asked:

> R. H. Case calls Shakespeare's "Antony and Cleopatra" "an extraordinarily vivid presentment in Elizabethan terms of events and characters of the ancient world." Would it be fair to describe DeMille's "Cleopatra" as "an extraordinarily vivid presentment in *American* terms of events and characters of the ancient world?" Justify your answer.[49]

Although DeMille's *Cleopatra* was closely bound, both in its production and packaging, to the representation of contemporary American social mores, the Egyptian setting and the Cleopatra narrative were not arbitrary points of historical reference. Reviewers placed the film's visual style—its exhibition of spectacular historical reconstructions and opulent production values—in the tradition of DeMille's biblical epics *The Ten Commandments* (1923), *King of Kings* (1927), and *Sign of the Cross* (1932). Those biblical epics had been made in a climate of ever-increasing concern about the moral content and effects of Hollywood films. According to the Republican reformer Will Hays, at the time of his appointment by the majors in 1922 as an internal regulator of the film industry, films had to be made "giving the public all the sex it wants with compensating values for all those church and women groups." DeMille is regarded as having found a shrewd film formula to meet Hays' requirements during the 1920s, namely romantic triangles, spiced with liberal displays of sex and consumption, and diluted by the triumph of marriage at the film's close.[50] The early years of the Depression, however, witnessed a proliferation of films visualizing (and *talking* about) divorce, adultery, prostitution, crime, and violence, despite the installation in 1930 of a formal Production Code which stipulated that the Hollywood studios should promote the institutions of marriage and the home.[51] When DeMille released *Sign of the Cross* in 1932, he might have anticipated that he could display sex, nudity, arson, homosexuality, lesbianism, mass murder, and orgies relatively uncontentiously, for they were all clothed in religious history and all marked as pagan depravities, nobly scorned or endured by the heroine and (ultimately) the hero, who are seen in the closing moments of the film virtuously conjoined as they ascend into the blazing light of Christian salvation. But, however pious the film's conclusion, and despite its enormous box-office success, the spectacular sex and sadism of *Sign of the Cross* exacerbated the already intensifying debate over the morality of motion pictures.[52] *Cleopatra* was released in July 1934, just three months after the Catholic Church had launched its pressure group the Legion of Decency, which pledged millions of Catholics to boycott films judged immoral. In the same month as the release of *Cleopatra*, the film industry felt compelled to appoint a lay Catholic as head of a new Production Code Administration, with considerably greater powers to police the content of Hollywood films and to enforce adherence to the Code.[53] In the face of a more restrictive Production Code, the historicity of *Cleopatra* provided DeMille with a less objectionable formula than that of *Sign of the Cross* with which to attract spectators.

In *Sign of the Cross*, Claudette Colbert had played Poppaea, the sultry and sadistic wife of the emperor Nero, who attempts to seduce the Prefect of Rome and kill off the Christian girl for whom the Prefect rejects her. By the following year, the persona of another Paramount star might have appeared better to embody the sexual revolution of the last decade. In her film roles, Mae West played a raucously independent woman, who initiated seductions and outsmarted men. But by 1934 West's earlier films were taken out of circulation, and her new ones, such as *It Ain't No Sin*, were rigorously vetted, turning her character into a moderately bad girl on her way to redemption.[54] In such a charged climate, the Cleopatra narrative offered DeMille and the Paramount studio an opportunity to display yet again the sexually transgressive behavior of a woman now dressed in the dignity of magnificent historical necessity and illustrious literary precedent, and safely distanced in the past and the oriental elsewhere.[55] The seductions of Colbert/Cleopatra were now displayed in a milder and more indirect form than those of Colbert/Poppaea, and they received their proper punishment at the film's close. Encased in a secular narrative, they were also less likely to aggravate the powerful lobbying forces of organized American religion.

Cleopatra was thus a highly appropriate vehicle for the exploration, without considerable censure, of contemporary concerns about gender, sexuality, and ethnicity in 1930s America.

The constituents of the Cleopatra narrative were also highly resonant and expressive points of historical reference for the 1930s. Between the two World Wars, with the increasing entry of women into the public domain and an associated intensification of debates about women's roles, there was a significant increase in the number of western reassessments of the queen's reign. For, in Cleopatra's representations, an active female sexuality *and* political power were problematically combined.[56] An academic redefinition of Cleopatra had already begun in 1864, with the publication of a biography defending the queen by the German historian Adolf Stahr. His work was followed by a series of histories and novels which ridiculed the Roman portrait of a wicked seductress, such as Arthur Weigall's *The Life and Times of Cleopatra* (1914). Following Stahr, *The Life and Times* drew attention to Cleopatra's political vision of a pan-Hellenic empire subsuming East and West.[57] During the course of the 1930s, among an array of plays, novels, and biographies about the queen,[58] a corresponding reaction to these revisions surfaced with, for example, Oscar von Wertheimer's *Cleopatra—A Royal Voluptuary* (published in an English translation three years before the release of DeMille's film). Included in the preface to Wertheimer's biography was the remark that "we judge men by their achievements and women by the love they have inspired."[59]

Paramount's *Study Guide* for the college-age audiences of DeMille's *Cleopatra* clearly engages with this historical debate and comes down expressly in favor of Wertheimer's cruel voluptuary. In the studio's promotional literature, despite references to Shakespeare, Dryden, and Shaw as source material, Wertheimer's becomes the master text against which to test the veracity of DeMille's film adaptation. Contestants for the "Cleopatra scholarship" are encouraged to read Wertheimer before responding to the set questions, passages from *The Royal Voluptuary* are quoted (including criticism of Weigall), and several scenes or characterizations in the film are justified as carrying out Wertheimer's conception of events. Following the historical model offered by Wertheimer enables Paramount's *Study Guide* to describe Cleopatra's political policies as an example of the "unbridled ambition of women to attain power," and thus to articulate contemporary anxieties about public roles for women.[60]

The orientalist structures of meaning which refigured the representation of Cleopatra from the time of the Napoleonic campaigns in Egypt, and persisted into her cinematic depictions in the silent era of the early twentieth-century, also bolster the expression of contemporary social concerns in

DeMille's *Cleopatra*. The film's first image is of two stones drawn back like curtains to reveal the action behind them, its last image that of the stones drawn together to conceal the preceding spectacle. Cleopatra's story is thus framed both as spectacle and as penetration of the oriental mysteries of Woman, for the stones first open to reveal Cleopatra in a desert landscape tied to a monument covered in hieroglyphs and close on an image of the queen silent, remote and majestic in death, enthroned in the royal palace at Alexandria.[61]

Before *Cleopatra*, however, orientalism had already suffused DeMille's cinematic practice, as a means to mark out not just a new and troubling feminine identity, but also a new and troubling ethnic identity. In sectors of the American urban communities of the early twentieth-century, concern about the arrival of new immigrants from outside Europe was assimilated to concern about the increased public authority of women, since both were construed equally as threats to the existing social formation. Both "modern" women and new immigrants were often figured cinematically in orientalist terms. As the collective urban Other, they were set in an exotic mise-en-scène and characterized as having a taste for sybaritic luxury or depraved sex.[62] In the first part of DeMille's *Cleopatra*, the Egyptian queen seduces Julius Caesar in Alexandria and then comes to Rome, where Caesar is planning to divorce his wife Calpurnia, set himself up as king, and make Cleopatra his queen. Interlinked with wider discourses of gender and ethnicity, DeMille's representation of the oriental queen's arrival in Rome and her impact on the Romans had a special hold on urban American audiences of the 1930s, for the United States is a society where ethnic composition and immigration exist at the core of its historical and cultural formation.[63]

In the Roman sequences of DeMille's *Cleopatra*, at the dinner party (which *Variety* scathingly compares to "a modern bridge night"), the gossip concerns Julius Caesar's rumored divorce and his designs to convert the republic into a monarchy. During Cleopatra's ensuing triumphal procession through the streets of Rome, when the more familiar images of Julius Caesar's Roman soldiers and chariots, trumpets and magisterial *fasces* are swiftly supplanted by the bizarre music, black attendants, animal iconography, and canopied sedan of the enthroned queen, cinema audiences are offered the opportunity to identify with the Roman crowds on screen who have cheered their Roman leader but observe the arrival of his Egyptian mistress in bemused silence. In subsequent scenes, at the Roman baths and in the house of Julius Caesar, first the conspirators and then Mark Antony express volubly their anxieties about the malign influences now exerting themselves on Caesar and the city at large. Rome, they protest, cannot become an oriental city ruled by a frivolous queen. Julius Caesar, they complain, has been domesticated and made ridiculous by a woman. In these film sequences, Rome is characterized as a republican, masculine world, where women are domesticated wives and only men have political authority. That world is perceived to be under threat from the tyrannical, feminine world of Egypt, where women are rulers of both the state and their menfolk.[64] The first half of DeMille's *Cleopatra* thus acts out an extreme version of a current fear that the social fabric of modern America is endangered.

The long-standing and widely disseminated practice of utilizing the virtues of the Roman republic to underscore the heroism of America's Founding Fathers[65] enhances the spectator's competence to read the film's appalled Romans as historical analogies for the old Anglo-aristocracy of America's cities now threatened by the arrival of an urban Other.[66] Set in antiquity, the urban Other is refigured as foreign, decadent, and dangerous, and any attempt to master the city as doomed to failure, since spectators already know that Cleopatra's stratagems will not succeed—Julius Caesar will be assassinated and the queen will be forced ignominiously to leave the city. Historical analogy thus fosters an hyperbolic articulation of gender and ethnic conflicts in terms of the rescue of a city and a civilization from corruption.

The second half of DeMille's *Cleopatra* increases and then appears to remove the fears articulated in the first half concerning the challenge posed to traditional gender roles by the advent of the New Woman. The Marc Antony who, in the earlier Roman sequences, had bitterly protested that both Caesar and the Roman eagle had been tamed by a woman, and who had concluded the first half of the film with a declaration that he would take vengeance for Rome on the Egyptian, is himself vanquished by her. Through the use of DeMille's visual system of objective correlatives,[67] Antony is represented as engulfed and unmanned by a woman's body in the sequence where the Roman visits Cleopatra's barge at Tarsus. When Antony enters the feminine ship, he passes between a double line of women waving soft fans to reach within a Cleopatra who reclines before a vulvaic mass of plumes. On the way to being sexually possessed by the queen—a "gorgeous piece of cinematic euphemism" involving the rhythmic thrusting and retracting of her ship's banks of oars[68]—Antony loses all the emblems of his Roman virility, namely his soldier's helmet, his huge wolfhounds, and his upright stance.

The conservative narrative drive of DeMille's *Cleopatra* later restores Antony reassuringly to full manhood and Cleopatra to a very traditionally conceived femininity. When news reaches Antony in Alexandria that the Romans have declared war, he springs to attention again as an aggressive Roman general. At that precise moment, Cleopatra falls to her knees and, with the camera looking down on her, declares "I've seen a god come to life.

I'm no longer a queen. I'm a woman."[69] Through dialogue, camera angle, and gesture, cinema spectators witness the empowerment of Antony and Cleopatra's submission to love. In the concluding sequences of the film, Cleopatra now works not in the interests of her country but of her man. The second half of DeMille's *Cleopatra* thus displays a minatory vision of the New Woman only to contain her eventually within the safe bounds of conventional romance.[70] Once again the message that social order could be disrupted by modern women's claims to political and sexual freedom is made more rhetorically pointed by the use of historical analogy. The lesson that New Women are dangerous but defeatable is lent an air of authority and venerability by its apparent antiquity.[71]

Off-screen Cleopatras

Filmic representations of Cleopatra cannot, nor would they want to, limit her significance to the espousal of imperialism or patriarchy. The cinematic tradition for depicting Cleopatra has often closed with the defeat of the oriental queen, but, at the same time, it has lingered lovingly over her attractions. Thus DeMille's *Cleopatra* (unlike Guazzoni's *Marcantonio e Cleopatra*) is framed as the story of the queen, not her Roman opponents. The characterization of Cleopatra through casting, dialogue and gesture, camera work and lighting, often invites audience identification with her.[72] In the barge sequence, for example, DeMille's "Rembrandt style" of film aesthetics provides highlighted close-ups of Cleopatra's face as we are made privy to a clever double bluff by which she entertainingly seduces a gruff and naive Antony.[73] At the end of the film, moreover, its diegetic world is left in suspended animation as DeMille's camera slowly recedes from the visually opulent image of a motionless Egyptian queen clothed in full Pharaonic costume, enthroned on high in the royal palace beneath a giant winged scarab. The closure of *Cleopatra* (1934) reveals an evident conflict between the film's narrative and stylistic codes. DeMille's distinctive visual style in this film, as in many of his earlier films, consists of furnishing rich details of glamorous costumes and decor, and in figuring the New Woman as herself a seductive spectacle, often through ritualistic moments of narrative stasis that permit voyeuristic access to her dressing or reclining in luxurious surroundings.[74] The historical film invites a gendered consumer gaze that visually appropriates the commodities showcased in the film and narcissistically apprehends the image of the woman on screen as an ideal of female beauty and of a consumer life style.[75]

Studies of American consumer culture have drawn attention to a progressive tightening of the bond between the institutions of Hollywood cinema and the department store through the second and third decades of the twen-

tieth century. The film frame came to function (in the famous phraseology of
Charles Eckert) as a living display window occupied by marvelous man-
nequins. Hollywood films showcased fashions and furnishings to a consuming subject largely envisaged as female, since the film and retail industries
were aware, in the 1920s and 1930s, that women were the primary motiva-
tors of cinema attendance and that they made between eighty and ninety
percent of all purchases for family use.[76] The DeMille visual style, in both his
comedies and his historical epics, is regarded as an exemplary model of the
commodification of cinema and the solicitation of a consumer gaze.[77]

The Cleopatra narrative could very easily submit to such DeMille treatment. In her tradition, Cleopatra was already a supreme embodiment of
Woman engineered as seductive spectacle. Essential topoi inherited from
Roman-oriented sources include her exposure to Julius Caesar from inside
a carpet and her self-presentation as Aphrodite/Isis to attract Antony's
Dionysus/Osiris.[78] Such accounts of the queen provide historical justification for film sequences where a woman poses self-consciously for the admiration of a male, on-screen audience. [illustration 4.5] Furthermore, the
oriental mise-en-scène required for the cinematic representation of Cleopatra had already been utilized as a retail strategy in department stores earlier in the century, and had gained a renewed modishness ever since the
discovery of Tutankhaman's tomb in 1922, after which American and European markets were flooded for some years with a vast array of Egyptian-
izing designs.[79] Framed within a consumer gaze, Cleopatra and the Orient
undergo a slippage in signification. By a metonymic process, they supply
showcased products and those tied in offscreen with the sheen of a mysterious and venerable eroticism and luxury.[80] For the consuming spectator,
mastery of the Orient involves not occupation but consumption.

In the 1930s, beyond the cinema screen, lay a massive apparatus to tie up
commodities with particular films.[81] In cinema shops and other retail out-
lets, Colbert/Cleopatra was deployed to sell a range of products such as hats,
cigarettes, shoes, and soap. Press books supplied by Paramount to theater
managers suggested ways of exploiting tie-ins with department stores. One
such studio press release, supplied to accompany the British exhibition of
Cleopatra, noted:

> The opening of the autumn style season brings into prominence the new style
> accessories which definitely reflect the "Cleopatra" motif that is so prominent
> throughout all the season's fashions. All over England, leading stores are
> primed to exploit the new coiffeur jewellry, and other "Cleopatra" items,
> such as ladies' belts, compacts and cigarette cases, and costume jewellry
> which are being made by a cooperating manufacturer.[82]

4.5 Poster advertising Claudette Colbert in *Cleopatra* (1934). [Photograph from private collection of Maria Wyke.]

Women in the audiences of DeMille's historical film were thus encouraged to identify with the Cleopatra on screen and to carry over that identification into their lives outside the cinema through the purchase of Cleopatra gowns and other "style accessories."[83] Such identifications constituted a useful vehicle for socializing ethnically diverse spectators into "a more homogeneous nation of consumers."[84] To that end, the features of the actress chosen to play Cleopatra, Claudette Colbert, adhere more closely to dominant American conventions for female beauty than to those required of an orientalized urban Other. Both the film's diegesis and consumer retailing, however, marketed a traditionally conceived femininity for the queen and her spectators. The narrative resolution of DeMille's *Cleopatra* and the extra-cinematic consumer discourses that surrounded the film deny the queen any political authority. Any societal concerns the female spectator may have are deflected onto an intensified concern with her own body and the need to dress it and shape it in line with the demanding requirements of the oriental glamor of Hollywood.[85] The Roman conquests that consumers might make, thanks to the Cleopatra-style accessories they can buy, belong purely to the domain of romance.[86] If cinema is a "technology of gender,"[87] film production and exhibition are not without their paradoxes and complexities. The narrative code, visual style, promotional literature, and marketing strategies associated with DeMille's *Cleopatra* do not necessarily offer a consistent lesson in gender politics for 1930s America. And, invited to read femininity as a mode of self-theatricalization, it was always open to viewers of the film to acknowledge thereby femininity's constructedness.[88]

Similarly, the infamous *Cleopatra* released in 1963 by 20th Century-Fox offers a heterogeneous set of appropriations of Roman history, a conflicting array of lessons in gender politics, and a range of different identifications as a result of the competing discourses of, for example, the film's diegesis and visual style, associated newspaper publicity, and studio press-releases and promotions. In the case of Fox's *Cleopatra*, even the diegesis itself is not a very stable entity. The film finally distributed by the studio in 1963 was a substantially cut version of that originally made by the director Joseph L. Mankiewicz. Mankiewicz's *Cleopatra* appears to have been conceived as a response to DeMille's, one more suited to the social and political climate of the early 1960s. A souvenir program from the film's charity premiere in Los Angeles (held on 20 June 1963) opens with a quotation from the historian Arthur Weigall that highlights the *difference* between ancient and modern codes of behavior. In a later section on the history and legend of Cleopatra, the program declares:

> Modern scholarship has pieced together a reasonable interpretation of events that for 2000 years had captured the imaginations of playwrights, biographers, novelists. Considerably altered now is the popular exaggeration of her as "the temptress of the Nile." Beautiful and seductive, Cleopatra was, but she was also a hereditary ruler, a woman of rare spirit and courage, cosmopolitan and yet superstitious.[89]

As the film's historical master-text, Wertheimer's depiction of a royal voluptuary is jettisoned in favor of a return to Weigall's political visionary. In the climate of the early 1960s, Cleopatra could be depicted more comfortably as a woman of considerable political authority, and her vision of world unity troped opportunely in the rhetoric of the United Nations.

Fears for the effectiveness of the UN were constantly aired during the 1950s and early 1960s, as it failed to resolve the problems of an enduring colonialism and a continuing antagonism between NATO and the Warsaw Pact. The election of President Kennedy in 1960 seemed, to some Americans, to hold out the hope of an end to the Cold War, but confrontations between the United States and the Soviet Union continued unabated.[90] A screenplay outline for Mankiewicz's *Cleopatra* (dated 1961) attributes to the director a description of the queen as "an early-day Kennedy."[91] In surviving footage of a scene at Alexander's tomb, Cleopatra attempts to persuade Julius Caesar of the merits of Alexander's grand design—that there should arise "out of the patchwork of conquests, one world, and out of one world, one nation, one people on earth living in peace." The characterization of Cleopatra as "a kind of Eleanor Roosevelt captivated by the ideal of one-world unity"[92] was apparently woven tightly through the original film shot by Mankiewicz. Although this visionary Cleopatra reappears briefly in some of the studio's press releases and in premiere programs, little survives of a coherent political diegesis in the film which was finally exhibited in 1963.[93] Moreover, what little did survive was swamped by the film's blockbuster production values and by extra-cinematic publicity concerning the quality of the film's spectacle and the life style of its female star.

A mass of extra-cinematic discourses began to accumulate around Mankiewicz's *Cleopatra* long before its release, as the film was in production on and off for almost two years. Shooting began in England in October 1961, and culminated in the loss of some five million dollars, a change of director, and a serious illness for its big-name star, Elizabeth Taylor. In September 1961, with a new director and a new one million–dollar contract negotiated for Taylor, shooting restarted in Italy. Having failed to meet a pressing studio deadline of June 1962 for completion, the film's producer was fired and the head of Fox resigned. Finally, under the authority of a new studio head, a considerably edited version of Mankiewicz's *Cleopatra* was premiered in June 1963.[94] Throughout this period, 20th Century-Fox fed huge amounts of detail about the production process into magazines and newspapers which, from early 1962, also began to fill with rumors about an adulterous affair between two of the film's principals, Elizabeth Taylor and Richard Burton. The *Motion Picture Herald* for 26 June 1963 thus claimed "never before in motion picture history, perhaps, has a film come to the public with a greater degree of expectancy than 'Cleopatra.'"

In the long and costly absence of a film on which to peg an advertising campaign, 20th Century-Fox solicited consumer interest during production through the star image of Taylor. Star images, such as Taylor's, had an important function in the economy of Hollywood in the 1950s and 1960s. The film star's persona entered into extracinematic circulation, in studio publicity and promotion, newspapers and magazines, in advertisements, on radio and television talk shows, then continued into the films themselves and subsequent commentary on them. Images of female stars, especially, were exploited by the studios and the associated retailing industries as a means of selling fashion and beauty products. Representations of the star's supposed personality and life style were organized around themes of consumption, success, and sex. The star was also defined, paradoxically, as being both an extraordinary and an ordinary individual, so that she might become a model of beauty and consumption to be imitated, on a humbler scale, by readers of her image. Simultaneously, Hollywood studios structured the images of their stars in extra-cinematic texts as a vehicle for describing forthcoming films—as an invitiation to readers to enter the cinema where they might expect to see those images vividly enacted.[95]

An article in an edition of *Vogue* from 1962, accompanied by photographs of Elizabeth Taylor both dressed in historical character and in some "non-cinema coifs," defined the star's image in terms of a "new Cleopatra complex":

> Cleopatra, at the height of her fascination and power, sailed with Caesar to Rome where, the record shows, her potent, volatile charms turned the *vox pop* decidedly pettish. Her experience, in fact, was quite the reverse of Cleopatra Taylor's. . . . To *this* Cleopatra the Romans seem anything but hostile; their designers are plotting some not-too-broody Cleo clothes; the papers are full of Liz; and the Queen of the Nile coiffure can be felt at least as far north as Paris. . . . To all challenges, Miss Taylor presents an on-location manner that's disciplined and direct. Off-set she's as languid as a cheetah, relaxing, cat-like, at her Via Appia villa with her husband, three children, four dogs, two Siamese cats, sipping champagne by the pool, letting the world come to her—and it does.[96]

By means of an elision between the Egyptian queen and the Hollywood film star, Taylor inherits Cleopatra's commanding power, her immense celebrity, and her legendary life style. The champagne and the pool take on the fabulous quality of Cleopatra's banquets by virtue of being sited at a Roman villa. The langor of a cheetah and the pose of a cat recall the animal iconography of Pharaonic Egypt and hint at a feral sexuality to match that attributed to the oriental queen. Dissolving the boundaries between historical character and film star considerably enriches Taylor's star image and, by extension, the fashions she promotes, as well as soliciting interest in the elusive film where the "new Cleopatra," it may be assumed, will act out all the extravagance and excess of the old.

As rumors broke about Taylor's affair with Burton, however, the rhetoric of an identity between star and Egyptian queen was explored in other extra-cinematic texts without any attempt to promote Mankiewicz's *Cleopatra* or its associated merchandising. On these occasions, a correspondence was observed not just between the fascination of the queen and the film star who was now playing her part, but also between their respective sexual relationships with their lovers. An article in *Show Business Illustrated* of 2 January 1962 noted parallels at length:

> MOVIE OF "CLEOPATRA" curious case of destiny at work. Film now underway again after series of appalling mishaps—e.g., near-death of Elizabeth Taylor, loss of $5,000,000. Why was unlucky project not abandoned altogether? Reason: Elizbeth Taylor fated to play Cleopatra. Parallels in life of two girls spooky . . . LIZ ALSO FOUND NEW REGENT. Also man whose wife was paragon of sunny domesticity. Eddie Fisher. Party boy like Antony. Left wife, married Liz . . . Both queens accused of stealing husband from nice wife. Liz replied: "What am I supposed to do, ask him to go back to her?" Cleopatra would have said the same. She and Liz are classic Other Woman. Can't help it. Metabolism.

Taylor, at the time when she was making *Cleopatra*, was already notorious for being seen to break up the marriage between Eddie Fisher and Debbie Reynolds, whose star image was that of America's perfect young wife. The assimilation of the film star to her film character now provides an opportunity to equate Cleopatra's enticement of Antony from Octavia bathetically with Taylor's past affair.[97] But it also permits a hint at a fresh sexual scandal, for the article concludes by insinuating tantalizingly that there are yet more parallels to come:

> But does small voice of Cleopatra whisper to Liz at night across the centuries: "You really *can* rule the world. Get a barge! Roll yourself in an Oriental rug and have it sent to . . ." But who? MANY FASCINATING possibilities. But no concern of scholarly work. Stick to facts. Future will reveal them in own time. Notes put aside until then.

More explicit and detailed reports of the affair between Taylor and Burton then poured forth in the European and American press from early 1962. By the spring, 20th Century-Fox had become concerned whether such massive and persistent press interest would provide good box-office returns or encourage the American public instead to boycott the film on its eventual release.[98] Both the couple and the film set were besieged by the world's press. In a letter dated 7 June 1962 (which was published in 1963 in a collected edition entitled *The Cleopatra Papers*), the Fox publicist Nathan Weiss wrote to his colleague Jack Brodsky on just such a press visit to the film's Alexandria set outside Rome:

After lunch there was a short but eloquent scene in which Antony divorces his wife after the fashion of the time—by proclaiming it three times to the multitudes. Partly because the writing is so overnight-contemporary, to coin a new period, there were regrettable connotations from the point of view of stirring up the press—regret that is from the puritan Fox viewpoint, but not damaging I suspect to the box office. It is, in just about every sense, a most peculiarly ambivalent production.[99]

Provided on set with such gloriously neat connections between Roman history and a modern sex scandal, the press continued to figure their accounts of the Taylor/Burton affair in the extravagant terms of a Cleopatran romance.[100]

Accounts of the production of Mankiewicz's *Cleopatra* published by insiders after the film's release suggest that the extra-cinematic discourses of film star adultery infected the film-making process itself, both the overnight revisions of the script and, in particular, the performance of the female star. On 12 April 1962, the Vatican weekly *Osservatore della domenica* printed an open letter in which Elizabeth Taylor was attacked for making a mockery of the sanctity of marriage and threatened with a future of "erotic vagrancy."[101] In *My Life with Cleopatra* (1963), the producer Walter Wanger duplicated his notes on the subsequent day's shooting:

Filmed one of the most dramatic scenes in the movie and one of the most dramatic real-life scenes I have ever witnessed. Again the parallel between the life of Cleopatra and the life of Elizabeth Taylor is incredible. The scene filmed in the Forum calls for Cleopatra to make her entrance into Rome sitting with Caesarion on top of a huge (more than thirty feet high) black Sphinx drawn by 300 gold-covered slaves. The entrance into Rome was Cleopatra's big gamble. If the Romans accepted her with an ovation, she had won Caesar. If they refused to accept her, she had lost him, and very possibly her life. There were almost 7,000 Roman extras milling about in front of the Forum. All of them presumably had read the Vatican criticism of Liz. Not only would these Roman extras be accepting Cleopatra, but they would also be expressing their personal acceptance of the woman who plays Cleopatra. . . . I saw the sense of relief flood through Liz's body as the slave girls, handmaidens, senators, guards, and thousands of others applauded her—personally.[102]

Wanger's description of filming (as well as Weiss's published letter) may have been a damage-limitation exercise, an attempt, after the events of 1962, to recoup for the benefit of the enormously costly film some of the worldwide notoriety that had accrued to it. But the publication of the producer's diary, along with the letters of the Fox publicists, would have further encouraged contemporary spectators of *Cleopatra* to read its representation of ancient history and its characterization of the Egyptian queen as an extension of the extra-cinematic discourses on Taylor's marriages and adultery. Criticism of Taylor's performance in reviews of the film—her perceived "commonness" and inability to know "the difference between playing oneself in an Egyptian costume and playing Queen of Egypt"[103]— exposes the contradiction between the role of Cleopatra as it may have been originally conceived (political visionary) and the star performance of it (cruelly hounded Other Woman). Thus, the extra-cinematic development of Taylor's star image from legendary bon viveur to legendary adulteress and her performance of that image in Mankiewicz's *Cleopatra* overwhelmed any attempt by the film's diegesis to characterize the queen as a state leader dreaming of world empire.

Star images often "embody social values that are in some sense or other in crisis."[104] Discourses of stardom are littered with the exploration, in particular, of sexual behaviors. Elizabeth Taylor's star image as a modern-day Cleopatra and her performance of it in Mankiewicz's film became a useful reference point in the early 1960s for discussion of problems attached to the institutions of heterosexual monogamy. The Kinsey reports of 1948 and 1953 on the sexual behavior of males and females respectively had aroused enormous interest and debate in an era that idealized the family as a refuge against social change. The president of the Union Theological Seminary observed that current interest in Kinsey's work (including his revelations of persistent adultery among middle-class American women) was symptomatic of "a prevailing degradation in American morality approximating the worst decadence of the Roman era."[105] Moral panics about the fragility of conventional sexuality, about the success of *Playboy* and the introduction of the oral contraceptive, about increases in adultery and divorce, thus came to be troped in the language of Roman history.

Roman Spectators

Hollywood rarely acknowledges the discursive operations of the star system, that the star personality is a construct built up and expressed only through films and associated extra-cinematic texts, that the person and the image are two separable entities.[106] Mankiewicz's *Cleopatra*, however, appears to offer a glimpse of that duality, and in doing so sets up an identification between the Romans within the film who looks at Cleopatra and the spectators in the cinema who look at the screen. Near the beginning of the Cleopatra/Antony half of the film, during the sequence where Cleopatra sumptuously entertains Antony on board her barge at Tarsus, she tantalizes the drunk Roman with a mock-Cleopatra, a scantily dressed and lascivious imitation, whom Antony grabs and passionately kisses only to turn and find that the real Cleopatra has left the shipboard banquet hall. Angrily, he abandons the fake queen and tracks down the real one to her boudoir. There he confronts Cleopatra directly, after having first slashed the diaphanous hangings that screen her from him. *Cleopatra* here hints self-consciously at the strategies of the Fox publicists and the press who, for many months before the release of the film, had been constructing the star image of "Cleopatra Taylor" for an avid readership. The dynamic between the characters on screen reproduces that between the film and its spectators. The play-acting on the barge suggests that there are two Taylors just as there are two Cleopatras, and that Antony's search for the real queen behind the gauzy curtain mirrors the spectator's search for the real Taylor behind the star image. *Cleopatra* shows us what Antony sees, first his blurred vision of the Cleopatra double, then, after the veil which fills the whole film frame is cut away, his direct uncluttered gaze on the sleeping queen. Thus Mankiewicz's *Cleopatra* encourages its spectators to believe that their desirous looks, like that of Antony/Burton, will cut through to and finally take possession of the elusive star.

A similar scene also occurs in the Cleopatra/Julius Caesar half of the film. During an early sequence set in Alexandria, Cleopatra is shown fully clothed, seated on a plain bench, drinking from an unassuming cup, as she listens to a recitation of Catullan poetry. Realizing that Julius Caesar is on his way to her palace-chamber, she declares:

> We must not disappoint the mighty Caesar. The Romans tell fabulous tales of my bath, and my handmaidens, and my morals.

The queen then stages a titillating spectacle of herself for the benefit of Caesar's gaze, posing supine and sensuous on a couch, now naked but for a sparsely decorated, transparent covering, surrounded by handmaidens who dance, or fan their seductive mistress, or paint her finger- and toenails. The scene not only hints self-consciously at the discourses of stardom that have shaped the Taylor image, but also foregrounds the way female stars have been made to function in Hollywood cinema, including past cinematic Cleopatras. The "fabulous tales" the Romans tell signify the sensational accounts of Taylor's star life style off set (her poolside champagne, her eight-hundred-dollar-a-week hairdresser, her perpetual debauch with Burton)[107] as well as the Roman histories of an oriental whore. Attention is also drawn to Hollywood cinema's mechanisms for fetishizing and objectifying

its female stars for the desirous spectator.[108] We are offered the double pleasure of a sophisticated laugh with Cleopatra at the hackneyed, DeMillean
tactic of "the bedroom scene," as well as the scopophilic act itself, when
the body of Cleopatra/Taylor is viewed admiringly by the approaching
Roman/camera.[109]

In the 1960s, at a time when a visit to the cinema had become only one of
a number of possible leisure activities, a large number of Hollywood films
exhibited such narrative self-consciousness about the artifices involved in
film-making.[110] The historical epic had always been a genre in which cinema could display itself and its powers through showpiece moments of
spectacle, such as (in the case of films reconstructing ancient history) chariot
races, gladiatorial combat, triumphal processions, land and sea battles, the
persecutions of Nero, or the seductions of Cleopatra.[111] The ancient world
of such Hollywood films was, as Michael Wood has argued, "a huge, many-
faceted metaphor for Hollywood itself" and, throughout the 1950s, the
spectacularly reconstructed ancient world (with its lavish production values,
and the visually enticing technology of Technicolor and widescreen) also
signaled the hope of salvation for a film industry suffering from the depre-
dations caused by the large-scale retirement of the American public into
do-it-yourself pursuits and domestic television viewing.[112] Mankiewicz's
Cleopatra, in particular, was widely discussed in its long pre-release period
as a last ditch (and ultimately unsuccessful) attempt by a Hollywood studio
to bring back audiences to the cinema following the by now outdated production techniques of the old studio system, and the generic codes of hugely
expensive historical construction which had last won the industry significant commercial success in 1959 when MGM released *Ben-Hur*.[113]

Aided by the intense expectation generated by pre-release discussion of
the film, Mankiewicz's *Cleopatra* positioned its spectators as Romans wait-
ing to see the oriental splendor that is Hollywood cinema itself. Details of
the magnificence of the Forum scene were fed to the press long before spectators had an opportunity to judge its visual pleasures for themselves. At the
moment when Cleopatra is finally seen arriving through a triumphal arch,
the crowd on screen express their amazement at the oriental spectacle of the
black, half-naked dancing girls, the emissions of brightly colored smoke,
the scattered rose petals, the birds released from false pyramids, the massive
sphinx float, and, finally, the queen and her son enthroned on high, dressed
in cloth of gold. The reaction of the Roman crowd on screen to Cleopatra's
spectacle attempts to solicit a similar reaction in contemporary spectators to
Fox's long=awaited historical epic.

Two alluring features of Cleopatra for Hollywood cinema were her legendary reputation as a creator of fabulous and seductive spectacle and the

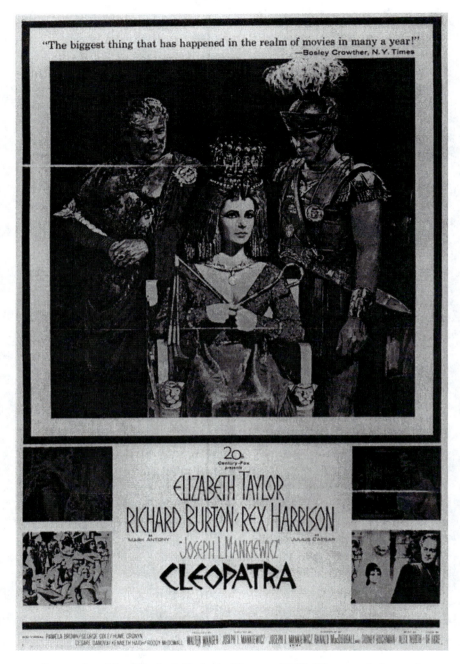

4.6 Poster advertising Elizabeth Taylor in *Cleopatra* (1963). [Photograph from private collection of Maria Wyke.]

long-standing association of her kingdom with the mysteries of moving-image projection. Through the representation of Cleopatra and the Orient both on screen and off (in film promotion, and in cinema architecture and foyer design), the Hollywood studios could proclaim cinema's own visual seductiveness to its awed "Roman" spectators. [illustration 4.6] But, given that the production of Mankiewicz's *Cleopatra* led to the financial ruin of the 20th Century-Fox studio and was ever after marked as having ushered in the end of the historical epic genre, it is perhaps unsurprising that one scene edited out of the exhibited version of the film shows the queen seducing Julius Caesar with a display of Egypt's extraordinary inventions, including the marvelous, moving images of a zoetrope.[114]

5

Nero:
Spectacles of Persecution
and Excess

The Attractions of the Antichrist

Nero was the instrument of considerable commercial success in 1951, as the result of his portrayal by Peter Ustinov in the Hollywood epic *Quo Vadis*.[1] American markets were saturated with publicity for the film and with a host of merchandizing tie-ins. The MGM campaign book distributed to cinema managers in the United States, for example, contained a sample advertisement for Munsingwear rayon boxer shorts which appealed to its potential customers with the intriguing caption "make like Nero in . . . QUO VADIS shorts." Beside the caption was drawn the figure of a modern American male who happily plays a fiddle while watched adoringly by his personal "empress." He sports a wreath and sandals, a vest, and a pair of rayon boxer shorts which are decorated with images of spears and Roman military uniforms—a design selected from among Munsingwear's "eight fiery patterns blazing with color."[2] [illustration 5.1] Nero had become a symbol of virility, luxury and the pleasures of consumerism for 1950s America.

Yet the opening voice-over of *Quo Vadis* heralds the Hollywood film as a simple narration of the rise of Christianity and its triumph over the evils of Neronian Rome:

This is the Appian way, the most famous road that leads to Rome, as all roads lead to Rome. On this road march her conquering legions. Imperial Rome is the center of the empire and undisputed master of the world, but with this power inevitably comes corruption. No man is sure of his life. The individual is at the mercy of the state. Murder replaces justice. Rulers of conquered nations surrender their helpless subjects to bondage. High and low alike become Roman slaves, Roman hostages. There is no escape from the whip

5.1 Poster advertising Munsingwear rayon boxer shorts, in association with *Quo Vadis* (1951). [From University of Southern California Cinema-Television archive.]

and the sword. That any force on earth can shake the foundations of this pyramid of power and corruption, of human misery and slavery, seems inconceivable, but thirty years before this day, a miracle occurred. On a Roman cross in Judaea, a man died to make men free, to spread the gospel of love and redemption. Soon that humble cross is destined to replace the proud eagles that now top the victorious Roman standards. This is the story of that immortal conflict. In this, the early summer in the year 64 A.D., in the reign of the Antichrist known to history as the emperor Nero, the victorious four-teenth legion is on its way back to Rome under the command of one Marcus Vinicius.[3]

While the MGM campaign book calls on consumers to "make like Nero" and includes advertisements for shorts and pyjamas decorated with such synecdoches of imperial rule as the Roman eagle, the film's prologue identi-fies the emperor as "the Antichrist" and speaks of the coming toppling of the Roman eagles by the cross of Christ. At the close of the film, Nero is dead and Galba is marching on Rome. The protagonist Marcus Vinicius, having assisted in the overthrow of the emperor, now casts off his soldier's uniform to make a spiritual journey out of the sinful city to which he had arrived at the film's opening. The final frame of *Quo Vadis* reveals that the passing stan-dards of the legionaries have been replaced along the Appian Way by Saint Peter's crook, miraculously rooted to the spot and in full blossom to mark a visitation from Christ and the future triumph of his Church at Rome.

The title of the Hollywood film and its depiction of Nero as an Antichrist thwarted by the courage of a Roman soldier who has converted to Christianity are both borrowed from Henryk Sienkiewicz's nineteenth-cen-tury historical novel *Quo Vadis?* Sienkiewicz's novel was initially serialized between 1894 and 1896 in the *Gazeta Polska* (in the original Polish) and sub-sequently achieved vast international success in numerous translations.[4] Within nineteenth-century conventions for the composition of historical novels set in the Roman empire, the Polish author sought authority for his representation of the Neronian age in his claimed reliance on ancient histori-ography such as that of Tacitus and Suetonius.[5] But his vision of a Neronian Antichrist in conflict with the early champions of the Christian faith was not inherited from the ancient historiographic tradition. According to the Roman historians, Christianity was one of many disruptive, distasteful and criminal superstitions at work within the Roman empire.[6] For Tacitus, Nero's persecution of the Christians was instigated to stave off accusations that he was responsible for the devastating fire that burned Rome for several days in the summer of A.D. 64, and constituted just another example of the emperor's corruption of the old public virtues of the Roman elite and an indication of his rapid moral decline into a vicious tyranny:

To suppress this rumor, Nero fabricated scapegoats—and punished with every refinement the notoriously depraved Christians. . . . First, Nero had self-acknowledged Christians arrested. Then, on their information, large numbers of others were condemned—not so much for incendiarism as for their anti-social tendencies. Their deaths were made farcical. Dressed in wild animals' skins, they were torn to pieces by dogs, or crucified, or made into torches to be ignited after dark as substitutes for daylight. . . . Despite their guilt as Christians, and the ruthless punishment it deserved, the victims were pitied. For it was felt that they were being sacrificed to one man's brutality rather than to the national interest. [*Annals* 15.44.][7]

Sienkiewicz's emplotment of the triumph of Christian faith over the Antichrist reiterates not the pagan assessments of Nero, but his incorporation into early Christian eschatalogical literature. Soon after Nero's downfall in A.D. 68, a number of pagan sources had reported rumors emanating largely from the Greek-speaking provinces of the empire that Nero had not died but fled East shortly to return at the head of a Parthian army. The *Revelation to John*, dated variously to the late 60s or 90s A.D.., appears to have adapted these rumors to construct a myth of the city of Rome and its resurrected emperor incarnated, respectively, as a woman "drunken with the blood of the saints" and "the beast" she rides "which had the wound by the sword, and did live." They make war on the resurrected Christ only to be utterly overcome by him. By the end of the first century, some Christian writers had integrated this apocalyptic vision with that of an Antichrist who would establish a reign of terror on earth before the second coming of Christ. Although no specific mention is made in *Revelation* of Nero or an Antichrist, for several centuries the legend of *Nero redivivus* seems to have been identified with that of the Antichrist by some Christian apologists, and both Nero and the Antichrist with "the beast" of *Revelation* 13 and 17.[8] Thus Commodianus states explicitly "for us Nero is the Antichrist," and Victorinus of Petau, in his commentary on *Revelation*, speaks of Nero as the Beast and the Antichrist.[9] The identification seems to have been shortlived, since there is little evidence for it beyond the fifth century, and by then many writers such as Lactantius, Sulpicius Severus, and Augustine had already distanced themselves from it or expressed misgivings about its validity.[10] In the late nineteenth century, however, the French humanist and scholar Ernest Renan reaffirmed the identification.

The fourth volume of Renan's *Histoire des Origines du Christianisme* was published in 1873. Concerned with the persecutions undertaken during the reign of Nero, it was pointedly entitled "The Antichrist." Renan's purpose, however, was to unpack the origins of the early Christian legends concerning the crucifixion of Peter and the decapitation of Paul in Nero's Rome, and to explain the sacred text of *Revelation* historically. Having witnessed and fled the atrocities of Nero, John swiftly took revenge, according to

Renan, by incorporating the emperor into the apocalyptic drama of *Revelation*. The history of Nero's fall quickly became, in the Christian imagination, the narrative of a final, fiery struggle between the bestial emperor and the apostles Peter and Paul, between the early Christian Church and the imperial power of Rome, between Christ and Antichrist:

> Already the idea had spread that the coming of the true Christ would be preceded by the coming of a sort of an infernal Christ who should be in everything the contrary of Jesus. That could no longer be doubted; the *Antichrist*, the Christ of evil, existed. The *Antichrist* was this monster with a human face made up of ferocity, hypocrisy, immodesty, pride, who paraded before the world as an absurd hero, celebrated his triumph as a chariot driver with torches of human flesh, intoxicated himself with the blood of the saints, and perhaps did worse than that. . . . The name of Nero has been discovered; it shall be THE BEAST. Caligula had been the *Anti-God*. Nero shall be the Anti-Christ, the Apocalypse.[11]

Although the anti-clerical Renan had already treated the divinity of Christ as an historical construct and pursued a rationalist exegesis of the biblical tradition (a method which had been initiated earlier in the nineteenth century by David Strauss's *Life of Jesus*), his lively telling of the formation of early Christian belief seems to have been read by Henryk Sienkiewicz as a confirmation of and justification for a satanic depiction of Nero. The novelist countered Renan's often ironic account of *Revelation* by expressly appropriating the fourth volume of *Origines du Christianisme* as an historical document of capital importance for the reconstruction of the Neronian age.[12]

Animating Early Christianity

One condition for the emergence of a cinematic historiography of Nero thus lies in a nineteenth-century popular tradition of historical novels and plays which, composed in opposition to contemporary religious skepticism, described or enacted a conflict between Christian and pagan ideals set in the ambience of the Roman empire.[13] Like Lytton's *The Last Days of Pompeii* (1834), Wiseman's *Fabiola* (1854), Wallace's *Ben-Hur* (1880), or Barrett's contemporaneous toga play *The Sign of the Cross* (1895), Sienkiewicz's *Quo Vadis?* attempted to substantiate and animate the poorly documented and much debated story of the early Christian Church by placing Christian believers and converts (both actual and imaginary) on the stage of well-documented Roman history.[14] So Sienkiewicz's novel begins towards the end of Nero's reign and follows the love story of a pagan soldier Marcus Vinicius and his Christian beloved Lygia, the progress of whose love is blessed by Peter, Christ's Vicar in Rome, but endangered by the Antichrist Nero. Pagan and Christian histories alike are personalized, domesticated and enlivened through the melodramatic representation of a star-crossed love. The reader of *Quo Vadis?* first encounters Nero, the Roman Antichrist, through the eyes of the fictive Christian maiden who has unwillingly been taken to his palace:

> Lygia, who, at the beginning of the banquet, had viewed the Emperor as through a mist, and thereafter had been led by Vinicius' words wholly to forget the monarch, now turned curious, frightened eyes in Caesar's direction. Acte had spoken the truth. Caesar, leaning forward across the table, was gazing at the pair with one eye half-closed and the other eye glued to an emerald monocle. As his glance encountered that of Lygia the maiden's heart seemed to turn to ice. . . . Like a frightened child she seized Vinicius' hand, while through her brain there whirled a series of swift, chaotic impressions. So *this* was Caesar, the terrible, the all-powerful Caesar! (49)[15]

Similarly, Peter, the Vicar of God, is observed furtively in the catacombs by the (as yet unbelieving) Roman soldier Vinicius who is in pursuit of his vanished beloved:

> The old man raised his hand, and, making the sign of the cross, blessed all present. . . . In this poor fisherman Vinicius saw, not an archpriest skilled in the performances of rites, but an old, simple, infinitely venerable man who had come to proclaim far and wide a truth which he had beheld and touched, and in which he believed as a man believes the testimony of his own eyesight. And Vinicius, who had no wish to succumb to the spell of the scene, felt, nevertheless, a feverish curiosity to hear what was about to issue from the mouth of this companion of the mysterious Christ. (135)

Following the initiation of the fire at Rome (which, in the novel, is revealed to be unquestionably Nero's responsibility, despite the doubts expressed by Tacitus), the emperor's persecutions include sending the innocent Lygia into the arena tied to a bull in one of his many morbid, mythological spectacles.[16] Her giant protector Ursus, however, rescues her and Vinicius (now a convert) appeals to the sympathy of the spectators to obtain pardon for his beloved. The novel ends by proceeding beyond the lovers' happy prospects to a description of Nero's consequent suicide and the foretelling of the eventual triumph of Peter's Church at Rome.

Part of Renan's project in the fourth volume of his *Origines du Christianisme* was to contribute to the intense and continuing debate initiated by the

Protestant theologians of the sixteenth century concerning the martyrdoms of Peter and Paul. He explored the accumulation of early Christian legend around the two apostles which had led, by the fourth century, to the construction at Rome of the basilicas of St. Peter and St. Paul-beyond-the-walls. What, for Renan, were matters of historically unverifiable conjecture became graphic matters of fact in Sienkiewicz's narrative.[17] The novelist further embellished *Quo Vadis?* with a miracle ultimately derived from the early Church fathers. The title of his novel refers to a Christian tradition in which the apostle Peter encounters a vision of Christ approaching him along the Appian Way as he flees from the Neronian persecutions at Rome to safety. When Peter asks "Quo vadis, Domine?" ("whither goest thou, Lord?"), he receives the reply, "Now that thou art abandoning my people, I am going to Rome—there to be crucified a second time." (424) So Peter turns back to tend to his growing flock and face a martyr's death, strengthened in the realization that Rome has become the city of Christ, the capital which will "rule over both the souls and the bodies of men" (425).

Within the novelistic framework, the restatement of such legends as authentic events of Nero's reign held an immediate and enormous appeal for their nineteenth-century readers. In 1899, the same year as the novel's first publication in an Italian translation, the Roman Catholic Church felt compelled by its enormously favorable reception to hold a conference in the Church of Saint Ambrogio at Genoa in which the clergy could debate the relative merits of *Quo Vadis?* as a serious Christian apology.[18] Popular interest in the novel continued to be stimulated by the excavations which were being conducted on a massive scale in the city of Rome in this same period, from 1870 on to 1914. Reports by the Christian archaeologists Giovanni Battista de Rossi and Rodolfo Lanciani, published in both scholarly volumes and newspaper articles, stimulated extensive interest in their attempts to support the theological doctrine that both Peter and Paul had been martyred at Rome at some point during Nero's reign. Surveying the current excavations in the catacombs and recently discovered Christian inscriptions, the archaeologists stated their support for many of the legends of martyrdom to be found in Christian writers from the second century onward. The writings of de Rossi and Lanciani inspired widespread religious fervor, and masses were held at the newly revealed underground basilicas.[19]

In 1900, the archaeologist Orazio Marucchi published a scholarly volume confirming the Petrine tradition (*S. Pietro e S. Paolo in Roma*) and, simultaneously, contributed a learned introduction on the history and archaeology of early Christianity in Neronian Rome to another Italian translation of Sienkiewicz's novel.[20] The excavations in the Roman catacombs appeared largely to authenticate the representation of the early Christian community set out in *Quo Vadis?* but the novel was also able to repair the fragmentary buildings, flesh out the skeletal remains, and bring to life the new historical accounts of the persecutions and martyrdoms in Nero's reign. As late as 1913, arguments concerning the Petrine tradition continued to be aired, when, for example, George Edmundson preached the eight Bampton lectures at the University of Oxford on the subject of "The Church in Rome in the first century." In the series of sermons, he drew on the work of Lanciani and de Rossi to declare that the presence and execution of Peter and Paul at Rome towards the end of Nero's reign were now facts of Christian history "practically outside controversy."[21] It is conceivable that the additional sympathy he expressed for the *quo vadis?* miracle may have arisen as the result of its apparent confirmation in the pages of numerous editions of Sienkiewicz's novel and by its visual portrayal in cinematic adaptations of *Quo Vadis?*—such as the Italian version, which was achieving vast international acclaim in the very same year as Edmundson delivered his sermons.[22]

Significantly for readings of the new cinematic tradition for Nero, Sienkiewicz's narrative of Nero's fall and Christianity's triumph, soon after its publication, was interpreted by some commentators as not just a Christian apology but also a patriotic manifesto for more contemporary concerns. Already Renan, in the *Origines du Christianisme*, had claimed that the overthrow of the tyranny of Nero by a revolt initiated in Gaul was "one of the glories of France."[23] Although *Quo Vadis?* is Sienkiewicz's only novel to be set outside Poland, its two entirely fictional main characters—Lygia and Ursus—are made to originate from "Lygia," an area of northern Europe between the Oder and the Vistula, which the author liked to think of as an ancient Poland. The innocent Christian child and her giant defender came to be understood by readers of *Quo Vadis?* as representing, respectively, Catholic Poland and the Polish people. The people, embodied in the shape of Ursus, rescue their martyred country from the horns of the terrible beast that is Poland's foreign oppressors, namely Germany, Russia and Austria:

In the arena there was passing an unprecedented scene. At the sight of his princess bound upon the horns of the savage bull, the Lygian, hitherto humble and prepared for death, had sprung forward like a man scorched with living fire, and, with back bent, was creeping, zigzag fashion, towards the maddened beast. Then from every throat there issued a short, a tremulous cry of amazement, followed by a profound silence. For with a single bound the Lygian had reached the beast and gripped its horns! (411). . . . At the sight of the unconscious maiden who, beside the huge body of the Lygian, looked like a tiny child, emotion seized upon knights, Senators, and the mob alike. Her frail figure, her unconscious condition, the frightful danger from

which the giant had just rescued her, and, finally, her beauty and the devotion of the Lygian all combined to touch the popular heart. . . . The people
had had enough of blood, of death, of torture. With voices strangled with
sobs they demanded that Lygia and Ursus should be forgiven. (413)

The subsequent, apocalyptic downfall of Nero (the novel's other "Beast")
and the triumph of the Roman Church operate as a warning to the oppressors of Poland—a symbol of the possibilities of popular vindication against
the tyrannies exercised by the empires of the nineteenth century. And in
Petronius, who is given a central role in the novel (rather than the more traditional Seneca) as bold commentator on and critic of the habits of his
emperor, might be seen a parallel for Sienkiewicz himself—the nineteenth-
century author's fears of artistic censorship and repression being expressed
through the hounding and final suicide of the ancient novelist in the narrative's interior.[24] These allegorical strategies at work in the novel *Quo Vadis?*
were then implemented more forcefully in the cinematic reconstructions of
Nero as a representation of present as well as past histories of persecution
and tyranny.

The novelistic myth of Nero the Antichrist, the orgiastic reveler, the
arsonist who sang the fall of Troy while Rome burned, the first persecutor of
the Christians, murderer of Peter and Paul, and symbol of tyranny over-
thrown by populist force, achieved a unique diffusion for a nineteenth-century literary work. Soon after its publication, *Quo Vadis?* became a world
bestseller, and in 1905 its author received the Nobel prize for literature. By
1933 more than one hundred translations of the novel had gone into circulation in many different languages. The novel's apocalyptic theme inspired
operas and was adapted for both the American and the European stage,
where it obtained long runs in the first years of the twentieth century at, for
example, the Teatro Manzoni in Rome. So popular did this religious and
political fable become that the names of the novel's ancient heroes were even
given to French racehorses, and so instructive did it seem that it was for
many years on lists of books recommended to American college students.[25]

The Cinematic Emperor

Just a few years after publication, *Quo Vadis?* was also seized on by the
fledgling film industry, and in 1901 Pathé studios in Paris produced a one-
reel short in which a selection of scenes from the novel were represented in
the form of fairly static tableaux.[26] The literary tradition of the historical
novel had great importance for the new film medium, for it provided a rich
narrative typology and spectacular visual possibilities for the screening of
history, and its popularity guaranteed directors an audience for their film

adaptations. Yet the representational strategies of early historical film borrowed additionally from a much broader repertoire of nineteenth-century aesthetic forms than the historical novel, drawing on the sensational technologies of circus shows and pyrodramas, theatrical and operatic codes, and the visual arts, in pursuit of audience pleasure, profitability, and the legitimation felt to accrue to a mode of high culture.[27] In all these nineteenth-century forms and more, Nero was ubiquitous.

Thus one of the first tentative experiments in the screening of Roman history made by an Italian production house, the one-reeler *Nerone* (Luigi Maggi, Ambrosio, 1909), displays the persecution of the Christians as, almost literally, an afterthought. The short film bases its plot on a vastly condensed synthesis of the Italian dramatic tradition for Nero—from grandiose productions of Monteverdi's opera *L'incoronazione di Poppea* (first performed in 1642) to recent stagings of Pietro Cossa's populist tragedy *Nerone* (first performed in 1871)—where the emperor figures not so much as an Antichrist but as the ruthless son who kills his mother Agrippina, the callous husband who rejects his wife Octavia, or the passionate lover who pursues mistresses such as Poppaea or Acte. Highly dependent still on the conventions of the Italian stage, almost every scene of *Nerone* (1909) operates as a self-contained unit within which the actors playing Nero, Octavia, or Poppaea, planted before papier mâché backdrops and facing their unseen film audience, gesture majestically. Towards the close of the film, the flight and suicide of Nero is preceded by a brief sequence in which the emperor is represented beset by a bad conscience. Superimposed on the wall of his bedroom, the terrified Nero sees a vision of Christian suffering and steadfastness in the arena whose static tableau closely recalls the composition of Jean-Léon Gérôme's famous painting *The Christian Martyrs' Last Prayer* (1883). Any celebration of the innovatory powers of cinema seems to be reserved for the display of the burning of Rome and the panic of its citizens. It was this red-toned sequence which vastly impressed audiences of the film on its release both in Italy and abroad.[28] According to the *Moving Picture World* of 6 November 1909, it possessed "such a marvelous realism of affect that as we sat and watched this colored part of the film, we seemed, as it were, to hear the cries of the victims."

In its recourse to near contemporary cultural artefacts for the articulation of ancient history on screen, early cinema effectively established nineteenth-century constructions of the Neronian age as the canonic instruments for Nero's popular dissemination in the twentieth century. The differing technologies and economic practices of the cinematic industry, however, inevitably reshaped the Nero of the nineteenth-century tradition into a new emperor for a new medium.[29] Historians of this period of historical film production generally regard Enrico Guazzoni's *Quo Vadis?* (Cines, 1913) as the first film to have formulated a specifically cinematic system for the projection of the past to a mass domestic, and international, audience. Borrowing from the whole gamut of nineteenth-century modes of historiography, Guazzoni's *Quo Vadis?* appeared successfully to match, or even to exceed, their power to reconstruct the past and the pleasure such reconstruction gave. Its cinematographic novelty has been said to reside in its feature length, its translation of the novel's complexity into a filmic structure that (through the use of both close-ups and long shots) alternated individual and collective experiences of imperial Rome, its naturalistic acting, its elaborate, three-dimensional set designs, and its exploration of depth of field (especially through the movement on screen of vast crowds of extras). Prompted partly by the arrival in Italian film companies of a new generation of entrepreneurs for whom filmmaking was a matter of cultural prestige as well as commerce, the innovative aesthetics of Guazzoni's *Quo Vadis?* swiftly became the model for subsequent productions in the genre of the historical film.[30]

Produced as a showcase for the Cines Company in Rome, and released on the national and international market in the early months of 1913, Guazzoni's cinematic adaptation of *Quo Vadis?* had the then unusual length of six reels (of approximately two hours duration), thereby allowing for a storyline that could do justice to the complexities of the novelistic narrative, at the same time giving the cinema audience a cultural artefact that lasted as long as a play or an opera. Two years later, while the film was still in circulation in Italy, its status as an artefact of high culture comparable to an historical novel was conveniently reinforced, when a new edition of Sienkiewicz's novel was published in Milan illustrated with stills drawn from Guazzoni's production. Simultaneously, the cinematic Nero was laying claim to the status of both literary and visual art.[31]

In the 1913 film adaptation of *Quo Vadis?* the new visual and aural potentials of cinema were fully exploited as the arena, in particular, became a focal point for the development of a new Neronian narrative. In the design of the mise-en-scène where gladiators salute Nero in the royal box, fight, and then die, Enrico Guazzoni appears to have been influenced by paintings such as Jean-Léon Gérôme's *Ave Caesar, Morituri Te Salutant* (1859) and *Pollice Verso* (1872). Audiences are said to have clapped every time they recognized the representation in the filmic medium of such popular neoclassical paintings as these.[32] [illustrations 5.2 and 5.3] The pleasure that Guazzoni offered his audiences, however, exceeds that of a simple, static reproduction of the Roman arena's most celebrated nineteenth-century iconography. Gérôme's *Ave Caesar*, in which gladiators salute the emperor Vitellius before they are about to die in combat, places the painting's viewer disturbingly as a participant on the floor of the arena. *Pollice Verso*, in which

5.2 Gérôme's painting *Pollice Verso* (1872). [Courtesy of Phoenix Art Museum.]

5.3 A gladiator stands over his victim, from *Quo Vadis?* (1913). [Photograph taken from postcard in private collection of Riccardo Redi.]

5.4 Program advertising Barnum Circus show *Nero, or the Destruction of Rome* staged in 1889. [Courtesy of Guildhall Library, Corporation of London.]

a ferocious crowd gestures for the death of a retiarius who lies prostrate beneath the foot of a victorious mirmillo, presents its viewers with a position even closer to the outcome of the bloody combat.[33] Guazzoni's film juxtaposes and animates Gérôme's paintings, expanding their spatial frame, endowing them with a temporal dimension, movement, and music, and multiplying their points of view. Placed first at the level of the gladiators, the camera pans around the arena with them as they march towards the royal box to salute Nero. During the fatal duel, the camera cuts from the gladiators up to Nero and his court in the royal box, and pans round the huge crowds to include in the film frame the excited response of the Vestal Virgins. When the mirmillo stands triumphantly over his victim, the editing of the shots allows the cinema spectator to share both the participatory view from the arena floor and the voyeuristic view from within the royal box. The arena sequence then draws closer to the climactic rescue of Lygia from the bull with the animation of Gérôme's painting of Christian martyrdom, *The Christian Martyrs' Last Prayer* (1883). A group of Christians are escorted into the arena by Roman soldiers. The vast spatial dimension of Guazzoni's film is emphasized by the amount of film time dedicated to a single long-shot of the soldiers relentlessly pushing the Christians to the back of the arena, where they remain at a great distance from the film spectator as the lions begin to appear in close-up from screen left. A range of points of view are made available to the spectator—close-ups of Christian victims are intercut with long-shots of raging lions and the steady gaze of the dreadful spectacle's author, Nero. Thus Guazzoni's *Quo Vadis?* challenges the stasis of the nineteenth-century picture frame by the fabrication of a whole sequence of movement-images.[34]

The arena sequence of Guazzoni's *Quo Vadis?* drew additional inspiration from other popular institutions of the nineteenth century—equestrian shows and circus spectacles. Barnum's circus, for example, had some twenty years earlier toured Europe and the United States with a show entitled "Nero or the Destruction of Rome," the centerpiece of which comprised the restaging of gladiatorial combats and chariot races, the slaughter of Christians, and the announcement of a revolt by Galba, all within the boundaries of a reconstructed Circus Maximus.[35] [illustration 5.4] The circus show had itself borrowed from the plot of Sienkiewicz's novel to include scenes of bull-baiting, and its "kings of force" took on names such as Francisco Ursus. Elaborating on the iconography and technologies of such circus spectacle, the arena sequence of *Quo Vadis?* (1913) departed in numerous ways from the nineteenth-century conventions of both the visual arts and theatrical practice. The film's use of an auditorium built in depth on a vast, open-air set broke the bounds of theatrical space with its confines of painted backdrops and a proscenium stage. The new emphasis on Nero's reign as *spectacle* was achieved by the employment of vast numbers of extras to play the slaughtered Christians and the Roman witnesses to their martyrdom. The whole sequence was enhanced by the specifically cinematic, and relatively new, techniques of expansive long-shots and brief pans around the crowd. The sympathies of the cinematic spectator were directed towards the Christians by the exploitation of point-of-view shots as they are led into the arena to the accompaniment, at the Italian premiere of the film, of a chorus of fifty singers from the churches of Rome. The film's audience found that it too was face-to-face with the lions.[36]

The new technologies for representing Nero as spectacular persecutor of the Christians were met with considerable enthusiasm by domestic and foreign reviewers of Guazzoni's *Quo Vadis?* and the arena sequence was widely acclaimed with the critical rhetoric of "fidelity" and "accuracy." *Bioscope* for 20 February 1913, for example, declared that

> They have given us, in this particular scene, an absolutely faithful portrait—complete and accurate down to the very stones of the amphitheatre—of one of the chief sights of the Roman Empire. It is a spectacle far surpassing the wonders that any modern tourist may see on an actual visit to the city, and it realizes the past for us as it has never been realized before. If the cinemato-

graph had been invented a thousand years ago and the film taken then had been preserved, we should have no more fascinating and invaluable possession than this picture devised by the Cines Company.[37]

The fire of Rome and the visitation of Christ to Peter also became highlights of the new narrative of Nero as the film's audience became witness to the use of real flames and saw divine visions, both achieved through the special effect of superimposition. The fire, the chariot races, the gladiatorial combats, the massacres, Christ and the Antichrist, all seemed to come alive on the screen and vividly engage the off-screen spectator. The new technologies of cinema thus helped to authenticate a spectacular history for Nero, while the representation of the emperor's spectacles helped to exhibit cinema itself and its innovative powers for projecting the past.

Church and State in Modern Italy

Historical film-making of the silent era exploited the new technologies of the cinematic medium to adapt the subject matter and often grandiose register of nineteenth-century historiography into a language accessible to a much broader and often less literate audience.[38] The screening in Guazzoni's *Quo Vadis?* of vast crowds of spectators massed at the arena, the display of the imperial eagles, the Roman salute and the *fasces*, and the exhibition of strength by the populist figure of the strongman Ursus, are often described by modern critics as having assumed for the mass Italian audience of 1913 the value of strong historical symbols—symbols capable of gelling the aspirations of the new Italian nation through the pleasurable reconstruction of the country's past Roman glories. According to Monica dall'Asta, for example, the public united in the Roman circus of *Quo Vadis?* represents perfectly the condition of jingoism prevalent in an Italy which had only recently undertaken the Libyan adventure. She recognizes, however, that a nationalistic reading of the arena sequence has to take into consideration the complex movement of identification required of the film audience from the Roman imperialists to their Christian victims.[39]

If a decisive push towards a meeting between Italian screenings of Roman history and nationalistic ideology may be said to come from the outbreak of the first Italo-Turkish war and the subsequent conquest of Libya, the narrative of Nero's fall which *Quo Vadis?* depicts does not seem to supply a neat union between the cinematic history of *romanità* and contemporary Italian aspirations to empire. In the film, the Roman eagles, the *fasces*, the salute, and the triumphal processions belong to a decadent emperor whose historically inevitable overthrow and death is instigated by the heroism of the persecuted Christians. The narrative of *Quo Vadis?*—in contrast to that of Guazzoni's subsequent production *Marcantonio e Cleopatra* (1913) or Giovanni Pastrone's *Cabiria* (1914)—was clearly not a wholly appropriate site for a cinematic exploration of the moral and political cohesiveness of modern Italy in successful confrontation with external opponents. Instead Guazzoni's *Quo Vadis?* appears to have appropriated Nero's fall as a metaphor for the possible outcome of the new state's internal dissensions.

Already in the nineteenth century, narratives of Nero's reign and Peter's martyrdom were inextricably bound up with wider political discourses concerning the battle then taking place in Italy over the temporal powers of the papacy. In his *Origines du Christianisme*, the anticlerical Renan argued against the theological doctrine of the supremacy of the Church at Rome. According to Renan, Jesus had not looked to Rome as the most appropriate location in which to base the government of the faithful, had not desired to establish an episcopal succession in a fixed city, and had not even intended to appoint a leader in his Church. Responsibility for the creation of "the holy city" was placed by Renan in the hands not of God but of Nero. The primacy of the Church at Rome was both an historical accident caused by Nero's massacres and a modern constraint in need of political redress. Thus in the *Origines*, Renan's rejection of a doctrinal belief in the Roman Church's absolute authority was coupled with praise for the "liberating" occupation of the papal state by the King of Italy, which had occurred only recently, in 1870.[40] The subsequent, graphic reenactment of the legend of *quo vadis* in Sienkiewicz's novel reads as a forceful response to such assaults on the temporal sovereignty of the papacy. After the visitation of Christ along the Appian Way, Peter is strengthened in his belief that "all the legions of Caesar could never destroy the living truth," that Rome has become the city of Christ destined to "rule over both the souls and the bodies of men" (425). In the discursive structures of the novel, Peter speaks for the Catholic Church, Nero for the secular state, and Christ's miraculous appearance on the outskirts of Rome provides both ancient and divine sanction for the renewal of the Vatican's temporal powers in modern Italy.

In Italy itself, throughout the nineteenth century, the political struggle between the papacy and the nationalists was conducted on both sides through the rhetorical tropes of *romanità*—as a contest between the cross and the *fasces*. While the *risorgimento* revolutionaries sought to secularize Italy through the resurrected image of an ancient Roman republic governed by triumvirs and consuls, the Vatican countered such symbolism for political authority with the image of Christianity triumphant over pagan Rome and, for example, programatically conducted the consecration of the Colosseum to the early Christian martyrs. The papacy thus attempted to transform the *risorgimento*'s virtuous Roman republic ascendant into an imperial tyranny historically destined to be brought down by the heroism of the early Church's Christian adherents.[41]

A curious scene occurs in the course of Guazzoni's film *Quo Vadis?* which seems to have warned its Italian spectators to look carefully for correspondences between the cinematic fable of the Neronian age and the condition of Italy in the first decades of the twentieth century. As in Sienkiewicz's novel, the Roman soldier Vinicius is converted to Christianity through his love for the innocent girl Lygia. When in the film, however, he kneels alongside Lygia in a humble Christian house to be blessed by Peter, a symbol attached to the room's back curtain is revealed framed centrally on the cinema screen—it seems to be an axe and sickle arranged in what would become a very familiar design in the twentieth century. [illustration 5.5] *Quo Vadis?* appears to offer itself thereby as an ancient allegory for the continuing conflicts between Church and secular state in modern Italy. Since the unification of Italy in 1861, the Vatican had refused to recognize the new secular state's existence and a mass movement had developed to reconquer national life for Catholicism. Towards the turn of the century, the Liberal government, lumping together the "clericals" and the partisans of the Socialist International as political subversives, had banned a large number of Catholic and Socialist organizations, and had arrested and imprisoned many of their supporters.[42] Through the film's simple symbolic iconography, spectators were being guided visually to equate the Christians of the Neronian age with those groups (Catholics and Socialists) who had been persecuted by the Liberal government in the repressions of 1898. Adapting the political rhetoric of Sienkiewicz's novel, Peter once again speaks for the Catholic Church, Nero for the secular government under whose authority the new persecutions had been taking place. In the spectacular climax to the film, the giant Ursus then wrestles the innocent girl, who is Catholic Italy, from the clutches of the beast who is the secular kingdom.[43]

By 1913, the year in which *Quo Vadis?* was released, the role of Catholics in Italy's national life had become a central preoccupation. A tacit truce, rather than a general reconciliation, between Church and state had furnished Catholic candidates for the national elections of that year and permitted the Catholic masses to vote in most constituencies.[44] The cinematic depiction of Nero's persecution of the Christians and his subsequent downfall was released by the Cines production house which, funded by Catholic banks, was organizing its film-making activities as a way of extending Catholic influence in Italian society.[45] The narrative drive of Guazzoni's *Quo Vadis?* places Roman and Christian culture in sequence as successively greater stages in the progress of Italian history. The financial backers of Cines, therefore, could take pleasure in seeing the contemporary claims of

5.5 Baptism of Vinicius, from *Quo Vadis?* (1913). [Photograph taken from postcard in private collection of Riccardo Redi.]

the Catholic Church to the renewal of its temporal power enhanced by a multilayered historical reconstruction of a Manichaean struggle between victimized Christians and a secular tyranny. The final victory of the Christian Church over the Roman state within *Quo Vadis?* might then signify to contemporary spectators the merit of reestablishing the value of the Catholic Church in the social and political order of modern Italy.[46]

The cult of *romanità* appears to have been homogeneous neither in Italy's cultural formation generally nor in its cinematic productions of Roman history. If *romanità* was an ambiguous concept, an invented tradition that was capable of assimilating modern Italy to the virtues of the Roman republic and the glories of the Roman empire as well as to the Christian values which were regarded as having destroyed the earlier pagan past, it is not surprising that such ambiguity seeped into the cinematic reconstructions of Italy's ancient history. Despite the use in *Quo Vadis?* of the *fasces* and other paraphernalia of Roman rule as contested national symbols, the exhibition practices and narrative image associated with the film on its release rendered it a glorious product both of the Italian nation and of the art of the cinematograph.

Guazzoni's film adaptation of the novel *Quo Vadis?* became an enormous international success, and its exhibition was everywhere packaged as a prestige event. In London, its premiere was held at the Royal Albert Hall in the presence of King George V. In New York, it was the first film ever to play in a Broadway theater usually devoted to the "legitimate" stage, where it ran for twenty-two weeks. In Rome itself, the premiere was held at the Teatro Costanzi in the presence of ambassadors, politicians, and literati, and it remained in circulation in Italy until the end of the First World War. Each opening was described in all the respective daily newspapers, and the relatively new publications dedicated to cinema, such as *The Motion Picture World*, filled page after page with details of these events.[47] In all these extra-cinematic discourses, more space was dedicated to aesthetic rather than political readings of the film. Thus *Bioscope* for 20 February 1913 mentions in passing the educational value of Guazzoni's *Quo Vadis?* as "an immense drama, dealing with the fates of a faith and a nation," but is otherwise far more concerned to detail the Italian film's brilliance as an example of the art of cinema:

> It will do more to promote the dignity and well-being of the film trade than any other production one has seen. A picture like this can be neglected by nobody. Once and for all, it establishes the right of the cinematograph to recognition as a serious and unique artistic instrument with infinite possibilities, to be esteemed accordingly.

Captured on screen, Nero's spectacles were lauded both in Italy and abroad, and the emperor came to embody the newfound artistry of cinema and the pleasures of the cinematic gaze itself.

The Italian practice of employing *romanità* as an instrument for the exploration of the modern state's national identity necessitated a troubled history for the representation of Nero on screen under the years of Fascist rule. Even before the March on Rome in 1922, the Fascist party had constructed its own identity and legitimated its actions through the tropes of an ancient Rome reborn. In its title the party claimed to have appropriated for itself the symbolic authority of the Roman *fasces*. The party's advocacy of national unity and strength was cased as a call for a return to the perceived discipline and militancy of Roman Italy, and when Mussolini finally marched on Rome his act of aggression was swiftly formulated as a glorious reenactment of Julius Caesar's crossing of the Rubicon.[48] The sequence of intertitles which open a remake of *Quo Vadis?* produced in 1924 demonstrates the uncomfortable fit between the cinematic Nero and the political rhetoric of the now recently instated Fascist regime. The first intertitle might have satisfied the Fascists: "Rome was capital of the world. Its eagles and standards, planted by the victorious legions, marked the boundaries of the known world." But the second and third intertitles could not have:

To Rome flowed an enormous mass of interests and forces, customs and religions, the vices and virtues of all the world. / Symbol of that mixture of
power and corruption, beauty and sin, was a man, an emperor—Nero.

Although it was not until the 1930s that the ideological connotations of
romanità became both more pronounced and more oppressive, already in
1924 the Neronian narrative was a wholly inappropriate paradigm for the
aspirations of the Fascist regime. It was redolent neither of national unity
nor of rightful dominion over foreign peoples, but of vicious dictatorship,
sadistic persecution, and widespread discord and dissent. Moreover, the
renewed representation on screen of a bitter struggle between the cross and
the *fasces*, between the generosity of Peter and the cruelties of Nero, might
now recall not only the turn-of-the-century persecutions of Catholic organizations instigated by the old liberal government, but also the present ruthless persecution of the Catholic Popular Party by Mussolini's blackshirts.
The Roman premiere of the new *Quo Vadis?* (which was directed by
Gabriellino d'Annunzio and Georg Jacoby) was held in March 1925. After
the bitterly contested elections of the preceding spring, Fascist violence and
intimidation against the Popular Party had continued unabated and intensified after Mussolini's declaration in January 1925 that the Fascists were
going to rule dictatorially. At the time when Roman audiences saw this latest *Quo Vadis?* opposition parties, the press, and labor organizations were
being repressed or dissolved, and anti-Fascists imprisoned.[49] Although the
regime at the same time was attempting to woo the Vatican through, for
example, the reintroduction of Christian teaching into primary schools, its
bloody destruction of the Catholic Popular Party would have facilitated for
cinema audiences the opportunity to equate the dictator Mussolini with the
tyrant Nero.

Quo Vadis? (1924) cannot have pleased the Fascist regime, but neither
could it have been entirely pleasing to the Church or the state's Catholic
opponents, for the film made by d'Annunzio and Jacoby gives far more
screen time to the imaginatively reconstructed vices of the emperor than to
the virtues of the Christian faith. The film opens, for example, in the
grounds of the imperial palace, with the Roman court amassed before an
extraordinarily grand fountain. The camera lingers lovingly over the brutal
but sensual image of a young girl's naked body as, on the emperor's whimsi-
cal command, she is fed to the vicious eels which lurk in the fountain's
depths. Following the characteristics of Weimar cinema with which the
German codirector Georg Jacoby and the German lead actor Emil Jannings
were particularly associated, this *Quo Vadis?* foregrounds specularity—the
pleasure and the anxiety of the look. Repeatedly, however, as Nero peers

through his emerald ring at a tortured slave girl, the innocent Lygia or the martyred Christians, the camera takes up his point of view, and the cinema spectator is permitted simultaneously to abhor *and* to enjoy the lustful or sadistic vision of the repulsive emperor.[50]

Distasteful to both state and Church, the *Quo Vadis?* of Jacoby and d'Annunzio could not even lay claim to the cinematic innovation of Guazzoni's earlier adaptation of the nineteenth-century novel. The remake was poorly received by both critics and the general public as a systematic and rather tiresome repetition of the mise-en-scène of Guazzoni's film, and its conservatism was considered to be unrelieved by any significant technical advance over the Italian film industry's earlier glorious achievement.[51] After the critical and commercial failure of *Quo Vadis?* (1924), only one Nero entered film distribution in Italy before Mussolini's fall, and that Nero belonged to an artistic tradition different from that of film spectacle.

From 1917, before the establishment of the Fascist regime, the comedian Ettore Petrolini began to include among the numerous sketches he performed on the Italian stage a parody of the Neronian court which was full of humorous anachronisms. Dressed in the guise of both Nero and clown—wearing a wreath, a red nose, and baggy pants—Petrolini sets light to Rome with a box of matches and explains to firemen on the telephone that he wants to rebuild Rome in fortified cement. The act clearly originated as a parody of the Italian rhetoric of *romanità*, including all its manifestations in the literary, theatrical, and cinematic versions of the *Quo Vadis?* narrative.[52] Petrolini continued to perform this sketch in Italian theaters throughout the 1920s, and in 1930 a film of one of his performances was released throughout the country. The film's title, *Nerone*, gave the parody of *romanità* pride of place in the actor's comic anthology.

It is still the subject of some controversy whether the *Nerone* which Petrolini played on stage in the 1920s had become a subversive critique of dictatorship under Fascism, for Petrolini in person expressed his admiration for Mussolini and received awards from the regime, while Mussolini himself was a great admirer of the comedian. On one occasion, the *duce* is said to have covered his face laughing when the Petrolinian Nero produced a speech reminiscent of one of his own. At the very least, the comic sketch gave theater audiences of the 1920s a momentary license to laugh at the enduring posturings of *romanità*, and perhaps even served the interests of the regime at the time by parading before the Italian public Fascism's apparent broad-mindedness.[53] However, by the time the Petrolinian Nero passed beyond the confines of Italian comic theater on to the cinema screen in 1930, the dangers of its incompatibility with the official rhetoric of the regime were openly recognized. On the release of the film *Nerone*, the *Giornale d'Italia* claimed indignantly that it was intolerable to display this sort of Nero—a Nero in rags, part despicable, part foolish—to the world at large.[54]

Even after the fall of Mussolini and the end of the Second World War, the Italian film industry did not again invest considerable capital in the production of spectacular Neros for mass, international audiences. It was only as late as 1985, at a time when television had taken over from cinema as the new medium for expensive historical productions, that Rai television coproduced a colossal, Felliniesque remake of *Quo Vadis?* as a six-hour miniseries. In the intervening sixty years, the Italian cinematic Nero had only resurfaced in small-scale ventures, cheap parodies, or the so-called "sexy" genre, designed for release in the less prestigious movie theaters. From the 1930s, Neronian film spectacle became the prerogative of Hollywood, and yet another Neronian narrative was constructed to suit the requirements of a different cinematic system and another continent's historical consciousness.

The Roman Eagle and the American Cross

The earliest versions of the Neronian narrative produced by the American film industry were largely based not on the Roman Catholic momentum of Sienkiewicz's novel *Quo Vadis?* but on the evangelism of a British toga play. When Paramount released Cecil B. DeMille's *Sign of the Cross* around Christmastime of 1932, it was already the studio's second version of the Wilson Barrett play of that name in which the Prefect of Rome, Marcus Superbus, is torn between loyalty to his depraved emperor and love for the pure Christian girl Mercia.[55] The play, performed extensively in Britain and America from 1895, begins when the persecution of the Christians at Rome is already under way, and ends not with the successful rescue of Mercia from Nero's arena and its political and religious consequences for the history of the "Holy City," but with the Roman soldier's conversion to the Christian faith and his personal salvation through martyrdom in the arena by his beloved's side:

> MERCIA: Farewell—Marcus.
> MARCUS: No, not farewell—death cannot part us—I, too, am ready. The light hath come—I know it now—Thou hast shown me the way—my lingering doubts are dead [*he takes Mercia's hand*]. Return to Caesar—Tell him Chrystos hath triumphed—Marcus, too, is a Christian—[*Drawing her closer to him*] Come, my bride—
> MERCIA: My bridegroom—
> MARCUS: Thus, hand in hand, we go to our bridal [*they ascend the steps*]— There is no death for us, for Chrystos hath triumphed over death. The light hath come. Come, my bride. Come—to the light beyond.
> [*Exit, hand in hand, into the arena*] [*Curtain*][56]

In his autobiography, DeMille described his film adaptation of Barrett's play as following on in a natural progression from his earlier biblical films (which had themselves also been based on melodramatic stage spectacles and Victorian pictorialism). For the director, *The Ten Commandments* (1923) narrated the Giving of the Law, *The King of Kings* (1927) the Interpretation of the Law, and *The Sign of the Cross* (1932) the Preservation of the Law. According to DeMille's own retrospective account, *The Sign of the Cross* and its representation of the Roman past was also highly relevant to the dark conditions of the American Depression in the months which preceded the launch of Franklin D. Roosevelt's New Deal.[57] In an interview given to *New York American* for 15 June 1932, DeMille had already expressed in a similar, but more hyperbolic mode the relevance for America of the film he was about to shoot:

> Do you realize the close analogy between conditions today in the United States and the Roman Empire prior to the fall? Multitudes in Rome were then oppressed by distressing laws, overtaxed and ruled by a chosen few. Unless America returns to the pure ideals of our legendary forebears, it will pass into oblivion as Rome did.[58]

DeMille's cinematic nostalgia for moral certitude, a sense of community and pure Christian values, was appropriately explored through an adaptation of the narrative structures of Barrett's *The Sign of the Cross*. At the time of the play's performances at the turn of the century, it was labeled "a sensational sermon" or "a Salvation Army tragedy" by its Victorian critics for its melo-dramatic representation of a corrupt empire (embodied in the arrogant Superbus) which is redeemed by a fresh infusion of Christian ideals (embodied in the compassionate Mercia).[59] In the well-defined metaphoric world of toga drama, the decadent Roman empire needing redemption inevitably recalled the contours of more recent empires. Barrett's play was capable of addressing both misgivings about the entrenched powers of the British establishment in its maintainance of empire and fears that American imperialism was undermining the nation's unifying Christian culture and leading it to Armageddon.[60]

Barrett's *The Sign of the Cross* provided DeMille with a more usable past than Sienkiewicz's *Quo Vadis?* For audiences of DeMille's film adaptation of the toga play, a parable was provided for the crisis of Depression America, in which the poor and oppressed are equated with Christian virtue and cat-astrophe is avoided and salvation attained by a rejection of worldliness and a deferral of pleasure to "the light beyond." No solution to the current crisis is made available in the temporal domain. The choice of the nineteenth-century play rather than the novel as source material for an American narrative of Neronian Rome also meant the absence from DeMille's film of the apostle Peter and the *quo vadis* legend which, in the Italian film versions of the novel, had sanctioned the supremacy of the Church at Rome and furthered the interests of Italian Catholicism. The nonsectarian, nondoctrinal evangelism of the play transferred well to American screens, becoming a vehicle to draw a mass audience of liberal Protestants and religious fundamentalists as well as urban Catholics. The purposes of religious parable and commercial profit were thus satisfied simultaneously.[61]

The rhetoric of historical accuracy—such as references to the employment of a huge research team—was a constant component of the publicity campaigns for DeMille's historical epics, but nonetheless there was also always an American quality to his cinematic reconstructions of antiquity.[62] The cinematic technology of sound, for example, was now applied for the first time to an American spectacular film, thereby assisting the process of establishing in the film's audience an alignment that differed substantially from that constructed for Italian audiences of earlier Neronian spectacles. The heroic protagonist Marcus speaks in the American cadences of the actor Fredric March, the hated emperor in the English accent of the actor Charles Laughton. This linguistic paradigm of American heroes pitted against British villains was subsequently inscribed into the narratives of the post-war Hollywood epics set in ancient Rome. In *The Sign of the Cross* (1932), the Neronian narrative of earlier Italian cinema is rewritten to render Nero the embodiment of essentially *foreign* evils against which a modern American crusade is to be fought. DeMille's historical film offers its audiences the satisfying cadences of a victory destined to be won. The cruel emperor is identifiable with British colonial rule, the innocent Christians with the American rebels against that rule, and all that is needed is a simple replay of the American Revolution to win Marcus and modern America back for God.[63]

In the fight for the soul of Marcus, *The Sign of the Cross* deploys a simple iconographic code to plot the victory of an Americanized Christianity over Nero's alien *romanitas*. The film's opening sequence includes a close-up of a cross which a Christian has drawn in the dust of a Roman street, only for it to be trampled on when Marcus disperses the passers-by. Later in the film, the symbol of a Roman eagle seen in relief on the wall of an underground prison (where the innocent boy Stephan is being tortured horribly in the name of Roman justice) is swiftly countered in the next scene by a simple cross of twigs which Marcus curiously examines after a Christian meeting in a woodland grove has been broken up. When his beloved Mercia is dragged off to the arena dungeons from the hero's home, Marcus is left leaning wretchedly against his door with arms widespread, but he backs away in alarm from the shadow of a cross which his posture thereby casts upon the floor. In the absence of an engaging Petronius or a forgiving Peter, the Americanized Neronian fable is focused even more exclusively on the arena as the site of a final, spectacular battle between the eagle and the cross, empire and individual, tyranny and religious devotion. The film's climactic sequence symbolically pitches a Nero dwarfed by the huge sculpture of an eagle with outstretched wings (which sits above his throne in the arena's royal box) against Marcus and Mercia, who walk up the steps of their dungeon to death swathed in a brillant and cherished light that falls on them in the shape of a cross. Throughout DeMille's *The Sign of the Cross*, the Roman eagle signifies an oppression and moral decadence which is quintessentially foreign, the triumphant cross a freedom and innocence which is quintessentially American. Americanism is thus associated with the dogmas of Christianity and gifted with the endorsement of God.[64]

How DeMille's Nero could be read as a cultural symbol of the evils against which modern-day America fights was made explicit on the film's reissue in 1944. At the time of the Allied campaign in Italy (when Mussolini had already been ousted from power in Rome), Paramount saw the possible appeal and commercial potential of a rerelease of *The Sign of the Cross*, and began preparations to add a costly new prologue to the film outlining its additional, suddenly acquired, relevance. Through the technologies and practices specific to film industries, the studio was able swiftly to disclose and to extend their Nero's engagement with developments in contemporary history. In the specially filmed prologue, two American army chaplains, one Protestant and one Catholic, are on board a Flying Fortress whose mission is to drop propaganda leaflets on Rome about the merits of the Allied invasion. They, in a group now representing a microcosm of Christian America, explain to the skeptical, secular turret-gunner and pilot the troubled history of the city. The prologue concludes, "Nero thought he was master of the world. He cared no more for the lives of others than Hitler does" and, as the plane turns back, the clouds of anti-aircraft smoke which fill the screen dissolve to be replaced by the smoke of the ancient city burning under Nero's orders, accompanied by the sounds of the emperor's demonic laughter. At the close of the film, after Marcus and Mercia ascend to death and salvation, a new epilogue briefly displays Allied bombers flying in the shape of a cross.[65] Through the addition of prologue and epilogue, the damage to the ancient city becomes the clear counterpart of its modern devastation, and the campaign to liberate Rome parallels the travails and victories of the early Christian martyrs. DeMille had once before used such a technique for making the past more overtly usable during a time of war. His *Joan the*

Woman (1916) contains modern prologue and epilogue set in the trenches of France and relates the enclosed narrative of the Hundred Years War to the pressing needs of contemporary, war-torn France.[66]

When, soon after the production of the new prologue and epilogue to *The Sign of the Cross*, Rome fell to the Allies, Paramount rushed the revised version of the film for early marketing, and distributed to cinema managers a pressbook that was able to extend even further the rhetoric of the film's engagement with the rapidly changing events of the war.[67] The pressbook included the following suggestion for a spot announcement to advertise the film locally:

> Eternal Rome—prize of conquest through the centuries—now freed by the might of Allied arms—in the flaming nights when the murderous tyrant Nero had it burned to the ground. Here is a picture which will show you why Truth can never be stamped out by a tyrant—why the sign of the cross will forever be the symbol of man's final triumph over brutality and barbarism and will shine in all its brilliance centuries after men shall have forgotten the broken cross of a later tyrant.

Similarly, a sample poster had superimposed over scenes of Neronian debauchery the bold caption, "You've added a glorious chapter, lads, to the greatest story ever told!" and above the caption was positioned a group of Allied bombers formed in the shape of a cross. [illustration 5.6] In the face of such bold strategies for establishing the new significance of the film, it comes as no surprise that *Variety* for 24 August 1944 recognized that, in the terms of the reissue, "the early Christians gave their lives like American soldiers are giving theirs today for the sake of tolerance and freedom." The array of signifying practices with which cinema can swiftly manipulate its audiences' readings of film narrative gave DeMille's historical film, and its Nero, great elasticity as metaphor for modern times.[68]

Notwithstanding the moralizing metaphors to which Paramount drew such heavy attention, DeMille's Neronian narrative was also produced as a self-conscious demonstration of cinema's virtuosity in the creation of spectacle. In the final arena sequence, for example, the spectator is regaled with a vast array of gladiators, wrestlers and boxers, elephants, bears, tigers and bulls, combats between a girl and a gorilla, amazons and pygmies, before ultimately reaching the display of Christian piety before hungry lions. During the era of the American Depression, when *The Sign of the Cross* was originally made and exhibited, cinema had become a showcase for the display of commodities. And, as box-office receipts plummeted in the years 1932–1933, Hollywood studios such as Paramount sought to attract lost

5.6 Sample poster advertising the reissue of *The Sign of the Cross*, from the campaign book of 1944. [From University of Southern California Cinema-Television archive.]

audiences additionally through a portrayal of sex and sadism that went some way beyond the strictures imposed on film representations by the 1930 Production Code.[69] In his narrative of the so-called "Preservation of the Law," DeMille translated the basis for extravagant consumption to ancient Rome and placed the appeal of lurid themes within a legitimating narrative of religious uplift. But his careful lighting set-ups imparted a brilliant sheen to the materialism and perversity of the imperial city. Seducing the eye with the pleasures of sensuous surfaces, the aesthetics of the film subverted its inspirational message.[70]

Despite severe budget limitations, *The Sign of the Cross* is a slice of cinematic showmanship, in which the luxurious palaces, the pomp, the stylish backless gowns, the erotic display of female flesh, the lascivious orgies—all the film's production values—belong to the oppressors. It is Nero, as Michael Wood succinctly puts it, who throws the party.[71] The consequent ambivalence of the Nero narrative as moral metaphor is disclosed by the marketing strategies of the campaign book for the 1944 reissue, which encourages cinema managers to sell the film's religious element to church-goers, its historical element to schools, but its *spectacle*—"the glitter, the excitement, the thrills which characterized Rome at the height of her power and the depth of her depravity"—to the masses. The film stimulated cries of outrage from various American religious groups and women's organizations, but supplied Paramount with millions of dollars just as it was facing bankruptcy.[72]

The conflicts of interest generated by *The Sign of the Cross* appear to have been partially resolved in the figure of the film director himself. He is the external constructor of the film's internal spectacle but whereas the ancient Nero directed scenes of horror, the modern Nero's spectacles are represented as more benign. In a lengthy article by Dorothy Donnell that was published in the *Motion Picture Magazine* of November 1932, DeMille takes on the role of a new, beneficent Nero. He puts Hollywood's extras, unemployed since the beginning of the Depression, back to work. Hungry Vestal Virgins and gladiators, the article continues, now order malted milks and ham sandwiches in the studio cafeteria, and DeMille tries to spare the destitute among his cast when he chooses those who must appear in only a single scene. Articles such as this, and the publication of illustrative photographs drawing attention to the process of *creating* the ancient world as cinema, demonstrate Hollywood's use of the film spectacle as a metaphor for the Hollywood industry itself. [illustration 5.7] Once again the rhetoric of the Neronian fable is changed to suit new extra-cinematic contexts, and new self-conscious cinematic practices. Hollywood films become the modern arena for spectacle, and narratives about them construct their directors as new, heroic Neros.

5.7 Cecil B. DeMille directs the filming of *The Sign of the Cross* (1932). [Courtesy of BFI Stills, Posters and Designs.]

Make Like Nero!

From the late 1930s, Metro Goldwyn Mayer planned the production of what was to become the last film to date to address the Neronian myth in spectacular style, namely Mervyn LeRoy's adaptation of the *Quo Vadis?* novel, which was finally released in 1951. At a cost of over seven million dollars, this colossal Technicolor production nonetheless achieved considerable commercial success and the prestige of eight Oscar nominations.[73] It too appealed to its audiences as a multifaceted and somewhat contradictory metaphor for contemporary America and, specifically, for America's own film industry.

The rhetoric for historical authentication which MGM employed to launch the film was remarkably extravagant, thus imparting to the action projected on screen an apparent ideological authority. Studio publicity drew attention in particular to one of the film's contributors, Hugh Gray, as an Oxford man, educated in classics, knowledgeable in both Greek and Latin, whose research for the film was claimed to originate in the close study of Ovid, Petronius, Tacitus, Juvenal, and Suetonius, and now filled four volumes which would be generously donated to the University of Rome (or, alternatively, the UCLA library) upon completion of production. Even the film's title was designed everywhere to signal the meticulousness of the studio's investigations. It did not carry a question mark since, according to publicity releases, "such punctuation was not an ancient phenomenon."[74] The voiceover which introduces the 1951 *Quo Vadis*, however, sets out Nero as the Antichrist of the apocalyptic tradition—in the manner of Sienkiewicz's historical novel. Following in the iconographic pattern established by DeMille, the spectator simultaneously is invited to witness the eagle of the Roman legionaries being overwhelmed by the filmic superimposition of the cross. And the wording of the voiceover (intoned in a median, male American accent), with its imprecise talk of A.D. 64 as a period in history when "the individual is at the mercy of the state, murder replaces justice, and rulers of conquered nations surrender their helpless subjects to bondage," exposes the connotative richness of the by-now highly conventionalized Neroes of the American cinematic tradition.[75]

As with *The Sign of the Cross*, the Hollywood studio practice of releasing pre- and post-production information to the press, often reproduced verbatim in newspaper and magazine articles, effectively prepared audiences to read the cinematic Nero as a reflection on the triumphs of modern America. As early as April 1943, for example, an MGM newsletter described its forthcoming historical spectacle as "never more timely," for it was said to deal with the beginning of Christianity and "an oppression that threatened its destruction through Nero, the despotic, brutal, ruthless Hitler of his day." Within *Quo Vadis* itself, national alignments were effected using the conventions of sound initiated by DeMille's *Sign*. The film's producer Sam Zimbalist claimed to have had the script rewritten in order to present the storyline clearly from the point of view of the film's hero, played by the American actor Robert Taylor, while the villain, played by Peter Ustinov, again speaks with an English accent now familiarly signifying a *foreign* autocracy.[76] In addition, by the time of the film's release in 1951, the choice of the nineteenth-century novel, rather than the nineteenth-century play, as the basis for the film's narrative drive might fortuitously appear to audiences to suggest a welcome and pertinent historical progression. Produced prior to the Second World War, and rereleased before the war's conclusion, *The Sign of the Cross* depicts a victory over Neronian tyranny achieved only through a personal, spiritual redemption, whereas the post-war *Quo Vadis* depicts a victory achieved by collective, military overthrow. At the conclusion of *Sign*, Nero's power is still intact; at the conclusion of *Quo Vadis*, the tyrant is satisfyingly dead. The latter film's narrative, therefore, replays America's past and its most recent (and now successful) opposition to European imperialism and dictatorship.

An MGM press release on the production of *Quo Vadis* notes that the post-war Italian government generously supplied the *Forma Urbis*, a plaster reproduction to scale of imperial Rome, for a scene in which Nero points out to the astonished Petronius his megalomaniac vision—a new city to be built on the ashes of the old. [illustration 5.8] Perhaps some of the American spectators watching this film sequence might have recognized that the model in question was originally made for one of the culminating moments in Mussolini's exploitation of *romanità*—the *Mostra Augustea della Romanità* (Augustan Exhibition of Roman Spirit) which commenced in 1937.[77] While the scale model of the imperial city was first placed on display in an Fascist exhibition that sought to associate the city of the *duce* with the monumental grandeur of Augustan Rome, *Quo Vadis* resituates the model within the narrative of a madman's idea of urban planning. Almost all of those, however, who in 1951 saw the paraphernalia of imperial rule that clutter this new screen portrayal of Nero—the spread eagles, for example, which adorn his monuments, his throne, even his clothing—could not fail to recall Mussolini's personal use of such potent images of *romanità*, including the decoration of one of his caps with a spread eagle. For, during the war, cinema goers, both in Europe and the United States, had become familiar with the Fascist appropriation of *romanità* through newsreel footage and documentaries concerning the *duce* and his spectacles of popular consent.[78]

By the second decade of the Fascist era (from 1932 to 1942), the regime's deployment of *romanità* had intensified, in particular, as an instrument to excite popular enthusiasm for Fascism's imperial ambitions. The Roman eagle and the *fasces* had become the symbols of the Italian state; the "Roman" salute and marching step had entered into party ritual, mass demonstrations, and public ceremonial, such as the massive military parades that moved from the Colosseum to the headquarters of Mussolini's government in the Piazza Venezia—from ancient to modern empire—once the specially built *via dell'impero* (the Road of Empire) was opened in October

5.8 Nero shows his court plans for rebuilding Rome, from *Quo Vadis* (1951). [Courtesy of BFI Stills, Posters and Designs. ©1951 Turner Entertainment Co. All rights reserved.]

1932.[79] Thus, according to one contemporary film critic, it was a special pleasure for the Italian spectators of *Quo Vadis* to identify the crowds massed on screen beneath Nero's balcony with those who had recently filled the Piazza Venezia.[80] In post-war Italy, such a scene was capable of providing pleasure because, placed strategically among the Roman crowds saluting and cheering their emperor, are a number of plain-speaking dissenters with whom spectators might momentarily and conveniently identify.

Among the witnesses in *Quo Vadis* who are troubled by Nero's spectacle of military might is the apostle Peter. Throughout the Second World War, the crypt of St. Peter's Basilica at Rome had been subjected to unprecedented archaeological scrutiny. Preliminary reports on these Vatican excavations began to appear in Italian periodicals from 1941 and, in the course of the next ten years, accounts of the discoveries were published in the newspapers and magazines of most western countries including the United States. Finally, at the end of the year in which *Quo Vadis* was released, the official reports of the excavations disclosed that beneath the papal altar had been found an ancient mausoleum at which St. Peter had been venerated from at least the latter part of the second century.[81] None of MGM's publicity releases, however, nor any of the American newspaper articles about the making of the film *Quo Vadis* refer to the Vatican search for St. Peter's tomb. Instead, the Roman Church's collaboration with the Fascist regime (which had occurred from the signing of the Lateran treaty in 1929 until the time in the late 1930s when Mussolini became committed to the policies of Nazi Germany)[82] appears to be touched upon within the film when a purple-robed Nero appears on the balcony in a setting that suggests not just Mussolini at Fascist headquarters but also the Pope at St. Peter's itself. The Scottish actor Finlay Currie plays the solemn white-robed apostle standing out among the crowd who observe Nero's triumph, and embodies not the tainted Roman Catholic Church but the purity of Protestantism. By separating St. Peter from the papacy, the narrative of *Quo Vadis* represents effectively not the victory of Catholicism over a secular state, but that of Protestant Christianity over a European tyranny.

In the self-reflexive publicity that MGM manufactured in the American press, the Hollywood studio itself was treated literally or figuratively as a conquering hero. Both the film script and the Italian studios in which *Quo Vadis* was made were represented in the manner of disputed territories wrested by the American film industry from the clutches of the Italian dictator. Mussolini was reported as having offered the studio in 1938 a significant sum for the film rights to the *Quo Vadis?* novel, which the studio patriotically refused.[83] Much was made of the circumstances of the film's production at the Cinecittà studios in Rome which, it was noted, were originally built by Mussolini as a threat to the world dominance of Hollywood.[84] Newspaper articles concerning the first American film to be produced in Italy since the war, headlined by resonant titles such as "Americans in Rome," constantly reinforced the studio's own attempt to establish a relationship between Hollywood film production and America's wartime military successes.[85] Similarly, the production notes MGM distributed on the release of *Quo Vadis* in 1951 were replete with military analogies: the marshalling of the thousands of people involved in the film-making process was claimed to be "as complex a problem of logistics as has ever faced a general in the field," while the construction of the film's spectacular sequences was claimed to have merited "the same attention to minute details that a modern army might employ prior to a full-scale land and sea invasion."

At the beginning of *Quo Vadis*, however, the conquering hero Marcus Vinicius has *already* come back home from war, only to find there is another war still to be fought by Christianity's humble cross against Rome's proud eagles. The voiceover that opens *Quo Vadis* and the subsequent narrative drive of the film resonate with both the rhetoric of America's wartime combat against European tyrannies and the strident terms of the more immediate and pressing conflicts of the Cold War era.[86] On 12 March 1947, President Harry Truman formally launched the anti-Communist objectives of American foreign policy with an address to Congress in which he depicted a far-reaching struggle between "free" and "totalitarian" ways of life, and argued that "it must be the policy of the United States to support free peoples who are resisting attempted subjugation."[87] The year in which *Quo Vadis* was shot, 1950, saw the full flowering of the anti-Communist crusade in America in which religion took on a patriotic significance. Membership of fundamentalist Protestant sects grew as charismatic leaders like the Reverend Billy Graham painted the Cold War in apocalyptic terms and assimilated Stalin to the Antichrist, while American Catholics reacted passionately to the persecution of their coreligionists in the eastern bloc. Church membership and attendance became a means of affirming "the American way of life" against a political system perceived, above all, as godless. Two years after the release of *Quo Vadis*, in 1953, President Dwight Eisenhower incorporated a "float for God" in his inaugural parade and declared that the "recognition of the Supreme Being is the first, the most basic expression of Americanism."[88]

Many of the biblical epics which were produced from then on in the 1950s—*The Robe* (1953), *The Ten Commandments* (1956), *Ben-Hur* (1959)—thus became privileged sites for the Hollywood film industry to display and give scriptural authority to the ideology of America's Cold War. Most notably and explicitly, in a prologue to *The Ten Commandments*, DeMille himself appears on screen to inform audiences that

> the theme of this picture is whether men ought to be ruled by God's law or whether they are to be ruled by the whims of a dictator like Rameses. Are men the property of the state or are they free souls under God? This same battle continues throughout the world today.[89]

The studio publicity for *Quo Vadis* (perhaps more than the film itself) brought out this additional facet of MGM's Nero—as contemporary cultural symbol of a pagan, dictatorial Stalinism that, in its cinematic translation, is overwhelmingly defeated by the Christian faithful. The 1951 campaign book contained an announcement that the world could well use the message of *Quo Vadis* "in the dark days that seem to be threatening us," that its storyline "cries out a creed of non-violence and a just resistance to a godless aggression."[90] The community relations department of the Motion Picture Association of America took up the studio's clarion call by mailing to appropriate community leaders a letter which defended the film against charges of brutality and historical inaccuracy in the following terms:

What is important is the overall, lasting and certain impression of revulsion against evil and against a dictatorship that denies personal security to everyone and precludes the freedom to worship one's deity according to the dictates of his own conscience.

"QUO VADIS" is the greater show, the better entertainment, because without seeming to do it, it draws the great lesson from the past that we never so much needed as in the present.[91]

Such Cold War didacticism rehearsed within the institution of cinema was evidently effective for, according to the *Gazeta Wyborcza* of 31 May 1991, the film was treated as a threatening weapon of enemy ideology by the Communist rulers of Eastern Europe, where its screening was out of the question for decades.[92]

In the engaging, ironic figure of Petronius, however, *Quo Vadis* attaches a slight qualification to this essentially conformist position, and reveals further the use to which the cinematic Nero was being put for Hollywood's own obsessive self-presentation. The hounding and suicide of the writer Petronius portrayed within the film seems to recall and to criticize the severity of the witch hunts which had already been undertaken, in particular, against Hollywood's own supposed subversives. In 1947 the House Un-American Activities Committee (HUAC) had initiated an investigation into the political makeup of the motion picture industry itself. Ten screen-writers or directors who refused to discuss their political beliefs and affiliations were sentenced to a year in prison and blacklisted from further work in Hollywood.[93] As Bruce Babington and Peter Evans have observed with regard to *The Robe*, *Quo Vadis* tends to "political equivocation." The film replays and reinforces the rhetoric of the Cold War by figuring Stalin as the sadistic, godless Antichrist Nero but it also, through the death of the true artist Petronius, appears in passing to mourn the repression of the film industry's creativity which constant vigilance against Communism has required.[94]

In the same year as the release of *Quo Vadis*, a second round of investigations of the Hollywood film industry began which was only concluded after three more years. In such a climate, with Hollywood fearing to generate political controversy and desiring to demonstrate its own political purity, *Quo Vadis* could be presented as a patriotic product of a patriotic studio. One of MGM's chief executives, Louis B. Mayer, for example, had already provided testimony as a "friendly" witness in the 1947 HUAC hearings and an assurance that MGM was continuing vigilantly to prevent the incorporation of subversive ideas into the studio's products. Robert Taylor, moreover, the actor who played the hero of *Quo Vadis*, was a member of the right-wing Motion Picture Alliance for the Preservation of American Ideals which had been responsible for inviting HUAC to investigate the industry in the first place, and Taylor also had appeared as a "friendly" witness during the 1947 proceedings.[95] The hidden agenda of *Quo Vadis*—to vindicate the responsible politics of the MGM studio and the Hollywood film industry itself—was also abetted by the rhetoric of its production details. Everywhere MGM disseminated representations of itself as having patriotically contributed in some small way to America's Marshall plan for the restoration of Europe's post-war economies. The stacking up of details of the film's vast expense in the process of creating spectacle, its manufacture of thousands of costumes, sandals, helmets, and goblets, its construction of costly sets such as the replicas of Nero's palace and the Circus Maximus, the employment of thousands of extras at the Cinecittà studios, all became images of the Hollywood industry's generosity to Italy's dispossessed and its contribution to an economic program designed to keep Communism at bay in Europe.[96] The campaign book boasted that seven hundred pounds of food from the restaged Neronian banquet scenes were subsequently distributed to five relief agencies for needy Italian children. Following in the tradition of DeMille's beneficent Nero, *Quo Vadis* was greeted by the *Hollywood Reporter* for 25 May 1950 as having "breathed new fire into the economic life of Italy."[97] Nero the mad architect of a new Rome becomes Hollywood the lavish architect of ancient Roman sets and generous provider for the modern, post-war city.

Through *Quo Vadis*, the cultural force of Hollywood disseminated into the popular imagination of the 1950s the myth of Nero the Antichrist as a figure for modern America's enemies, whether Mussolini, Hitler, or Stalin. However, the appeal of Nero to Hollywood was that he could also display on screen the film industry's own spectacular excess and the seductive pleasures of consumption. At stake in the lavish production values of *Quo Vadis* were the reputation of MGM and the institution of cinema itself. As a showcase production in Hollywood's fight against the impact of television on cinema's box-office revenues, *Quo Vadis* was launched in MGM's press book and associated newspaper and magazine articles as the greatest and costliest picture of all time, comprising more sets, more actors, more costumes, more props, more principals, and more animals than any motion picture before—all generously paid for by MGM to give the film industry a much needed lift. A special campaign was also initiated to exhibit *Quo Vadis* in a carnival atmosphere and to exploit every product tie-in imaginable.[98]

The showmanship techniques deployed to exhibit *Quo Vadis* in 1951, despite the film's narrative of Christian spirituality triumphant, encouraged spectators to identify Neronian Rome positively as a site of superlative visual spectacle, grandeur, luxury, and eroticism, and to associate the experience of those pleasures with the practice of cinema-going itself. According

to the MGM campaign book, for example, the management of the Astor
Theater in New York erected above its cinema front an image of Deborah
Kerr tied to a stake which rose eight stories above Times Square, while
neon flames, lamps, and live steam simulated the burning of Rome. At the
televised premiere, models wearing imperial costumes handed out souvenir
programs while praetorian guards trumpeted the arrival of the opening
night's celebrities. Neronian Rome, as signifier not of persecution but of the
pleasures of excess, was thus taken out of the film frame and placed in the
cinema foyer and on the streets of New York and other major cities on the
exhibition circuit.

The MGM campaign book also provided theater managers with examples of an enormous variety of tie-ins to exploit in the marketing of the
spectacular and costly film. These product promotions read *Quo Vadis*, and
called on shoppers to read it, in a manner largely at odds with the film's
devices for the construction of historical analogy. Both in the 1930s and the
1950s, the "exploitation" section of Hollywood campaign books isolated a
particular scene from a film, immobilized it into a publicity still designed
for display in shop windows, and suggested an affiliation with an appropriate (if sometimes highly tangential) product.[99] Among samples of the satu-
ration merchandizing for *Quo Vadis*, a still of Peter Ustinov pointing to the
Forma Urbis [illustration 5.8] is accompanied by the following caption:

> It is an exciting moment when Emperor Nero and part of his court see the
> planned model of a new Rome in M G M's "QUO VADIS". If you're tired of
> your present living quarters and wish to move to the very latest in modern
> dwellings, come out today to *Crest Manor*. See for yourself what we have to
> offer in up-to-date one and two family houses of the very latest design.

Similarly, in the MGM campaign book's commodification of Rome, the
spread eagles that elsewhere signified European dictatorship and tyranny
were redesigned as the eagles of the American dollar and reproduced as a
pattern on a pair of *Quo Vadis* pyjamas. In the case of its final Nero,
Hollywood sold to a mass audience its self-absorbed vision of its own pleasurable excesses. Designs associated with *Quo Vadis* were used to sell to the
American consumer everything from raincoats, fire insurance, sports shirts,
wallpaper, tablecloths, slippers, pyjamas, jewelry, tie clips, and, of course,
Munsingwear rayon boxer shorts. If these advertisements called on the consumer to "Make like Nero!" it was the Hollywood film industry that was
the first to answer the call.

6

Pompeii:
Purging the Sins
of the City

Rediscovering Pompeii

A brochure of the mid-1990s advertises a range of family adventure destinations in the United States—"taking you where you've never been before."[1] In particular, a Virginia theme park promises that "the magical wonders of old world Europe" will be revealed by a trip through "nine authentically re-created villages" and recommends further that visiting families

> take off on a wet and wild expedition through the ruins of Pompeii. You'll board a 20-passenger boat which ascends mechanically to study sites inside the ruined structures . . . till a tremendous rumbling brings debris, flame and lava crashing around you.[2]

The invitation to experience at Williamsburg, Virginia the thrills, spills, and natural wonder of an "Escape from Pompeii" demonstrates the lasting fascination with and commercial pull of the ancient Italian city which was buried by the eruption of Vesuvius on 24 August A.D. 79. It also suggests that the modern consumers to whom the brochure is addressed are more likely to be drawn by a realistic reenactment of Pompeii's dramatic burial than by any detailed reconstruction of the buildings and artefacts buried. Study of the city's ruined structures is here swiftly supplanted in entertainment value by the thrill of braving and escaping simulated volcanic eruption.[3]

Some eighty years earlier, however, when the ancient city of Pompeii was made available to Americans as cinema rather than theme park, promotional literature spoke in terms of history, archaeology, reality, actuality, and art, and described the attractions of seeing earlier modes of representing the ancient city—its life as well as its death—now superseded by the new technologies of the moving image. When George Kleine distributed in the United States the Italian film *Gli ultimi giorni di Pompei* (Eleuterio Rodolfi, Ambrosio, 1913), the publicity boasted:

> The treatment of the story follows Bulwer-Lytton's novel closely. It visualizes historical romance—that is to say, romance is interwoven with history. It is antiquity re-enacted in the Twentieth Century. A critic has said of the book, "the archaeology of "The Last Days of Pompeii" is so sound that visitors accept as a matter of course, the identity of the houses of Diomed and Glaucus." This sense of reality is greatly intensified in the film. The characters are living and breathing human beings instead of shadows, and the scenes and happenings are actualities.
>
> The destruction of Pompeii is far more impressive in film than in books. We think that we hear the shrieks of terror-maddened multitudes amid the collapse of temples and hail of smoking cinders and blasts of flame.
>
> Before the great catastrophe the beautiful, idle, slumbrous, luxury-loving life of the doomed city has been painted with a master's brush.

The American film distributor appeals to and competes with a pre-existing historiographic "topography" of Pompeii to promote the cinematic resurrection of the buried city and the depiction of its citizens' voluptuous life and agonizing death. Kleine presents his Italian film as a faithful and vivid adaptation to screen of Edward Bulwer-Lytton's historical novel *The Last Days of Pompeii* (1834). The thrilling terrors of the cinematic eruption of Vesuvius are set up explicitly to surpass those provided by the novel, and are thus made implicitly to match those afforded by the spectacular, realistic strategies of Victorian pyrodramas. The closing metaphors of paint and brush interlink the cinematic iconography of Pompeian daily life with the visually rich, sensuous conventions of nineteenth-century classical-subject painting and stage designs, while the earlier invocation of archaeological realism draws on the continuing cultural hold of the ancient city which the excavations were constantly stimulating.

The drive to reenact antiquity in the twentieth century, to which Kleine draws attention, had been significantly motivated by the archaeological investigation of Pompeii itself. The excavations uncovering the ancient Italian city, its public monuments, domestic artefacts, and the skeletons of its citizens had begun in 1748.[4] Early antiquarian publications of finds from the site, such as *Pompeiana: The Topography, Edifices and Ornaments of Pompeii (1817–1832)* by Sir William Gell and John Gandy, created a fascination for the objects and interior decoration of the ancient city, and later influenced and facilitated the introduction of Pompeian motifs into the silver, porcelain, pottery, furniture, and domestic ornamentation of the neoclassical revival.[5] As the site continued to be cleared in the course of the nineteenth century, the discoveries revealed simultaneously both the antiquity and the ordinariness of the Pompeian objects and the buildings which had housed them and thus gave literal force to the dominant myth of Romantic historiography—that the past should and could be resurrected in the present.[6]

Already by the 1800s, the ruins of Herculaneum and Pompeii had become fashionable stops on the Grand Tour, inspiring in their numerous visitors both an antiquarian sensibility and melancholic reflections on the uniqueness of the locale, the appearance of "time arrested in its tracks," of "life in the shadow of death," of a "tomb to the vanity of the world."[7] On visiting Pompeii in 1845, for example, Charles Dickens wrote:

> Stand at the bottom of the great market-place of Pompeii, and look up the silent streets, through the ruined temples of Jupiter and Isis, over the broken houses with their inmost sanctuaries open to the day, away to Mount Vesuvius, bright and snowy in the peaceful distance; and lose all count of time, and heed of other things, in the strange and melancholy sensation of seeing the Destroyed and the Destroyer making this quiet picture in the sun. Then, ramble on, and see, at every turn, the little familiar tokens of human habitation and every-day pursuits. . . . Furniture, too, you see, of every kind —lamps, tables, couches; vessels for eating, drinking, and cooking; workmen's tools, surgical instruments, tickets for the theatre, pieces of money, personal ornaments, bunches of keys found clenched in the grasp of skeletons, helmets of guards and warriors; little household bells, yet musical with their old domestic tones.
>
> The least among these objects, lends its aid to swell the interest of Vesuvius, and invest it with a perfect fascination.[8]

The dramatic juxtaposition of ancient daily life and the volcanic eruption that ended it—"the Destroyed and the Destroyer" observed by Dickens, the "slumbrous, luxury-loving life" and "the great catastrophe" mentioned by Kleine—had already had a moralizing dimension imposed upon it in the ancient narratives which appeared around the time of the disaster. The fourth book of the Sibylline oracles, for example, interpreted the devastation as a divine punishment inflicted on Rome's cities to avenge the emperor's persecution of the Jews and the destruction of the temple at Jerusalem which had taken place in A.D. 70. Similarly, the early Christian writer Tertullian recalled the overthrow of the sinful cities of Sodom and Gomorrah when reflecting on the annihilation of the ancient Campanian towns—a view that appeared to receive sanction in 1885 when the graffito *sodoma gomora* was found scratched on the wall of a Pompeian dining room.[9] In the nineteenth century, the rediscovery of the buried city of Pompeii also suggested irresistible historiographic metaphors for the narration of recent political upheavals such as the French Revolution. Pompeii thus contributed significantly to nineteenth-century political discourse (and its extensions into the novel and the theater), such that Thomas Carlyle's *The French Revolution, a History*, published in 1837, elaborated its narrative through the exploitation of an array of geological metaphors.[10]

The traces of individual lives and deaths left by the skeletons found at Pompeii also disturbed and moved many of the city's nineteenth-century visitors. In 1875, after touring the Mediterranean as a journalist, Mark Twain wrote of a trip to Pompeii:

> I saw the skeletons of a man, a woman, and two young girls. The woman had her hands spread wide apart, as if in mortal terror, and I imagined I could still trace upon her shapeless face something of the expression of wild despair that distorted it when the heavens rained fire in these streets, so many ages ago. The girls and the man lay with their faces upon their arms, as if they had tried to shield them from the enveloping cinders. In one apartment eighteen skeletons were found, all in sitting postures, and blackened places on the walls still mark their shapes and show their attitudes, like shadows. One of them, a woman, still wore upon her skeleton throat a necklace, with her name engraved upon it—JULIE DI DIOMEDE.[11]

Soon after its rediscovery, Pompeii became a locale for fictions of love and death in which either modern characters are transformed by their encounter with such ancient tragedy (in, for example, Madame de Staël's novel *Corinne* of 1807) or biographies are provided for the bodies found in the houses, temples, and streets of the city.[12] In the almost complete absence from ancient literary sources of any association between Pompeii and particular historical figures, however, the archaeologically detailed recreations of the city's last days and its citizens' deaths which began to appear in nineteenth-century operas, novels, plays, paintings, and pyrodramas had to be peopled with fictional characters, such as the Sallustio, Ottavia, Menenio, and Appio of Giovanni Pacini's enormously successful opera *L'ultimo giorno di Pompei* first performed in 1825.[13]

Animating the City of the Dead

Edward Bulwer-Lytton (the novelist whose historical romance was later to be visualized on screen) visited the ruins of Pompeii in 1833 when Vesuvius was again active and threatening the nearby city of Naples. In the following year, he published *The Last Days of Pompeii* in which, for the deaths of his fictional characters, he drew on those of the skeletons he had inspected in the villa of "Diomed," the temple of Isis and the streets of the excavated city.[14] In the preface to the novel, the author set out his objective of romantic recreation of the past that (in his view) transcended the archaeological project of simple rediscovery:

> It was not unnatural, perhaps, that a writer who had before laboured, however unworthily, in the art to revive and to create, should feel a keen desire to people once more those deserted streets, to repair those graceful ruins, to reanimate the bones which were yet spared to his survey, to traverse the gulf of eighteen centuries, and to wake to a second existence—the City of the Dead![15]

It was through the by-now established conventions of the historical novel that Lytton achieved his purpose of reviving, creating, peopling, repairing, reanimating, traversing, and awakening the ancient past, and thereby he effectively popularized the archaeological discoveries of the preceding century and ultimately gave to early silent cinema the narrative foundations for its own resurrection of the buried city.

In addition to the constant expansion of archaeological knowledge of Pompeii, the emergence of the historical novel in the early nineteenth century also provided one of the conditions for the subsequent birth of a cinematic form of Pompeian historiography.[16] The historicity of Sir Walter Scott's Waverly novels, on which the conventions of later historical novels such as those of Lytton were based, required the construction of a framing device to authenticate the text with respect to an external model from the past.[17] In the case of *The Last Days of Pompeii*, the external model in relation to which the fictive narrative required authentication was the fragmentary remnants of the ancient city itself. Whereas Scott was more concerned with the flavor of his chosen historical period than with detailed documentary evidence, Lytton closely matched the setting of *The Last Days of Pompeii* to current knowledge of the excavations. He used as his source material the first work in English on Pompeii's domestic antiquities, the *Pompeiana* of Sir William Gell and John Gandy; from the accurate drawings they had made with the aid of a *camera lucida*, and from the detailed descriptions of individual houses they had catalogued, the novelist placed his characters in seemingly authentic and recognizable settings for the enactment of their last melodramatic moments—the Pompeian amphitheater, the "House of the Dramatic Poet," the "Villa of Diomedes," the temple of Isis, the forum.[18]

The pleasures which the novel was able to generate out of its convincing reconstructions of Pompeian architecture are manifold. Both at the opening and close of the novel, where the author describes the homes of his fictive protagonists, the Greek Glaucus and his beloved Ione, the reader is invited to experience what the contemporary tourist could no longer see or touch—the full glories of Pompeian domestic habitation in its original condition and usage. Towards the opening of *The Last Days*, Lytton speaks of the ancient home of his fictive hero Glaucus thus:

> His retreat in Pompeii—alas! the colours are faded now, the walls stripped of their paintings!—its main beauty, its elaborate finish of grace and ornament, is gone; yet when first given once more to the day, what eulogies, what won-der, did its minute and glowing decorations create. (34)

Similarly, towards the close of the novel, the author speaks of the home of his fictive heroine Ione in the following terms: "You may tread now on the same place; but the garden is no more, the columns are shattered, the foun-tain has ceased to play" (249). The reader is doubly blessed. For the histori-cal novel can take you back not only to the moment of archaeological rediscovery, when Pompeian wall-paintings were still brilliantly visible within their ancient dwellings rather than displayed (as now) in fading fragments on the walls of the Naples museum, but also even further back to the original moment when Pompeian gardens still blossomed, columns were complete and standing, and fountains still flowed. Thus the novelistic representation of the ancient city charms its readers by offering them anti-quarian pleasures substantially superior to those available to the latter-day tourist. Readers are invited to walk, see, and touch with the characters in the novel and, therefore, to regard such celebrated objects as the mosaic of the guard dog, the painting of Ariadne abandoned by Theseus, or the bronze seats in the *tepidarium* with a casual familiarity.[19]

The novel also flatters its readers when it invites them to identify the homes of the fictive protagonists Glaucus and Ione with the visible ruins of specific Pompeian houses. As George Kleine was to boast in his film public-ity some eighty years later, readers of the novel on visiting Pompeii "accept as a matter of course the identity of the houses of Diomed and Glaucus." According to Lytton, the archaeologists and historians of the ancient city had mistakenly inferred that a Pompeian house adorned with scenes from ancient Greek poetry must have belonged to a professional poet rather than to "Glaucus," the sophisticated man-about-town whom the author sites within it: "and still (though the error is now acknowledged) they style in custom, as they first named in mistake, the disburied house of the Athenian

Glaucus 'THE HOUSE OF THE DRAMATIC POET'" (34). Readers of the historical novel are attributed with a special, conspiratorial knowledge of Pompeii that supposedly elevates them above the ranks of the antiquarian pedant and, in the case of the house of Ione, above the ranks of the commonplace tourist:

> Let the traveller search amongst the ruins of Pompeii for the house of Ione. Its remains are yet visible; but I will not betray them to the gaze of commonplace tourists. He who is more sensitive than the herd will discover them easily: when he has done so, let him keep the secret. (249)

Reading *The Last Days of Pompeii* is thus rendered an act of joining a sensitive and knowledgeable community bound together by their shared, secret intimacy with the ruins of the ancient city and the characters with which the novel peoples it.[20]

Encased in its antiquarian "authenticities," *The Last Days of Pompeii* brings the ruins to life by narrating a sensational, melodramatic love story set against the backdrop of the doomed city. Glaucus, an Athenian gentleman resident in Pompeii, falls in love with another Greek resident of the city, the beautiful Ione. Jealous of their love, the evil Egyptian priest Arbaces—who presides over the local worship of Isis—murders Ione's Christian brother and contrives to have Glaucus accused of the crime. When Vesuvius erupts and overwhelms the corrupted city, a blind flower girl, Nydia, hopelessly in love with her patron Glaucus, organizes his rescue from the amphitheater where he has been condemned to the lions, and drowns herself only after she has conducted the lovers to the safety of an escaping ship. The religiously sentimental outcome finds Glaucus and Ione now happily ensconced in Athens, married and converts to Christianity.[21] The Manichean collision between good and evil which the novel delineates, the conflict between Athenian and Roman, Christian and pagan, is brought to an agonizing climax by the one clearly recognizable historical event that annihilates the villainous—the eruption of Vesuvius and the destruction of Pompeii in A.D. 79.[22]

The nineteenth-century historical novelists made the past widely accessible by depicting it in present-day terms, assimilating the fictive or historical characters of bygone ages to their own world: "the past was present, the present past."[23] Ostensibly for Lytton, the principal bond which united the Pompeians of the first century A.D. with his own day was the tie of shared emotions: "We love to feel within us the bond which unites the most distant eras—men, nations, customs perish; THE AFFECTIONS ARE IMMORTAL!—they are the sympathies which unite the ceaseless generations" (170). The author also points to many other correspondences between the

Pompeian past and the Victorian present. The lower classes of the ancient city are expressly compared to modern Italians and their outdoor life style to that of Paris, while the Pompeian elite evoke the beau monde of nineteenth-century London. The *via Domitiana*, we are told at an early stage of the narrative, "exhibited all that gay and animated exuberance of life and motion which we find at this day in the streets of Naples" (22), the house of the hero Glaucus is described as "a model at this day for the house of 'a single man in Mayfair'" (37), while the "mincing" Pompeian aristocracy recall "the beardless flutterers of the saloons of London thronging round the heroes of the Fives court" (110). But a deeper "presentist" structure can also be read out of the text, even though the absence of any explicit, fixed code for interpreting its operations renders it only loosely attached to the melodramatic narrative of past events. From the outset, Pompeii is explicitly described as a model or miniature of the whole avaricious, bloated Roman empire (29). Embodied in the handsome hero Glaucus, Athens is depicted nostalgically as a glorious democracy now enslaved to Rome:

> He felt, it is true, the impulse of nobler thoughts and higher aims than in pleasure could be indulged: but the world was one vast prison, to which the Sovereign of Rome was the Imperial gaoler; and the very virtues, which in the free days of Athens would have made him ambitious, in the slavery of earth made him inactive and supine. For in that unnatural and bloated civilization, all that was noble in emulation was forbidden. (117)

When, at the close of the novel, a robust Christianity is given the role of redeeming the Greek hero and heroine from the city's inevitable punishment, then *The Last Days of Pompeii* represents an amplification of the reformist, Whiggish stance of the author's plays—democratic principles and Christian charitable values offering salvation from the potential corruption that lurks within nineteenth-century European empires.[24]

Within twenty to thirty years of its publication, Lytton's *The Last Days of Pompeii* had become established as the canonic narrative of the ancient city's supposed fall from grace. The novel was immediately adapted for performance on the European and American stage as play or as opera.[25] Its representational strategies also stimulated the depiction of classical subjects by painters such as Lawrence Alma-Tadema and Edward John Poynter. So strong was the pictorial element in Lytton's descriptions of Pompeii, that the novelist was described by William Makepeace Thackeray as having "illustrated the place by his text, as if the houses were so many pictures to which he had appended a story."[26] The melodramatic narrative of love won, lost, and won again was frequently stopped in its tracks so that its protagonists could be set in a vividly delineated, archaeologically detailed Pompeian

6.1 Alma-Tadema's painting *A Roman Garden* or *A Hearty Welcome* (1878). [Courtesy of Ashmolean Museum, Oxford.]

landscape. Both the historical novel and the classical revival in European painting shared a scenographic exactitude of interest in the domestic architecture, furnishings, costume, and daily life of Pompeii. Jean-Léon Gérôme was inspired to paint gladiatorial combat by pieces of armor found at the site. The classical buildings and artefacts so lovingly visualized in works by Alma-Tadema were based on archaeological precedent, their fine detail aided by their creator's close scrutiny of hundreds of photographs taken at the excavations themselves.[27] But the historical novel further inspired classical-subject painters to illustrate some of its fictive scenes—as in Poynter's *Faithful unto Death* (1865) or Alma-Tadema's *Glaucus and Nydia* (1867)— and, more broadly, to place on canvas a fully credible classical world in which ancients appeared as "ordinary" people experiencing trivial incidents and enjoying everyday sentiments—as in Alma-Tadema's *The Discourse* (1865) or *A Favourite Custom* (1909). Although both representational forms, the historical novel and classical-subject painting, reconstructed the ancient world as humanized, domesticated, and glamorized, the visual depictions were not usually overshadowed by the literary work's inexorable narrative progression towards destruction and redemption, for their scenes were focused on a single, frozen moment in time. Consequently, the paintings often depicted a classical past that was arrested in a golden age, simpler, nobler, and more inspiring than the modern world of industrialization and ugly urban slums.[28] And, in face of the disorientation generated by industrialization, the painters frequently offered a comforting sense of continuity with Greco-Roman culture by locating in classical settings recognizably Victorian figures. Alma-Tadema, for example, even positioned himself or members of his own family in the Pompeian gardens of *A Hearty Welcome* (1878) and *In the Peristyle* (1866).[29] [illustration 6.1]

These visual images, displaying realistic antiquarian scenes which were focused on everyday events such as talking, courting, and bathing, achieved an extraordinary diffusion into mass culture from the 1850s onwards and lie

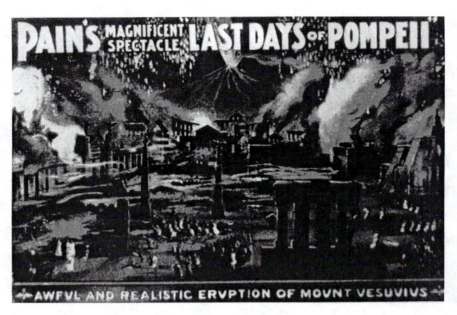

6.2 Poster advertising the pyrodrama *The Last Days of Pompeii*, c. 1890. [Courtesy of the Pain Archive.]

behind the artistic metaphors which George Kleine deployed in 1913 to launch an Italian film version of Pompeii's last days on the American market. The brilliantly colored pictures provided a form of nonliterary aesthetic pleasure that did not necessarily demand of their spectators any hermetic knowledge of the Pompeian excavations, and were patronized accordingly by the newly rich mercantile classes who could readily grasp a portrayal of "Victorians in togas" and, through the purchase and display of such paintings, thus appear to possess a familiarity with classical culture. Through technological advances in the manufacture of cheap reproductions, moreover, classical subject paintings introduced Pompeii and its art to an audience that increased dramatically over the course of the nineteenth century. First through the process of engraving, then through electrotyping, and finally, towards the end of the century, through photographic reproduction, Pompeian imagery circulated in a progressively wider public domain until its decorative motifs permeated the fashion, advertising, interior decoration, and household products of the 1880s and 1890s.[30] At the beginning of the twentieth century, therefore, when cinema took up the Pompeian narrative and its visual recreation, its audiences (particularly in Britain and America) were already equipped with an array of reconstructions of Pompeii and conventions of "presentist" interpretation to which they might expect the scenography to correspond.[31]

By the late 1880s, *The Last Days of Pompeii* had also been adapted for performance as a pyrodrama, and it proved to be the most popular and enduring example of that particular form of mass entertainment. Staged at vast outdoor locations such as the grounds of Alexandra Palace or the seaside resort of Manhattan Beach, enacted for an audience of up to ten thousand spectators on a huge stage with a cast of nearly three hundred, the performances offered both an abbreviated rendition of Lytton's fulsome narrative and momentary realizations of paintings which had been inspired by the novel. In addition to the pyrodrama's focus on collective identification with a spectacularly conceived past, this form of entertainment made several other significant contributions to late nineteenth-century modes of reconstructing the life and death of the ancient city. Historical narration was achieved through a transfer of emphasis from the verbal to the visual. Action was largely mimed to orchestral music and centred around spectacularly designed events, such as collective rituals at the temple of Isis, games, parades of circus animals, confrontations with real lions, the eruption of Vesuvius, the collapse of the city buildings, and finally the death of the villainous and the escape of the innocent on boats, which sailed away on a real lake. "Realism" was an essential feature of the productions. The city of Pompeii was constructed in the form of three-dimensional buildings hinged to simulate their collapse. Bonfires and magnificent firework displays were exploited to create the effect of an eruption, the flow of lava, and the burning of the city. As George Kleine was to comment about the superiority of filmic representations of Pompeii over those of the novel, here "the characters are living and breathing human beings instead of shadows, and the scenes and happenings are actualities."[32] [illustration 6.2]

These spectacularly staged events and special effects were witnessed by a new, mass audience of the working class which had been created by the processes of industrialization and urbanization, and had been attracted to exhibition halls, pleasure gardens, parks, and peoples' palaces by their affordable prices. For this new audience, the performance of a Pompeian pyrodrama was structured and marketed as pleasurably realistic, educational, and scrupulously moral: decadent Romans and their sinister Egyptian priests die, the decent Christians survive. Thus the historical vision of the pyrodrama, which continued to be performed successfully into the first decade of the twentieth century, conditioned its mass audiences to observe historical narrative through action, minimal facial expression, gesture, music, and spectacle, and further established nineteenth-century literary and visual codes, typological conventions, and possibilities of aesthetic pleasure in realistic resurrections of the past as the structural foundations on which cinematographic representations of the ancient city could be based.[33]

Purging Italy of the Orient

Matching the emphases of the modern Virginian theme-park ride through Pompeii, the earliest appearance of the ancient city on screen was as a prestigious pretext for the reconstruction of volcanic eruption and destruction. In 1900, in the same period as George Méliès released *L'éruption de la montaigne Pelée* and Ferdinand Zecca produced *La catastrophe de la Martinique*, William Booth made *The Last Days of Pompeii* (1900) as a four- or five-minute "reconstructed actuality" in which pagan sinners are punished by an illusionary apocalypse of fire. More spectacularly still, when Vesuvius was erupting again in 1906, filmmakers from the only recently established Italian production houses in Rome and Turin rushed into competition with each other to produce documentary footage of modern Italian houses with their abandoned rooms and gardens, this time submerged under real lava flow.[34] The display on screen of the cataclysmic wonders of Vesuvius was soon superseded in Italy, however, by a drive to re-enact antiquity. As the ambitious financiers of the swiftly expanding Italian film industry began to seek legitimation for the art of cinema and establish middle-class markets at home and abroad, their production houses turned to representations of history and, especially, re-enactments of the new nation's glorious Roman past. Drawing on nineteenth-century modes of historiography—the novel, play, opera, and painting—the studios sought to match the aesthetic pleasures and perceived educational value of high culture's most familiar and accessible historical genres.[35]

Pompeii became the focus for the Italian film industry's first experiment in screening ancient history, swiftly followed by the emperor Nero. With interest stimulated by the recent eruption and by widespread press coverage of the excavations and the constant discoveries being made there, the production house Ambrosio released Luigi Maggi's historical film *Gli ultimi giorni di Pompei* in 1908 to great domestic and international acclaim. Although Italy had produced its own operatic and poetic response to the tragic destruction of the ancient city in the form of, for example, Giovanni Pacini's opera *L'ultimo giorno di Pompei* (first staged in 1825) or Giacomo Leopardi's poem *La ginestra* (published in 1836), it was Lytton's fictive romance of Glaucus and Ione, the jealousy of the Egyptian priest, and the blind flower girl's rescue of the couple from the volcanic eruption that was appropriated by Ambrosio to become the canonical narrative for Italian cinema's representation of the Pompeian past in the twentieth century. Widely known throughout Europe and the United States, a translation of the novel had circulated in Italy from 1865, and already by 1858 the novel had been adapted for performance at Milan's La Scala. The opera *Jone, o l'ultimo giorno di Pompei* by Errico Petrella, with a libretto by Giovanni Peruzzini, had a long and successful run in Italy right up until the First World War.[36] Maggi's film of 1908 condensed the novel's narrative into a brief number of scenes, drew on the Italian operatic tradition for its grand mise-en-scène, rich sense of historical spectacle, elaborate costumes, acting style, and even some of its cast, and culminated in a scene of Pompeii's destruction which astounded audiences with its terrifying realism.[37] After its simultaneous release throughout Italy, and its wide international distribution shortly thereafter, both the popular press and specialist magazines recognized the cinematic innovation and achievement of *Gli ultimi giorni di Pompei*. According to a *Moving Picture World* of April 1909, the film was a model by which anyone interested in cinematographic production should be inspired.[38]

Two years later, the French director Victorin Jasset published an influential article in the Parisian *Ciné-Journal,* which looked back at the rapid evolution of cinematography and cited Maggi's *Gli ultimi giorni di Pompei* as a master work that had revolutionized the market for films by its artistic sense, its accurate mise-en-scène, the cleverness of its special effects, the grandeur of its conception and execution, and the exceptional quality of its photography. He also observed that the historical film had given Ambrosio a foremost place among film producers and the Italian film industry its first international success, and predicted accurately that, as a result, Italy would now monopolize historical filmmaking and Italian production houses would vie with each other in the grandeur of their Roman spectacles.[39] Thus, in 1913, as part of the industrial competition between the Italian studios to realize expensive, spectacular historical films that could match the artistic ambitions and box-office returns of earlier examples of the historical genre, such as Ambrosio's *Gli ultimi giorni di Pompei* (1908) and *Nerone* (1909), and the more recent and immensely popular *Quo Vadis?* of Cines (1913), the production of three remakes of *Gli ultimi giorni di Pompei* were announced one after the other in the American trade press.[40]

The trade advertisement which appeared in the American *Motion Picture Daily* to herald the production of an *Ultimi giorni* by the Turin studio Film Artistica Gloria makes clear the industry's appeal to cinematographic conventions for the production and reception of historical films which had now been institutionalized by the outstanding success of the feature-length *Quo Vadis?*:

> 1000ft, 30 lions, 50 horses, 1000 people. Directed by Mario Caserini. Costumes by Samperoni of Milan and Gentil of Rome. Sets built from original documents. Scenes that faithfully reproduce history. Shot on the slopes of

Vesuvius. Roman games, acquacades, the imperial galley, the destruction of Pompeii. WE FEAR NO COMPETITION.[41]

The film was never made. Despite the advertisement's boastful rhetoric, Gloria pulled out of production in the face of immediate and fierce competition from two other Turin studios: from Ambrosio, who had made the original Italian adaptation to screen of Lytton's novel, and then from Pasquali, who attempted to shoot its version within a single month in order to reach the American market first and exploit Ambrosio's prior publicity.[42] The advertisement for the Gloria version appealed to American distributors (somewhat prematurely) by locating the anticipated product in relation to the recently formulated cinematic aesthetics of its feature length, vast scale, huge casts, elaborate costumes, accurate scenography, historical realism, outdoor locations, visual spectacle, and clever special effects. In the context, however, of the Italian reception of such films, the appeal of the cinematic reconstruction of Pompeii's last days was far more substantial, complex, and wide-ranging than the American advertisement might suggest.

Since the unification of Italy, the excavation and rediscovery of the buried city of Pompeii had become a part of Italy's nationalistic imperatives. For the preceding century and a half, both the ancient sites of Pompeii and of Herculaneum had been treated as a quarry for works of classical art by the various dynasties which had ruled Naples. Under the occupation of the Austrian, Spanish, and French administrations, the Campanian cities had provided prestigious archaeological treasures for royal residences and foreign museums. Pompeii had been a place of entertainment for members of these occupying countries, and visitors to the ruined city were shown the ancient architecture and artefacts as attractions which were the property of foreign realms.[43] At the time of unification, in December 1860, the new king Vittorio Emanuele II appointed Giuseppe Fiorelli to oversee future excavations in order to reclaim Pompeii as the cultural property of Italy. The king's visit in 1869 further supplied much needed publicity and international recognition for a site that could insure a strikingly tangible historical legitimacy for his new kingdom.[44] Similarly, in 1903, a British archaeologist had proposed that an international commission should run the excavations, but the Italian government withdrew its support for the project when it was rumored that the head of the commission was to be the president of the United States rather than the Italian king himself. By 1907 the government had decreed that the city of Pompeii was to be excavated under exclusively Italian auspices, and, from 1910 on into the period of the Fascist regime, Vittorio Spinazzola ran the excavations meticulously, bringing to life the *via dell'abbondanza* by preserving or reconstructing the upper stories of its shops, their windows and balconies, signs and notices, and by leaving furniture and wall-paintings intact in the houses in which they had first been disclosed.[45] Thus, from the end of the nineteenth century, the rediscovery and restoration of Pompeii's ancient monuments as well as the fashion for decorating new buildings with Pompeian motifs had taken on a nationalistic, proprietorial imprint.[46]

Two adaptations of Lytton's Pompeian fiction were released in August 1913—*Gli ultimi giorni di Pompei* directed by Eleuterio Rodolfi for Ambrosio, and *Ione, o gli ultimi giorni di Pompei* directed by Giovanni Enrico Vidali for Pasquali.[47] They were praised frequently in the Italian press for their detailed archaeological reconstruction and lively animation of the ancient city. *La vita cinematografica* of 15 October 1913 claimed that the Pasquali film

is in its entirety a faithful and impressive reevocation of wealthy, pleasant and full surroundings. In them even the most expert eye knows only reluctantly how to discern the truth of the pictorial fiction, so great has been the meticulous and almost unceasing care for the slightest details. . . . No one ever had dared to reconstruct here in our Turin, a complete and very accurate area of one of the most formidable architectural monuments of the Roman spirit.

Pasquali dared, and was right to dare.

While earlier *Il giornale d'Italia* of 26 August 1913, commenting on the Ambrosio film, remarked:

This drama concerns the life in Roman antiquity of a Campanian city which is full of movement and of passions. The now silent streets of the disburied city are animated like the city streets of today. . . . Thus in little more that an hour you penetrate the secrets of that very distant life better than studying a hundred treatises of Greco-Roman antiquarianism.[48]

The technologies of film production employed in both films to reconstruct and animate Pompeii, and to adapt Lytton's fiction to screen, offered their contemporary Italian spectators a unique visual pleasure. For they were able to witness vividly, subjectively, and collectively not only the repairing of the ruins and the reanimation of its skeletons, but also the replacement of famous ancient artefacts (which were by now dispersed throughout European and American museums) in their "rightful" locations—that is in the houses and hands of the Pompeian citizens themselves. [illustration 6.3] In viewing and recognizing the films' careful reconstructions of the city's architecture and domestic furnishings, and in identifying with the point of view of the films' hero and heroine, the Italian spectators could enact the

6.3 Domestic interior, from the Pasquali version of *Gli ultimi giorni di Pompei* (1913). [Courtesy of BFI Stills, Posters and Designs.]

reclamation of Pompeii and its people as part of their own national heritage.

Such a cultural appropriation of Pompeii through cinematic historiography, however, was not without its paradoxes. For the ancient city which was being reclaimed for the Italian nation had, from the very moment of its catastrophic destruction, been locked into narratives which read its burial as a sign of divine vengeance on a sinful people. While Lytton's lovingly detailed delineations of Pompeian art and architecture might readily be translatable into visual instruments for the glorification of modern Italy, his inexorable narrative progression towards the disgrace and punishment of the city was less evidently so. *The Last Days of Pompeii* became a very well known and popular historical work in Italy around the time of unification and the birth of the new nation, but in the novel Lytton had made quite explicit how he proposed the downfall of Pompeii should be read by the Italians of his day:

> Italy, Italy, while I write, your skies are over me—your seas flow beneath my feet, listen not to the blind policy which would unite all your crested cities, mourning for their republics, into one empire; false, pernicious delusion! your only hope of regeneration is in division. Florence, Milan, Venice, Genoa, may be free once more, if each is free. But dream not of freedom for the whole while you enslave the parts. (117)

6.4   The Egyptian priest Arbaces, from the Ambrosio version of *Gli ultimi giorni di Pompei* (1913). [Photograph from private collection of Vittorio Martinelli.]

Thus for Lytton, the destruction of Pompeii (a city which operates in his terms as a model of the whole bloated Roman empire and its enslaved communities) carries a political warning against the most fundamental aspirations and achievements of the subsequently constituted Italian kingdom—namely unity, freedom, and empire.

Various repressions and alterations of Lytton's historical novel were clearly needed for both the Ambrosio and the Pasquali adaptations to mesh more comfortably with the cultural identity that was being formulated for the Italian nation in the period around 1913. Thus Christianity has no place in either film as a set of values to be opposed to and esteemed above those of its pagan persecutors. Nor are sensitive, democratic Athenians set against avaricious, decadent Romans.[49] Instead Pompeii is represented as a community endangered by a *foreign* evil that the eruption of Vesuvius must expunge. Justice is meted out to the hero Glaucus in the Roman senate house by the togaed representatives of imperial authority. But if an innocent man is condemned, the cause lies in the machinations of the evil priest of Isis, Arbaces, whose villainy is swiftly exposed and terribly punished.

Once the central characters have been introduced in the opening sequences of the Ambrosio and Pasquali films, it is the priest Arbaces and his
vile lust for Ione which propel the narrative proper. He is visually demarcated as Other, a non-Roman. His elaborate headdress and costume, the
architecture and religious artefacts of the temple of Isis within which he
attempts to initiate his disciple into the cruel impostures of the foreign cult,
identify the priest within the terms of Orientalism as belonging to the
racially inferior, decadent East, to the older superceded culture of the
Pharoahs.[50] [illustration 6.4] Constantly framed on screen by black slaves
and Egyptian props, Arbaces is described in Ambrosio's intertitles as a bird
of prey who sweeps down on the innocent dove Ione. The priest thus conforms to western stereotypes of Egyptian savagery, deceitfulness, immorality, animality, and perverse sexual dominance.

In the ensuing film narratives, there unfolds a multiple colonialist rescue
fantasy in which innocent western women must be rescued from the lascivious predations of eastern aggressors. In the Ambrosio film, Arbaces entices
Ione into his exotic terrain only to have his attempted violation of her body
thwarted by her brother. Temporary safety from assault is provided in the
recognizably Pompeian home of Glaucus. After the hero's contrived arrest,
the blind flower girl is similarly imprisoned in the vaults of the temple of
Isis and, on her escape, requires the assistance of a Pompeian aristocrat to
denounce the Egyptian priest publicly in the arena. The Pasquali film
intensifies the colonialist narrative drive by differentiating markedly
between the behavior of a black and a white slave towards the imprisoned
flower girl. It is only the sympathies of the white slave that prevent Nydia
from being mercilessly beaten on several occasions by the vicious African
servant of Arbaces, and it is the white slave who helps her send a plea for
help to Glaucus' friends. As Ella Shohat has observed, such rescue fantasies
manufacture a role for the western male as liberator from oriental aggression and thus provide an apparent justification for colonial domination.[51]

The spectacular and climatic sequence of the Ambrosio film, in which
Arbaces is denounced in the arena, was much admired both in Italy and
abroad. The reviewer for the Chicago magazine *Motography* wrote, on 18
October 1913:

> One little scene, alone, in this arena spectacle, is worthy of the highest
> praise—it is that one in which we behold not hundreds, but thousands and
> thousands of excitement-mad spectators, demanding the life of the high
> priest: their arms are raised in angry protest and every face is lit with passion.
> The reviewer has seen thousands of films, but cannot recall ever having seen
> a more convincing mob scene than [the] one in question.[52]

Such devices for the construction of a cinematic orientalism and a colonialist narrative drive had particular potency in the period around 1913. For, only a few years previously, audiences in Italian cinemas had watched documentaries on the history and habits of Egypt such as *Paesaggi egiziani* and *Regno dei Faraoni*, in the context of Italy's imperialistic ambitions to conquer territories in North Africa. The cult of *romanità* had frequently been deployed by Italian imperialists before, during, and after the North African campaigns of 1911–1912 to legitimate the new Italian nation's geopolitical ambitions. The Roman past was structured as a period of national unity, cultural supremacy, prosperity, and empire whose civilizing mission required renewal under threat of the oriental decadence of the Ottoman empire. The denunciation of Arbaces which occurs in the climatic moments of both Italian films thus conforms with the racist sentiments of Italian imperial policy in the early 1910s. Barbarism was a pressing and constant nightmare to be countered only by the establishment of a new Roman empire, by making Italy the mistress of the Mediterranean.[53] From the period of the conquest of Libya until the outbreak of the First World War, many Italian films set in the Roman past accordingly celebrated the glorious triumph of western civilization over the barbarism of the Orient and, in the months that followed the release of both the Pompeian films, the *Marcantonio e Cleopatra* of Cines (1913) and the *Cabiria* of Itala (1914) were to revel in the display of Roman troops winning victories on the shores of Africa itself.[54]

Both the Ambrosio and Pasquali films, therefore, simplify and reshape the narrative of Lytton's novel to offer their spectators a cinematic history of Pompeii that takes their audience on a voyage of purification and redemption from oriental contamination. Within this new filmic narrative, the eruption of Vesuvius functions to cleanse an Italian community in danger of degradation and violation by external agencies. The spectacular movement of the Pompeian crowds through the collapsing fabric of their city communicates cinematographically the collective racial fears generated by Italy's pre-war imperial ambitions. Only those can attain salvation who have escaped the corrupting influence of the East.[55]

The Last Days of Italian Cinema

On their release in August 1913, both versions of *Gli ultimi giorni di Pompei* met with considerable critical and commercial success in Italy.[56] When they opened in New York in October 1913, the Ambrosio and Pasquali films were also much admired by American reviewers for their grand theme, scenic wonders, superb acting, educational value and wide appeal. A critic for *The Moving Picture News* even noted that such great qualities were "typical of Italian picture-making art" and could not possibly be reproduced by

American films of the time.[57] By the end of the First World War, however, Italian films were no longer held in such high esteem on the international market, and the industry was beset by crisis. It faced a Europe-wide economic recession, a substantial increase in costs, the loss of foreign markets for export and an invasion of imported American and German films. Incapable of adapting production to the new audiences and life styles of the post war period, the Italian film industry suffered a massive decrease in the numbers of consumers of the national product. Accordingly, a sector of the industry attempted to monopolize production and control the Italian market through the formation, in 1919, of the consortium Unione Cinematografica Italiana (UCI), but with little success. In 1921 the bank supplying UCI with a substantial part of its credit failed, and Italian film production overall continued to decline from some 415 films in 1920 to no more than forty in 1925.[58]

In its attempts to reverse the disintegration of indigenous production, the Italian film industry looked back to the critical and economic success of its earlier historical films, particularly those exploring the concept of *romanità*. Accordingly, remakes were issued of *Messalina* (1923), *Quo Vadis?* (1924), and *Gli ultimi giorni di Pompei* (1926). However, it is precisely to this form of cinematic conservatism that much of the failure of the industry during the 1920s has been imputed. Italian spectators were now far more attracted to the allure of Hollywood imports since they seemed better equipped to touch on the concerns of modern audiences, and their otherness in foreign markets increased European audiences' sense of the modernity and fashionableness of Hollywood cinematography. Comparison between the products of the Italian and the American film industries exposed the apparent poverty and provincialism of Italian historical film-making in the 1920s, which seemed to manifest scarcely any response to the new editing techniques, camera movements, or acting styles of films such as Cecil B. DeMille's *The Cheat* (1915) and D. W. Griffith's *Intolerance* (1916), nor even any advance over its own cinematic aesthetics and innovative technology established in the early 1910s by Enrico Guazzoni's *Quo Vadis?* (1913) and Giovanni Pastrone's *Cabiria* (1914). Instead Italian historical films of the twenties privileged narrative repetition and a strong sense of déjà vu.[59]

It was in this context of the stagnation and collapse of the Italian film industry that *Gli ultimi giorni di Pompei* was produced in 1926, through the assistance of UCI, for Grandifilm at Rome. The company had been newly established by the film's directors Carmine Gallone and Amleto Palermi (in association with the Turinese producer Arturo Ambrosio) for the purpose of making another film version of Lytton's historical novel as successful as the earlier Ambrosio adaptations. The opening of the film parallels the preface to Lytton's novel when it directs its audience to read this new cinematic reconstruction of the Pompeian past according to an antiquarian aesthetic. An intertitle first ascribes a moral purpose to the resurrection and animation of the ancient city with which the film is subsequently concerned:

> Pompeii. City of joy for imperial Rome, in the year 79 after Christ was buried beneath a hail of ashes and fire. After 19 centuries, it rises again today, a marvel and a warning to men of the alternations in the human condition.

The camera then tracks through the excavations at Pompeii as they would have looked to the tourist of the 1920s. Monumental public architecture and private dwellings which will form the canonic sites for the film's fictive narration appear in fragmented ruins before the gaze of the Italian spectator—the *via dell'abbondanza,* the temple of Isis, the forum, the amphitheater, the court house, the street of tombs, the baths, and the house of "Glaucus." The camera now returns to a long-shot of the ruined forum. Through a brief and progressive series of disjunctive cuts, the ruined forum is suddenly replaced by a reconstructed one and it, in turn, is immediately replaced by one alive with people. The film's spectator, like the novel's reader, is permitted to enter into the life of the ancient city resurrected and animated, this time, by the magic of moving images.[60]

The visual resurrection of Pompeii which follows in *Gli ultimi giorni di Pompei* of Gallone and Palermi is undeniably marvelous. The reconstructions of Pompeian buildings which the camera lovingly explores demonstrate an extraordinarily fine archaeological detail, and the mise-en-scène is littered with recognizable reproductions of famous Pompeian artefacts—fountains, statuary, urns, tables, bowls, jewelry, wall-paintings, shop signs, mosaics.[61] [illustration 6.5] This pleasurably precise recreation of the ancient city, and the realistic depiction of its destruction, were frequently commented upon in reviews after the film's launch. *La rassegna del teatro e del cinematografo* of February 1926, for example, declared the film to be

> a grandiose reconstruction of Pompeii, at the epoch in which the city, cradle of every pagan pleasure, was overwhelmed by the terrible eruption of Vesuvius. One can say, without fear of unnecessary and unsuitable exaggerations, that on the level of the architectural reproduction of the city and of the realization of the volcanic marvel nothing could achieve greater perfection.

This latest cinematic resurrection of Pompeii evidently provides spectators with the marvel heralded in the first intertitle. What is less evident is the nature of "the warning to men," the preciseness of the presentist strategies, which this adaptation to screen of Lytton's historical novel proceeds to disclose.[62]

6.5 Arbaces visits Ione and finds her with Glaucus, from *Gli ultimi giorni di Pompei* (1926). [Photograph in private collection of Riccardo Redi.]

According to the film historian Mira Liehm, *Gli ultimi giorni di Pompei* of 1926, like the earlier historical films of the 1910s, exalts nationalistic feelings, is permeated with "the glorification of the Roman superpower," and establishes a "continuity between the Rome of Caesar and that of Mussolini."[63] Certainly the film continues and enlarges on the orientalist strategies of the Ambrosio and Pasquali versions, with the heroine Ione structured as the object of competition between the loving Glaucus and the lustful Arbaces. West is pitted against East, decency against villainy, the archaeologically precise replication of the hero's small and safe Pompeian house against the fantastically Egyptianized, vast, and demonic art deco palace of Arbaces—"the mysterious Egyptian, master of magic, feared for his occult power throughout Pompeii."[64] The Pompeian architecture and artefacts carefully reproduced on screen could easily be read by Italian audiences of the 1920s as metonymic evocations of the glories of Rome (ancient and modern) because, in the years immediately preceding the release of *Gli ultimi giorni*, excavation policy and publication concerning Pompeii converged ever more closely and openly with the discourse of *romanità* so favored by the Fascist regime.

After September 1924, when Amedeo Maiuri was installed as the new director of the site, research began to privilege the public monumental architecture of the ancient city, while attempts were made to resurrect out of the ruins the atmosphere of domestic interiors and the apparent elegance and serenity of Pompeian peristyles. Newly disclosed frescoes, furnishings, and utensils were left in place, and walls and ceilings repaired, while plants were replaced in gardens and water restored to fountains. In 1927, a year after the release of Gallone and Palermi's film, Mussolini announced a plan to reopen excavation of the (conveniently richer and more elegant) neighboring site of Herculaneum, and by the time the *duce* made a well-publicized visit to see Maiuri's work at Pompeii in 1940, its archaeological investigation was being lauded as a quasi-military operation and as a science serving to celebrate the civilization of Italy throughout the world. During the entire decade within which *Gli ultimi giorni di Pompei* was produced and distributed, Maiuri presented his discoveries of Italy's glorious heritage in newspapers and popular magazines, as well as academic journals. The Pompeian scenography designed by the architect Vittorio Cafiero for the film of 1926 could thus partake of a widespread and intensifying cultural investment in the ancient city as a material sign of Roman greatness.[65] The strategies deployed by the film to glorify Rome were recognized and approved in an otherwise qualified review which appeared in the Fascist press. *L'impero* for 13 February 1926 declared that

> Our newspaper, forecaster of a cinema of the future, ought to speak with moderate praise of this effort that concludes, even if it perfects, the cinema of the past. But there is so great an artistic vision in the work of Gallone and Palermi, there is so vigorous a remembrance of the Latin classical spirit, that we cannot exempt it from our convinced, and even moved, approval.[66]

The grandeur of Rome's authority receives moving and explicit tribute towards the climax of the film's narrative, after the devastating eruption of Vesuvius. Following the famous description in Lytton's novel and the equally famous depiction of the scene in Poynter's painting, a Roman soldier is seen still on guard duty by a gateway of the crumbling city. The two intertitles at this point read: "Pompeii is abandoned. Only the legionary stays immobile beneath the fury of the fire and ash, faithful to duty, symbol of the majesty ... of THE IMPERIAL RULE OF ROME." Between the two intertitles, the screen is filled with a drawing of the eagle and the *fasces*, those symbols of Roman authority which had served so potently for the legitimation of the Fascist party and which, by the end of 1926, were to be established as the official symbols of the Italian state.[67] Within the narrative drive of *Gli ultimi giorni di Pompei* (1926), however, the dutiful soldier can represent only a passing moment of glorification of Rome's majesty, swiftly to be buried under the moral vengeance of volcanic lava. Adhering closely to the structures of Lytton's novel, the innocents who achieve salvation are identified unequivocally as Athenian or Christian. Those who die are marked out as Roman aristocrats and attributed with the vices of decadence, effeminacy, disloyalty, cruelty, avarice, or arrogance. Furthermore, within the course of the film's narrative progression to the final catastrophe, the Christian proselytizer Olinthus calls the eruption "a warning from God to the idolators who live in corruption." The opening "warning to men of the alternations in the human condition" is clarified by the film's close—any city dedicated to pleasure is bound to be punished in an inferno, in the manner of Sodom and Gomorrah. The moralizing narrative structures of *Gli ultimi giorni* (1926), therefore, qualify the glorification of Rome, and limit the exaltation of nationalistic feelings, precisely at a time when the Fascist press was beginning to acknowledge cinema as a highly appropriate instrument through which to legitimate the state, and when the Italian film industry was beginning to reshape its products better to match the rhetoric of the Fascist regime.[68]

The conception of *romanità* which *Gli ultimi giorni* (1926) offers its audience is doubly ambiguous. If Italian spectators are invited to identify briefly with the stoic heroism of a Roman soldier, or to assimilate themselves comfortably to the moral purity of the first Christians, they are also given an opportunity to revel in the brutality and sensuality of the cultural patrimony of which they are the inheritors. Spectacular displays of naked women painting their toenails, dancing at orgiastic banquets, being flagellated or sexually violated—all these were the visual ingredients employed to sell the film. The cinematic reconstruction of Pompeii as a sinful city in whose pleasures modern audiences might be permitted to take momentary gratification was regarded with distaste in the Italian press reviews of the period. According to the same review in *La rassegna del teatro e del cinematografo* partially quoted above, the film was artistically perfect on the level of its architectural fidelity, but morally defective in its representation of pagan life. In particular, shots early in the film of male and female nudity in the Pompeian baths appeared to exceed any narrative function as examples of pagan decadence in their leisurely, voyeuristic displays of flesh. Such a troubled and contradictory cinematic image of *romanità* could not wholly be translated into an appropriate historical tradition for the legitimation of the newly installed Fascist regime or pass the increasingly restrictive censorship of the Catholic Church.[69] After *Gli ultimi giorni di Pompei* (1926), only one other film history of ancient Rome was produced in Italy until the end of the Second World War. That film, *Scipione l'Africano* (1937), unsurprisingly sought inspiration not in the Roman empire as represented in the cinematic histories of the 1920s but in the more accommodating territory of the

Roman republic, conceived as a site of dutiful citizenship, political morality, and military victory.[70]

Despite some limited commercial success and foreign exhibition, Grandifilm's adaptation to screen of Lytton's novel did not match the largely unqualified, fulsome critical acclaim achieved by its two predecessors in 1913. Italian reviewers, at any rate, while admiring the care expended on its Pompeian mise-en-scène and the realism of its volcanic eruption, were disdainful of both its conservative style and its eroticism, and were scandalized even further by the intrusion of a considerable foreign dimension into a supposedly national film genre. Driven by the commercial need to seek financial backing in Vienna and Berlin, Palermi had been compelled to cast stars of Hungarian, Austrian, and German cinema in leading roles. Of the film's principals, only the romantic heroine Ione and a priest of Isis, Caleno, were played by Italian *divi*—respectively, Rina De Liguoro and Emilio Ghione. Accordingly, when Ghione (an actor who was also a Fascist activist) published a profile of Italian cinema at the end of the 1920s, he applied to Gallone and Palermi's film the deprecatory title of "the last days of Ital-ian cinema."[71]

A Depression Gangster

In Italy, production of a cinematic historiography of Pompeii was not taken up again until after the Second World War, yet only nine years after the release of Gallone and Palermi's *Gli ultimi giorni di Pompei* (1926) the destruction of the ancient city and the deaths of its citizens became the subject of an American film directed by E. B. Schoedsack for the RKO studio. Although set in the same historical time and place as the Italian versions of the 1910s and the 1920s, Hollywood's *The Last Days of Pompeii* (1935) evinces a considerable rupture from the earlier, Italian conventions for the portrayal of Pompeii in moving images. The representational map of the city was redesigned to suit the requirements of a different film system and different conditions for the reception of the Pompeian past on screen.

The cultural force of Pompeii in America differed significantly from that in Italy. From the time of Italy's unification, the excavation of Pompeii had been taken under exclusively Italian control and the site appropriated as a remarkable material index of the country's glorious classical past. The United States had had recourse to an invented tradition much like that of the Italian nationalistic conception of *romanità* during the Revolutionary era and after the formation of the new federal government, but there had been no role to play in it for Pompeii. The Founding Fathers could have found in the history of Pompeii neither model nor anti-model for the new nation, for no documentary record survived in the city of either republican heroes or imperial villains.[72] The majestic public monuments of Rome were also more imitable as markers of American statecraft than the architecture and art of Pompeii, for the latter were less familiar and more intimately linked with unwelcome displays of the erotic.[73] Moreover, by the time of the release of *The Last Days of Pompeii* in 1935, Italy's deployment of *romanità* and its cultural investment in Pompeii had intensified considerably, whereas a significant gulf now lay between Hollywood's resurrection of antiquity and the earlier urgency with which the classical past had been pressed into the service of America's self-definition.

A detailed reconstruction on screen of Pompeii's architecture and artefacts could not have constituted for American audiences the collective reclamation of a cultural heritage viewed as utterly America's own nor could it have offered even a particularly familiar set of visual images. When collecting on a grand scale began in America in the nineteenth and twentieth centuries, Roman antiquities were far more easily obtained and exported than the jealously protected paintings and sculptures of Pompeii. Only finds from the villas in the surrounding countryside, such as those from Boscoreale or Boscotrecase, might find their way into the private collections and public museums of the United States.[74] Thus, looking at moving images of the ancient city was unlikely to generate the intense pleasures of recognition and ownership which the Italian film histories had been capable of providing for their own national audience. In Depression America, moreover, relatively few could afford to visit Pompeii itself (except, perhaps, for film producers on honeymoon like Merian C. Cooper, who inititated the RKO project immediately on return from a European trip).[75] Archaeologically precise recreations of Pompeii, therefore, would not have had the same tight grip on American historical consciousness as their earlier Italian counterparts had had in Italy, and would not have been received by the American public with the same degree of interest or cognition.

From the outset, American fascination with the excavations undertaken at Pompeii was focused rather more on the city's tragic burial than on the society or the objects buried by Vesuvius.[76] When George Kleine distributed Ambrosio's cinematic reconstruction of the ancient city throughout America in 1913, his promotional literature attempted to sell the film on more than its impressive replay of Pompeii's destruction. Yet it was to spectators' novelistic knowledge of the city that he was able, additionally, to appeal. The Italian film was marketed as a visualization of historical romance which brought to life not the ruins of Pompeii so much as Lytton's novel. In 1913, Kleine's publicity could presume on the wide cultural circulation and prestige of Lytton's Pompeii (disseminated in paintings and pyrodramas as well as editions of the novel) and could boast that the historical novel closely

structured visitors' experience of the excavations themselves. In 1935, however, the foreword to an educational guide published by RKO to accompany
the release of its film was considerably more circumspect:

> Bulwer Lytton's *The Last Days of Pompeii* is a literary classic of a paradoxical
> character: critics have refused to admit that it is particularly literary or much
> of a classic. But it continues to be widely read, and the title is familiar to
> everyone. No visitor to Italy would consider his tour complete unless he vis-
> ited the excavations at Pompeii and regarded them with vague memories of
> Bulwer Lytton's famous narrative.

With the Pompeian homes of Lytton's protagonists Glaucus and Ione fast
becoming "vague memories," the RKO film salvages only the title from the
novel's diminishing popularity and almost totally jettisons any dependency
on Lytton's nineteenth-century work for the construction of its ancient
landscape or narrative drive. Although, in the context of the educational
guide, grand claims are made to archaeological authenticity and historical
truth for the architectural backgrounds, ancient costumes, and customs of
The Last Days of Pompeii, the Hollywood film offers its own historical
authentication on screen through the replication of only two Pompeian
public monuments—the amphitheater and the temple of Jupiter at the
north end of the forum. *Last Days* also abandons the earlier Italian adaptations' melodramatic tale of love locked into and beset by a doomed, orientalized community, in favor of an original story that concerns individual
self-discovery, familial responsibility, and personal redemption. Marcus, a
hard-working blacksmith, is embittered after the accidental death of his
wife and son, and takes up the more profitable (if morally suspect) profes-
sions of gladiator and slave trader, but at the moment of Vesuvius' eruption
he learns the Christian values of human life, liberty, and paternal care, and
sacrifices himself to aid the escape of his adopted son and some runaway
slaves, dying in the comforting glow of a visitation from Christ himself.[77]

In crossing the Atlantic, not only had the cultural force of Pompeii radi-
cally altered but so had the mode of its cinematic reconstruction. By 1930,
despite the serious financial difficulties of the Depression, the Hollywood
film studios were producing over five hundred films per year for an audience averaging ninety million people per week. The standardization of
Hollywood's products, at which the studios aimed to ensure cost-effective
production, involved the modified repetition of popular narratives at the
same time as accompanying publicity differentiated each film as both original and unique. Film genres, cycles, and serials were institutionalized, and
even historical films were often structured in ways that corresponded to and

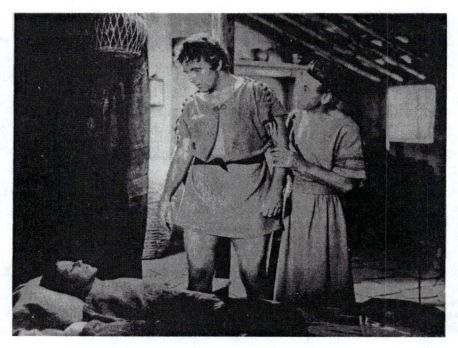

6.6 Marcus grieves over his wife's death, from *The Last Days of Pompeii* (1935).
[Courtesy of BFI Stills, Posters and Designs.]

gained some of their appeal from narrative genres set in the present.[78] Thus
Cecil B. DeMille's *Cleopatra* (1934) drew on the success of the director's earlier social comedies, while Schoedsack's *Last Days* (1935) borrowed from the
narrative strategies of a film genre grounded in the era of the Depression,
namely the gangster film.

The arrival of sound film, Capone's Chicago, Prohibition, and the Depression combined to inaugurate the genre of the gangster film with *Little
Caesar* (1930), and by the time of the production of *Public Enemy* in 1931 the
genre was already thriving. This cycle of "success tragedies" narrated a conflict between two fundamentally opposed conceptions of Americanism,
namely that America was a land of opportunity yet also a democratic and
just society. Modern city life's inducements to self-advancement, by which
the gangster is lured, are graphically demonstrated to create moral strains
and to lead potentially to criminality. The Hollywood gangster functions as
a scapegoat for contemporary desires for wealth and power as his pursuit of
them leads ultimately to punishment and even death. These films constituted implicit, and sometimes even explicit, acknowledgment of the problems besetting America in the early 1930s. The hero's fall in the last reel and

his recognition of the futility of the materialistic values he has adopted (like that of the business tycoon in the newspaper melodramas) provided a cinematic form of catharsis for Depession audiences. They were able to experience by proxy the dangerous excitement of fast cars, expensive clothes, flashy men, and seductive women, while being nonetheless morally vindicated in their failure to achieve the American dream—for the rich were irresponsible, criminal, and punishable with death, the poor at least survived, their dignity intact.[79]

The intertextual pleasures of *The Last Days of Pompeii* reside less in a familiarity with the current excavations at Pompeii, or with the nineteenth-century representational systems for resurrecting the city, than in the narrational codes of the contemporary gangster film. Especially in its opening sequences, the film reflects the hardships of the Depression era and the widespread questioning of traditional American values that it encouraged. Initially, Marcus the poor but honest blacksmith proudly declares: "I have a wife who loves me and a baby son. I work hard, eat hearty and sleep sound. What more could I have?" But he is cruelly robbed of his faith in rewards for hard work and the fairness of the social system, when he loses both wife and son through his inability to pay a doctor's fees. [illustration 6.6] Marcus learns from his bereavement, and chastises himself when comforted by a neighbor:

NEIGHBOR: My poor friend.
MARCUS: Poor, poor and a fool! I've lost all I loved because I was poor. A year ago, a week ago, I could have saved them. All my life I've been a fool.
NEIGHBOR: Steady, Marcus.
MARCUS: It cost me this to learn what the world is really like. Money is all that matters. Well I can get money. It's easy to get money. All you have to do is kill.

Lured by money and its gain through the violent killings of the arena and an illicit trade in horses and slaves, the "Pompeian" Marcus thus takes on the recognizable features of Hollywood's gangsters. In its dialogue, narrative development, and visual style (such as the montage sequence of Marcus' growing greed and bloodlust), *Last Days* draws deeply on cinematic rather than historical knowledge. Prominence is everywhere given to its presentist strategies of restaging in the past the hardships of the Depression and in reproducing a contemporary urban tale like that of *Little Caesar*.[80]

All through the early 1930s, civil and religious pressure groups staged public protests against Hollywood's representations of moral and political issues and, in particular, accused gangster films of a glorification of violence and a disrespect for the law. Already in 1930, the film industry had formally adopted a Production Code (composed by a priest and a Catholic layman) which had proposed that criminals and sinners should not be portrayed sympathetically on screen and that narratives might close with happy endings only if wrongdoers were seen to reform.[81] Underlying the Code, according to the film historian Gregory D. Black, lay the objective of turning films into "twentieth-century morality plays that illustrated proper behavior to the masses."[82] But few groups were satisfied that the Code was being implemented properly and, in 1933, the Legion of Decency was launched to continue the campaign against "immorality" in cinema through the threat of large-scale Catholic boycotts. The board of the Motion Picture Producers and Distributors of America (MPPDA) swiftly endowed the Production Code administrators with greater powers to police the film industry. No film could now be screened by members of the MPPDA unless it carried the Production Code seal of purity.[83] A new moralism accordingly emerged in Hollywood such that stars of the earlier gangster films, like James Cagney and Edward G. Robinson, now played incorruptible enforcers of American law and justice.[84]

As a highly moralistic gangster film dressed in classical costume, *The Last Days of Pompeii* clearly met the stringent requirements of the newly enforced Production Code—that any film depiction of crime or sin must contain compensating moral value. The education guide associated with the film piously declared of its hero Marcus that he

> represents humanity. Succumbing to greed, but eventually triumphing over himself, he is the symbol of humanity's many falls, but gradual progress toward a shining goal where men not only preach but practice the pure principles of unselfishness and self-sacrifice taught by Christ.

Similarly, in a letter dated September 1935 and addressed to friends of "better films," the president of RKO, Ned E. Depinet, announced that in his studio's latest production ministers would find a powerful sermon. According to a subsequent circular addressed to theater managers, such letters were part of a direct-mailing campaign designed to attract the approval of influential figures, such as clergymen and teachers, for the coming attraction.[85] On the release of *The Last Days of Pompeii*, one somewhat qualified American review at least welcomed the film's omission of all "the traditional party stuff" associated with Hollywood's past Roman epics:

> Picturization omits even a small allusion to Pompeii's sex angles. This film has no romance. In the last reel or so there are a few chaste kisses between the

lovesick boy and girl who are, however, just figures in the multitude. A Roman story without a single orgy, without even a glimpse of the public baths or a hint that the town was devoted to amorous dalliance is in itself something.[86]

But the moral and spiritual high ground claimed for the film by its omission of "sex angles" and its provision of Christian values (as well as a visitation from Christ) sinks under the extraordinary manipulation of the past which was undertaken by the film's makers in pursuit of a crudely constructed moralism—the hero Marcus witnesses both the crucifixion of Christ in Judaea and the eruption of Vesuvius in a time span perceived as totally implausible by most of the film's reviewers. While the *Motion Picture Herald* considered such tampering with historical events merely ill advised, the *New Yorker* of 26 October 1935 described it as both pretentious and impertinent. Failing to fulfill the religious and educational value that RKO had claimed for it, *The Last Days of Pompeii* could satisfy few spectators. Although *Last Days* drew on DeMille's *Sign of the Cross* (1932) for its representation of arena fighting and the persecution of innocents, it forsook the visual riches offered by DeMille's hugely elaborate imperial sets, costumes, and props, and the director's infamous displays of extravagant and sensual consumption. It further jettisoned the use of a visually seductive female character like those played by Claudette Colbert in *Sign* and *Cleopatra*. The women of *Last Days* are humble, homely, and pure, not power-hungry, exotic temptresses. In thus conforming to the Production Code, *The Last Days of Pompeii* displayed an ancient setting now deprived of the supposedly pagan violence and eroticism that had made the histories of antiquity directed by DeMille so appealing and substituted for it a Christian moralism that lacked any historical credibility.

Two years before the release of RKO's *Last Days*, United Artists had produced the musical comedy *Roman Scandals,* in which a hobo in the Oklahoma city of West Rome comes to realize its endemic corruption after he has been transported back to a more overtly corrupt ancient Rome. The cruelty of the imperial court could be read as a mirror in which was reflected and magnified the iniquities of modern America because the Founding Fathers had structured their new nation as the inheritor of a Roman cultural patrimony. America *was* Rome. *Roman Scandals* then deploys the trope of ancient Rome to suggest that Depression America is now heir to the tyranny and slavery of imperial Rome rather than the civic virtues and liberties of the Republic. Liberation comes in the form of social protest and the removal of the wrongdoers.[87] Such analogical mechanisms also operate in *Last Days* to provide a more conservative articulation of the present urban crisis, in which the rich are punished by volcanic eruption and the poor find salvation in Christian charitable values and an escape to pleasanter shores. Yet the latter film also suggests paradoxically (but more comfortably) that freedom may lie in America and corruption in a European elsewhere.

It was within the cultural competence of American spectators to read the decadent and doomed Pompeian city as a metaphor for the perceived decadence of modern Europe, precisely because Italy was currently defining itself in terms of an imperial *romanità* that encompassed its Pompeian past. Such an analysis of *The Last Days of Pompeii* as willfully turning the tradition of *romanità* against the very community which had invented it is supported by a question that was posed to school students in the educational guide that accompanied the release of the film. It reads: "What form of salute was used by the Romans? In what countries are similar salutes now demanded by the government?" Such a question requires of the respondent the acknowledgment of a continuity between the Roman past and Fascist Italy or Nazi Germany and opens up the possibility of extending that sense of historical continuity beyond the moments in the film where Pompeians salute. In *Last Days*, it is not the fear of orientalism that is buried by Vesuvius' eruption, but the fear of Fascism—metonymically represented by the huge statue of a militant male athlete in the Pompeian arena. [illustration 6.7] The anachronistic presence in the Pompeian amphitheater of a mammoth male statue invokes the giant statues of sports heroes which had recently been set up over the *Stadio dei Marmi* in Rome's *Foro Mussolini*. At least in Italy, regular newspaper articles and film bulletins had charted the progress of this architectural celebration of Fascist physical education through the years of its development between 1928 and 1932. Similar attention was subsequently paid to the construction of a colossal statue of Mussolini designed by the sculptor Aroldo Bellini in 1934 to dominate a vast new Fascist parade ground.[88] Yet while film critics were enthralled in 1913 by the climactic accusation and death of the orientalized Arbaces displayed in *Gli ultimi giorni di Pompei*, reviewers were less kindly disposed in 1935 towards the collapse of the Fascist colossus in *The Last Days of Pompeii*. One reviewer observed that the statue struck a phony note, looking like "something the pastry chef whipped up for a testimonial banquet."[89]

At one significant moment in *Last Days*, Marcus's adopted son, Flavius, speaks to fugitive Pompeian slaves of his vision of escape from the evils of the city to an unspoiled world which is still free, where the people are not enslaved or subject to torture, because they are out of reach of the Roman Empire. A reading of that "unspoiled," "free" world as a reference to modern-day America was also within the cultural competence of the film's

6.7 Destruction of the arena, from *The Last Days of Pompeii* (1935). [Courtesy of BFI Stills, Posters and Designs.]

spectators because America had conventionally dissociated itself from the evils of imperial Rome and aligned itself with the virtues of the Roman republic. Given that, from 1933, large numbers of Jewish émigrés were arriving in the United States from Nazi-occupied Europe,[90] the circumstances of the film's release would have provided further encouragement to read the historiography of *Last Days* as an integrative aspect of the historical text America was then writing about itself and its relationship to the violent conflicts now surfacing on the European continent. Given the long-standing association in the nineteenth-century historiography of Pompeii between its survivors and the values of Christianity (which is extravagantly supported in *Last Days* by having Marcus witness the crucifixion and achieve redemption through the acknowledgment of Christ), the safe haven of America could even be read as receiving the endorsement of God. Pompeii's cinematic reconstruction was capable of reminding a heterogeneous national audience of the virtues, the pleasures, and the security of being American. Yet this presentist strategy in *The Last Days of Pompeii* also failed to engage the interest of American audiences. At the time of the film's release, Sinclair Lewis was writing the novel *It Can't Happen Here,* which describes the rise of a Fascist dictatorship in America that puts intellectuals into concentration camps, adopts anti-Semitism as a national policy, and returns African Americans to slavery. On publication in December 1935, the book became a runaway bestseller.[91] Its grim vision of a Fascist takeover in the United States better matched current anxieties about the rise of the American Right than the sanctimonious escapism of *The Last Days of Pompeii.*

The Last Days of Pompeii* was a commercial flop. The setting of the film could not draw American audiences as successfully as had the Roman imperial courts and Egyptian boudoirs of DeMille's earlier Roman films. The lack of famous historical figures associated with Pompeii may have partially necessitated the film's implausible importation into the city of Pontius Pilate (played by Basil Rathbone as the film's only star of note). The attention and the expenditure of the RKO studio seems to have been focused largely on the anticipated drawing power of the film's special effects—the miniatures, glass paintings, double exposures, and stop-motion techniques directed at the realistic display of the volcanic eruption and the collapse of the ancient city. But even here reviewers compared the effects of *Last Days* unfavorably with the earlier work of the same RKO team (Merian C. Cooper/Ernest B. Schoedsack/Willis H. O'Brien) on the enormously successful film *King Kong* (1933).[92]

Post-war Pompeii

In the immediate post-war period, Pompeii once again provided Italian filmmakers with a usable past, for the ancient city had now become a viable symbol for wartime persecution and destruction. In his war diaries *Tagebuch aus dem Kriege*, for example, the German writer Felix Hartlaub had seen in the ancient city's devastation a parallel for the fall of Paris in June 1940.[93] The site itself had also suffered repeated bombardments and damage during the Allied campaign of 1943, and many of its precious artefacts had been dispersed for safe-keeping or even lost—in May 1945 American troops found in a German salt mine a number of crates of Pompeian antiquities which Goering had taken from their Vatican haven.[94] Three years later Paolo Moffa, aided by Marcel L'Herbier as artistic supervisor, shot an Italian/French coproduction of *Gli ultimi giorni di Pompei* at Cinecittà under the auspices of the Catholic production house Universalia. Released finally in 1950, the film loosely adapted to screen Lytton's historical narrative as a glorification of Christian suffering and endurance at the hands of pagan persecutors.[95]

Although few historians or archaeologists would now argue that unequivocal proof is available of the presence of a Christian community in Pompeii at the time of its destruction, Moffa's film could draw for its historical authentication on finds that had been widely publicized before the Second World War. In November 1936, work on the sports ground adjacent to the Pompeian amphitheater had disclosed a perfect palindrome inscribed on a pillar within which the word TENET was repeated in the form of a cross. In February 1939, at the House of the Bicentenary in Herculaneum, excavators found what appeared to be the shape of a crucifix impressed in a stuccoed wall. Christian archaeologists interpreted such finds as clear traces of the religion's presence in the ancient cities, and Italian newspapers of the period repeatedly responded with emotive articles entitled "Christians at Pompeii."[96] Thus the Universalia film opens not with the introduction of Pompeii's ruins or Lytton's fictive protagonists but with the ancient city's competing religions. The camera rapidly tracks past statues of Roman gods to move into the dark interior of the temple of Isis. The sequence climaxes with the superimposition on the scene of a single large cross which gradually blocks out the spectator's vision of the Egyptian priest and his sinister rituals as the cross radiates the screen with light. Simultaneously a voiceover declares that "only the poor were listening to the warnings of a new religion, that of Christ." Then, momentarily paralleling the antiquarian aesthetic of the earlier Italian versions of *Gli ultimi giorni di Pompei*, the camera pans through the contemporary ruins of the city only to single out the remains of a shop which the voiceover claims was the first site where Pompeian Christians were persecuted by Roman imperialists, arrested, and thrown to the lions.

Like *Fabiola* (1948) before it and *Spartaco* (1952) after it, Moffa's cinematic history of the classical past reshapes that past to address concerns about the Second World War and Italy's role in it. The film's narrative focuses on the trial at Pompeii of a Greek youth whose rescue from persecution and escape from the devasted city is achieved through the courage of an underground Christian community. An easy equivalence is established between the rubble of the ancient city and the modern ruins of war-torn Italy or France, between the cruel pagans and the Nazi army of occupation, between the early Christians and wartime resistance heroes. The Universalia production of *Gli ultimi giorni di Pompei*, backed by Christian Democrat financiers, offers a cultural patrimony for post-war Italy more appropriate than that promulgated under the defeated Fascist regime. Through the cinematic resurrection of Pompeii, audiences were provided with a victorious *romanità* of early Christian compassion, bravery, and sacrifice that achieved a conspicuous commercial success in Italy when the film was released in 1950.[97]

Ten years later, however, yet another Pompeii appeared on Italian cinema screens in Supertotalscope and Eastman Color that transposed to a classical past many of the conventions of the Western. Directed by Mario Bonnard with the assistance of Sergio Leone, the generically hybrid film *Gli ultimi giorni di Pompei* (an Italian/Spanish coproduction released in 1959) adapted the resurrection of antiquity to the physique of the bodybuilder Steve Reeves. The hero bends iron bars, fights alligators, strangles lions, and protects homesteaders from marauding villains on horseback before rescuing his Christian beloved from the arena and escaping the eruption of Vesuvius.[98] The poster designed by United Artists to advertise the peplum film on the American market carried a caption that appeared to usher in a new era for Pompeii as a signifier of pure spectacle and, eventually, theme park thrills:

> SEE! The Yawning Jaws Of The Flesh-Ripping Alligator Death Pit! SEE! The Awesome Eruption Of Mt. Vesuvius As It Avalanches Down Into A Boiling Inferno! SEE! The Martyred Christians Thrown To The Gaping Fangs Of Hungry Lions! SEE! The Dungeon Of A Thousand Tortures For The Shrieking Damned! The Slave Girls at The Mercy of Their Bestial Conquerors! SEE! The Shameless Orgy As Drunken Pompeii Abandons Itself To The Goddess Isis!

According to *Variety* for 15 June 1960, the film's crude dramatic approach and shallow characterizations were only a minor flaw—the simple promise of seeing sin, blood, and volcanic ash would be sufficient to guarantee box-office impact.

7

A Farewell to Antiquity

The Fall of Rome's Film Empire

This book has attempted, through its case studies of ancient Rome on screen, to bridge any division between classics and popular culture, between the serious work and the commodity, but this perceived disjunction between classics and cinema has already been addressed by cinema itself. In 1963, Jean-Luc Godard directed a film that self-reflexively narrates an attempt to make a cinematic adaptation of the *Odyssey* at the Italian film studio Cinecittà. *Le Mépris* (or *Contempt*, the English title) expresses contempt for, among other things, the brash commercialism that Godard regarded as having now taken over the Hollywood film industry. The economic power and commercial goals of the crass American producer who appears within the film (played by Jack Palance) interferes with the shooting by a German director of an *Odyssey* which is far removed from the then-recent pattern of blockbuster epics set in antiquity. While the American producer assumes the fickleness of Odysseus's abandoned wife Penelope, and relishes the appearance on screen of some naked bathing beauties, the German director attempts to make an *Odyssey* which confronts the concepts of divinity and fatalism and which, in execution, is painterly, austere, and abstract. At issue was also the production of Godard's film about the making of a film. Godard's own sour relations with the commercial producers Carlo Ponti and Joseph E. Levine were famously paralleled within *Le Mépris* by the interaction between the Hollywood producer of the *Odyssey* and its scriptwriter, director (played by Fritz Lang as himself), and assistant director (played by Godard). The narrative closure of *Le Mépris* then playfully marks the triumph of Godard himself over his own film's production constraints, for the irksome American producer is conveniently killed off in a car crash, to leave at the film's close the real artists Lang and Godard giving free rein to their directorial skills.[1]

In *Le Mépris*, the disjunction that operates is never between classics and cinema, but between two different kinds of cinematic production. Contempt is not expressed for the attempt to adapt Homer to widescreen, but for the commercialism that drives Hollywood's productions and the debasement of classical antiquity which, for Godard, inevitably ensues. The question for Godard would not be *whether* cinema should have a place in the classical tradition, but *whose* cinema. The realignment of the binary oppositions high/low, classical/popular, serious artwork/commodity, which *Le Mépris* effects, limits contempt to one sub-category of cinematic production—the "classical" Hollywood style. Even that contempt, however, is the one to which Hollywood itself attempted to respond in the studio crises of the 1960s.

In the early 1960s, the dominant Hollywood style for resurrecting ancient Rome on screen began to fail drastically at the box office and was falling into the kind of critical disrepute demonstrated by Godard's characterization of the vulgar American film producer in *Le Mépris*. *Variety*'s annual list for 1963 of all-time box-office champions included *The Robe* (1953), *Ben-Hur* (1959), and *Spartacus* (1960), but critics were already speculating that the economic success of such films could no longer be sustained. The commodification of the production and consumption of blockbuster epics was now emptying them of their initial novelty. Widescreen had become the norm, and the spectacular commonplace. With the success of each new blockbuster, rival studios had sought comparable profits by constantly revising upwards the size and cost of their next prestige epic film. The immense industrial undertaking required by individual studios for the production and exhibition of these films could no longer be justified after the catastrophic financial failure of *Cleopatra,* which was finally released in the same year that Godard brought out his critique of the Hollywood film industry. The consequent bankruptcy of 20th Century-Fox (which had produced *Cleopatra*) marked the final decline of the old studio system whose infrastructure had, in the past, been capable of supporting spectacular historical reconstructions on screen. As a function of economics and industrial competition, and to attract as large and heterogeneous an audience as possible, the Hollywood studios had created a relatively standardized, sanitized, and glamorized conception of ancient Rome that relied heavily on the star system, conventionality of narration, and visually clichéd production values—fabulous costumes, huge sets, and the requisite battle or arena sequence. But the family audiences for whom Hollywood's spectacular Rome had been designed were fast disappearing. The younger, and increasingly secular, audience still attending the cinema in the 1960s was likely to find a film such as *Cleopatra* reliant on a now-outmoded narrative form and ponderous visual style that created an uncongenial, too-distant world entirely at odds with the more sexually explicit and violent youth culture already visible on screen since the mid-1950s.[2]

The release of *The Fall of the Roman Empire* (1964) in this climate has come to be regarded, in hindsight, as a final attempt to restake a claim for Hollywood's vision of Rome on domestic and international markets through the exploitation of cinematic devices which challenge, at the same time as they draw on, the conventions of the classical Hollywood style. In its title and initial voiceover, Antony Mann's *Fall* declares a significant distance between itself and the earlier Cold War narratives of Christianity triumphant. For a "higher" level of authenticity, it appeals to eighteenth-century secular historiography rather than the nineteenth-century religious fictions, which had provided the narrative outlines for the films *Quo Vadis* or *Ben-Hur*. Like its source in the earliest chapters of Edward Gibbon's *History of the Decline and Fall of the Roman Empire* (1776–1788), Mann's film locates the onset of the Roman empire's decline around the period 180 A.D., when a seemingly happy and prosperous age was cruelly disrupted by the death of the humane emperor Marcus Aurelius and the accession of the tyrant Commodus. Audaciously, for a Hollywood film set in the Christian era, its depiction of a struggle to achieve equality, freedom, and peace in the empire is not cast as a conventional conflict between virtuous Christians and oppressive Romans and, in the course of the entire film, Christianity receives only the most fleeting visual evocation when a chi-rho pendant is found hanging on the corpse of the old emperor's advisor.[3]

The narrative of *The Fall*, however, fails to live up to the historiographic complexities promised by its opening voiceover. In the Gibbonesque tones of the British historian Will Durant, the voiceover proclaims: "The fall of Rome, like her rise, had not one cause but many. It was not an event, but a process spread over 300 years." Nonetheless, the suggestion of a vast time scale and a subtle exploration of historical causation is immediately replaced by a simple personalized conflict for leadership at Rome between Commodus and his fictive rival Livius. The cinematic conventionality of such a conflict between boyhood companions is underscored by its similarity to the opening antagonism between Roman and Jew in *Ben-Hur* and by the casting of Stephen Boyd (who, in the earlier film, had played the dark-haired villain Messala) as the blonde-haired hero Livius.[4]

Equally perplexing for the spectator of *The Fall of the Roman Empire* is its manipulation of mise-en-scène and spectacle. As Martin Winkler has observed, in radical denial of viewers' generic expectations, the first quarter of the film displays a Roman world which is visually bleak. The death of Aurelius and the opening of hostilities between Commodus and Livius are

7.1 Fortress on the Roman empire's northern frontier, from *The Fall of the Roman Empire* (1964). [Courtesy of BFI Stills, Posters and Designs.]

located on a wintry frontier of the Danube, before and within a drab, unprepossessing military fortress which is encircled by a dark forest swarming with barbarian hordes. [illustration 7.1] Immediately juxtaposed with this strikingly innovative set, however, is a sequence where a panning camera slowly follows the new emperor in sun-lit triumphal procession at Rome, approaching the Temple of Jupiter through an astonishingly spectacular and architecturally imposing forum. In terms of the diegesis, this scene might signal the luxury and claims to divine power of Commodus, framed as it is by the forbidding austerity of the frontier fortress and the republican simplicity of the Roman Senate house. Yet studio publicity (frequently reproduced in trade journals, newspapers, and magazines) isolated the scene from the film's narrative drive, immobilized it into publicity stills, and catalogued at length the technical superiority of its design over all the previous Hollywood recreations of the Roman forum from *The Robe* to *Cleopatra*: twenty-seven full-scale three-dimensional structures, three hundred and fifty individual statues, eight victory columns, one thousand hand-sculpted bas-relief panels, twelve tons of nails, three hundred and twenty miles of tubular steel, one thousand one hundred workmen, seven months to assemble, the biggest and most expensive Roman set ever made. . . .[5]

Conversely, several of the action sequences of *The Fall of the Roman Empire* also fed off the clichés of earlier epic films, while markedly diminishing their spectacular cinematic exhibitionism. An early chariot race between Livius and Commodus replays the famous and Oscar-winning equestrian competition of *Ben-Hur*, yet it includes only two chariots, is set along narrow country lanes on the Danube frontier, is overseen by no witnesses, lasts only three minutes, and has no accompanying music. Similarly, the final hand to hand combat between the two antagonists is boldly confined to a tiny section of the huge forum set, within a narrow space created by a make-shift arena of shields to which spectatorial access is frustratingly restricted. Such sequences have been described by Michael Wood as "the signature of a movie wanting to be different."[6]

The past/present axis of *The Fall of the Roman Empire* also recalls and undercuts the complacent historical parallels between the classical past and the American present set up by the religious epics of the 1950s. Films like *Quo Vadis* (1951), *The Robe* (1953), and *Ben-Hur* (1959) had frequently been interpreted in the press as capable of providing salutary lessons for their contemporary audiences about the outcome of the Cold War, for they appeared to demonstrate by familiar analogy the historically inevitable victory of American godliness over the Soviet Antichrist. The trade paper *Motion Picture Herald* plucked a similarly satisfying history lesson out of the narrative of *Fall*. In an early sequence of the film, Marcus Aurelius reviews the Roman empire's assembled kings and chieftains and in a rousing speech declares that the political future holds in store a *pax Romana*, "a family of equal nations." According to the *Herald*'s reading of the presentist strategies adopted by the film, the Roman empire fell because it lacked what the world possesses today—a United Nations.[7] Valuing the institution of the United Nations (which was established by the Allies in 1945) could easily be equated with valuing the international stature of America, for it was in New York that the headquarters of the UN had been established, and it was the United States who had taken the initiative in implementing the authority of the UN in the post-war period.[8]

Yet *The Fall of the Roman Empire* persistently burdens the aspirations of Aurelius and his heirs with a sense of futility and doom, from the opening sequence, where the auspices taken for the old emperor are unfavorable, to the concluding moment when Livius walks away from power knowing that his goals of political unity, tolerance, and peace cannot be achieved. A less selective reading of the film's traffic in historical analogies finds in them not a celebration of America's success but a warning of its impending fall. After the Second World War, the United States had rapidly risen to the status of a superpower, pre-eminent technically, economically, and militarily until the mid-1960s, but with the assassination of John F. Kennedy in 1963, the continuation of an arms race between the United States and the Soviet Union, the increasingly belligerent interventions of the United States in Vietnam, and the continuation of internal civil rights struggles, America had come to seem for many an empire on the brink of decline.[9] *The Fall of the Roman*

Empire thus offers to its spectators a disconcerting warning against the complacency of the Eisenhower years which the earlier Hollywood histories of Rome had made so manifest.[10]

The various mechanisms adopted by *The Fall of the Roman Empire* to challenge the dominant Hollywood style for representing Rome did not generate good box-office returns for the film. The trade press resolutely overlooked the film's innovative strategies, describing *Fall* instead as a blockbuster in the grand DeMille tradition, combining lavish and gigantic sets, mammoth battle sequences, power struggles, and an ill-fated love story, all of which it unwisely viewed as guaranteed to make moviegoers flock back into the cinemas.[11] Contemporary critics equally saw the film only as an old-fashioned spectacle and denounced it, accordingly, as "all pomp and poppycock."[12] After its commercial and critical failure, *The Fall of the Roman Empire* has since become synonymous in cinema history with the fall of the Hollywood film industry's own empire of Roman films.[13]

A Farewell to Antiquity

Godard's graphic depiction of the death of Hollywood's commercialized strategies for resurrecting classical antiquity on screen and their usurpation by a European art house alternative appeared to receive confirmation in the 1960s and early 1970s with the production of films like Federico Fellini's *Fellini-Satyricon* (1969), Pier Paolo Pasolini's *Edipo Re* (1967) and *Medea* (1970), or Michael Cacoyannis' Trojan trilogy *Electra* (1961), *The Trojan Women* (1971), and *Iphigenia* (1976). As the Hollywood mode of film production became fragmented, European film industries began successfully to counter the former preeminence of Hollywood's products on domestic markets by producing alternative forms of cinematic language and a revisionist approach to depictions of the past on screen. Such films were enthusiastically welcomed even in the United States by the younger film audiences who flocked to the newly opened art houses in which such European films came to be exhibited.[14] *Fellini-Satyricon*, in particular, offered an extraordinary challenge to Hollywood's cinematic vision of Rome and, both in the structures of the film itself and in extra-cinematic accounts of the film's making, its director Federico Fellini directly addressed questions of cinema's relation to classics and cinema's value as a means of reconstructing and consuming ancient Rome in the present.

While Hollywood's Cold War epics had taken modern religious fictions about early Christianity as their source material, Fellini appropriated as his originary text an ancient satirical novel by Petronius that told a disjointed tale, in a variety of literary styles, about the erotic adventures of two young friends. In marked contrast to the traditional Hollywood practice of privileging narrative and continuity of plot, *Fellini-Satyricon* imitates the episodic character of the Petronian novel, providing not a story but a collection of episodes with no, or only a tenuous, causal link between events. But, more disturbingly still, *Fellini-Satyricon* also takes up the accidentally fragmentary condition of the ancient text. In the film, even the slightest sense of narrative linearity is interrupted in seemingly arbitary places—as when Encolpio, engulfed by the collapse of a Roman tenement building, immediately reappears touring an art gallery without any further reference to his presumed escape, or when, at the close of the film, Encolpio's voice-off stops abruptly in mid-sentence: "On an island covered over with high, perfumed grass, a young Greek introduced himself and told us that in the years. . . ."[15] For Fellini, his lacunar narrative constituted a structural principal designed to mark the lacunar status of antiquity today. In an account published in the preface to his screenplay (and frequently repeated in the press and international film journals), Fellini argued that when screening antiquity the director's task, like that of an archaeologist, is to put the surviving pieces of antiquity together in a form that can never be completed, and the fragmentary images of the film so made then constitute "the potsherds, crumbs and dust of a vanished world."[16]

Fellini-Satyricon also rejects the traditional concentration of Hollywood's historical films on heroic characters possessed of clear-cut traits and objectives. Reproducing the Petronian parody of mythic heroism, Encolpio's quests are both ignoble and humiliating—first to regain his boy-lover Gitone, and then to obtain a cure for his sexual impotence.[17] Furthermore, although the speeches of this emasculated hero at the opening and close of the film provide it with a minimal narrative unity, *Fellini-Satyricon* privileges the visual image over a psychologically motivated story. Fellini's use of CinemaScope generates a wide frame that encloses a flattened space like that of an ancient fresco or wall-painting. The slow movement of the camera frequently gives precedence to the visual exhibition of the bizarre images which fill these scenes, rather than to the narrative development of the characters who pass through their margins and often first enter the frame as shadows before they appear as rounded bodies. In the critically acclaimed and much discussed sequence when Encolpio and Gitone walk through a brothel in the Roman Suburra, for example, the camera does not track them or display their point of view. Instead, as they wander in and out of shot, the camera surveys a grotesque parade of drunks, whores, and freaks and their shabby, quotidian existence.[18] The film defamiliarizes antiquity and self-reflexively draws attention to the artifice of the world it has created by constantly blurring distinctions between the "real" and the "illusory" in the conduct and the display of its characters. Thus, after the

7.2 Performers in Vernacchio's theatre, from *Fellini-Satyricon* (1969). [Courtesy of BFI
Stills, Posters and Designs.]

initial loss of his beloved Gitone, Encolpio rediscovers him as an actor on
the stage of Vernacchio, while in the art gallery which he later visits Gitone
reappears as a painted figure in one of the gallery's frescoes. [illustration 7.2]
Even within the film itself, antiquity takes on the illusory qualities and artificiality of a stage play or a painting.[19]

Any attempt by spectators at emotional engagement with the film's characters is further discouraged by the employment of a dubbing technique
which deliberately leaves the actors' lips out of synchrony with the dialogue
and by the utilization of disturbing musical accompaniment (such as odd
metallic sounds produced electronically) which were designed, according to
Fellini, to explain nothing. Similarly, almost all the sequences of *Fellini-
Satyricon* were shot in the studio Cinecittà, thus allowing for an elaborately
stylized scenography full of strange and exotic sets, colors, costumes, and
make-up, which together generate a hallucinatory, inhuman atmosphere.
The Rome and the Romans of *Fellini-Satyricon* recall neither the splendors
and sentimentality of the Italian silent films witnessed by Fellini in his
childhood, nor the contemporary tones of the Hollywood Cleopatras and
Neros of the sound era, nor even the comic-strip pleasures of the "spaghetti
epics" or pepla in which the Italian film industry had so recently invested
production.[20]

Again, in extra-cinematic discussion about the making of his film, Fellini offered theoretical justification for the range of cinematic techniques he had deployed to defamiliarize ancient Rome and to alienate spectators from the oneiric creatures he had placed in it. He wanted, he claimed, to strip the image of ancient Rome of its cultural accretions—the vision of it promulgated through the institutions of the school and the cinema, or the discipline of archaeology. Pre-Christian Rome was as unfamiliar and distant as another planet or the world of dreams, and his representation of it and its inhabitants on screen should consequently be equally distant and as indeciferable.[21] Fellini held to this view despite suggesting, paradoxically, that

> If the work of Petronius is the realistic, bloody and amusing description of the customs, characters and general feel of those times, the film we want to freely adapt from it could be a fresco in fantasy key, a powerful and evocative allegory—a satire of the world we live in today. Man never changes, and today we can recognise all the principal characters in the drama.[22]

Associated production releases and press reports concerning the casting for *Fellini-Satyricon* appeared to sustain the director's explicit identification of the principal characters with itinerant hippies of the late 1960s' "counterculture." One of the young unknowns was described as a hippie plucked from the streets of London's Chelsea, another as recently a sensation in the Broadway production of the musical *Hair*. The "evocative allegory" for modern times was generally regarded as culminating in one of the last sequences of the film—just as the Romans of the older generation were seen within the narrative of the film to be left to cannabalize a corpse on the seashore while the young sailed away in search of new adventures, so the rebellious youth of the late 1960s were turning away from the moribund religious beliefs and sexual constraints of the past in a never-ceasing pursuit of new freedoms and the next pleasure.[23]

While such readings of the film were likely to receive a welcome among the crowd of ten thousand who saw its premiere after a rock concert in Madison Square Garden, and in the pages of *Playboy* where Fellini was regularly interviewed, Alberto Moravia also drew attention to the very end of *Fellini-Satyricon* as confirmation of another narrative—the film's farewell to antiquity. For, in the closing moments of *Fellini-Satyricon*, the camera suddenly freezes on a close-up of Encolpio's face, which dissolves into a painted face on a half-obliterated fresco that stands scattered across a deserted plain. Both he and his companions are returned to the faded fragmentary condition of the ancient novel and of our modern knowledge of the society which it depicted.[24]

For Fellini then, a certain kind of cinema can be truer to the present
fragmented condition of classical antiquity than more conventional historical scholarship. Cinema can offer a visual archaeology of the past and,
moreover, bring it to vivid life before the eyes of its fascinated spectators:

> Another very tempting aspect of this cinematic procedure is one of evoking
> this world not through the fruit of bookish, scholastic documentation, a lit-
> eral fidelity to the text, but rather in the way an archeologist reconstructs
> something alluding to the form of an amphora or a statue from a few pot-
> sherds. Our film, through the fragmentary recurrence of its episodes, should
> restore the image of a vanished world without completing it, as if those char-
> acters, those habits, those milieux were summoned for us in a trance, recalled
> from their silence by the mystic ritual of a séance.
>
> What is important, it seems to us, is not descriptive precision, historical
> fidelity, the complacently erudite anecdote, or elegant narrative construction,
> but that the characters and their adventures live before our eyes as though
> caught unawares.[25]

The question, for Fellini, would not be *whether* cinema should have a place
in the classical tradition but *what else* could best capture the mysterious,
obscure and ethereal quality of the ancient world today.

Notes

Notes to Chapter 1

1. Cf. Winkler (1995), 140–2.
2. For *Roman Scandals* as a film of social protest, see Thompson and Routt (1987).
3. On this opening sequence of *Roma,* see Bondanella (1987), 246–7, and (1992), 193–205; Foreman (1993); Verdone (1994), 84–8.
4. See Bondanella (1992), 195, and Foreman (1993), 156. Cf. McBride (1978) on a similar reminiscence of childhood film-going in the earlier television documentary, *Fellini: A Director's Notebook.*
5. On Eliot's address in particular, see Ziolkowski (1993), 129–34, and Kennedy (1995).
6. See Gamel (1991), 220; Kennedy (1995), 74–7. Note that Highet (1949), 3, refers to the survival of the Latin language as "one more proof that classical culture is an essential and active part of our civilization."
7. Benjamin (1973), 223. For which, see Elsaesser (1984), 77, and Storey (1993), 108–9.
8. Knox (1994), 305.
9. Bloom (1987), 344 and cf. 64 and 304–12. On Bloom, see Taplin (1989), 186–8 and 196; Hawkins (1990), 109–10; Rose (1991), 18.
10. On Arnold's distinction between Culture and Anarchy, see Turner (1981), 17–36; Prickett (1989); Storey (1993), 21–7.
11. Calder in Reinhold (1984), 10.
12. Knox (1994), 12–4.
13. Martindale (1993), 24, remarking on the work of Terry Eagleton.
14. See, for example, Storey (1993) for a survey of cultural theory and its analysis of high/popular distinctions. Cf., more briefly, MacCabe (1986).
15. For the importance and the impact of this aspect of Bernal's otherwise highly contentious work, see for example Edith Hall (1991).
16. Kennedy (1995), 75. On disclosing "the contemporary horizon of interest" of the interpreter who investigates the classical tradition, see Gamel (1991), 220, who quotes the work of the reception theorist Hans Robert Jauss.
17. See Griffin (1992), 141, and Ziolkowski (1993), 129–34.
18. Highet (1949), 389. I am indebted to Max Schaeffer for drawing my attention to this passage in his undergraduate dissertation.
19. Beard and Henderson (1995), 6.
20. Beard and Henderson (1995), 107.
21. Beard and Henderson (1995), 105–6.

22. Storey (1993), 15, 155, and 160.

23. The following two sections, at various points, draw on and extend material first discussed in Wyke (1996).

24. See Bann (1984), 138; Costa (1989), 3; Williams (1990), 4; Nowell-Smith (1990), 163; Belton (1992), 30–1; Lant (1992), 88–9.

25. See Grindon (1994), 3–4, and Gori (1994), 12, on Griffith's comments in, for example, *Motography* for January 1915. Cf. Higashi (1994), 27, on the views of Cecil B. DeMille.

26. From the review of *Cabiria* in the Naples journal *Film,* 23 April 1914, quoted in Martinelli (1992), 75. All translations are my own unless otherwise stated.

27. See, generally, the discussions of historical film in Sorlin (1980); Ferro (1988); Ortoleva (1991); Gori (1994); Grindon (1994).

28. Heath (1977), 37–43, on which see Rosen (1984), 17–34. Cf. Sorlin (1980), 21–2; Grindon (1994), 5–16.

29. *Cinema* 6.119 (1941) quoted and translated in Fink (1974).

30. Fink (1974), 119–20.

31. Hirsch (1978), 12 and 29–32; Babington and Evans (1993), 1–3; Rosenstone (1995), 3–4.

32. Houston and Gillett (1963), 69.

33. Durgnat (1963), 11–12.

34. Major contributions to the cinema/history debate are conveniently collated in Gori (1994), and the debate's development is surveyed in Ortoleva (1991).

35. See Ferro (1988), 84, discussed in Gori (1988), 9–10 and (1994), 13–15, and Rondolino (1994), 164–5.

36. As Ortoleva (1991), 80–4.

37. Nowell-Smith (1977). Cf. Rosen (1984) and Ortoleva (1991), 80–3.

38. White (1973); Bann (1984) and (1990). Cf. Martindale and Martindale (1990), 141; Martindale (1993), 18–23; Rosenstone (1995), 3–4.

39. On the importance of Sorlin's work to the cinema/history debate, see Williams (1990); Ortoleva (1991), 37–42; Fledelius (1994), 118–20; Rondolino (1994), 165–6 and 177–9; Grindon (1994), 1–26; Rosenstone (1995), 3–13.

Notes to Chapter 2

1. Cf. Pearson and Uricchio (1990), 243–4.

2. Hobsbawm and Ranger (1983). They locate the proliferation of such "invented traditions" specifically in the period between 1870 and 1914. Cf. Lowenthal (1985), 35–73.

3. Hobsbawm and Ranger (1983), 279–80; Reinhold (1984); Bondanella (1987), 115–50; Vance (1989), esp. 1–42; Richard (1994), 12–84.

4. Kennedy postscript in Reinhold (1984); Vance (1984); Bondanella (1987), 152–71; Galinsky (1992), esp. 53–73; Richard (1994), 85–122.

5. Vance (1989), esp. 30–67; Ziolkowski (1993), 146–93; Mayer (1994), 1–20.

6. See Mayer (1994), 189–290, which includes a script of the play. Cf. Solomon (1978), 126–34; Hirsch (1978), 105–12; Elley (1984), 130–5; Smith (1991), 22–7; Babington and Evans (1993), esp. 177–205.

7. Lowenthal (1985), 112–6.

8. Lovett (1982), 20; Springer (1987), esp. 65–74 and 136–57; Bondanella (1987), 158–65.

9. Quoted in Hobsbawm and Ranger (1983), 267.

10. As Lopez–Celly (1939), 212–6. Cf. Croce (1914), 152–7; Calendoli (1967), 70–4; de

Tommaso (1975), 110; Ghigi (1977), 733; de Vincenti (1988), 12–4; Brunetta (1993), 151–7; Parigi (1994), 67–9.

11. Bondanella (1987), 165–6, discusses the significance of the postcard. See, more generally, on pre-Fascist *romanità*, Cubberley (1988), xii; Cagnetta (1979), 15–34; Canfora (1980), 39–40; Visser (1992), 7–8; Moatti (1993), 128; Wyke (1994), 16.

12. See, for example, Brunetta (1986), 57; (1990), 123; (1991a), 64–5; (1993), 143–6.

13. Hay (1987), 12–3 and 151–2. Cf. more generally on the social function of early American cinema, Belton (1992), 31–2; Pearson and Uricchio (1990), 260–1; Higashi (1994), 28.

14. Brunetta (1991a), 64–5, and (1991b), 13–16; Bernardini (1982), 34, and (1986), 34–40; Cardillo (1987), 25–37; dall'Asta (1992), 19–20. Cf. Wyke (1996), 143 and (1997).

15. Paolella (1956), 166–70; Calendoli (1967); Cary (1974), 7–9; Elley (1984), 81–4; Usai (1985); Bondanella (1987), 207–8; Leprohon (1972), 30; dall'Asta (1992), 20–32; Dalle Vacche (1992), 27–52; Mayer (1994), 312–4. Contrast Parigi (1994), 69, who argues that *Cabiria* is not designed to express a colonialist nationalism.

16. Quoted and translated in Bondanella (1987), 176.

17. Cagnetta (1979); Canfora (1980), 76–146; Bondanella (1987), 181–206; Braun (1990); Visser (1992); Ziolkowski (1993), 15–7; Moatti (1993), 130–40; Benton (1995); Fraquelli (1995).

18. Cardillo (1987), 158–62; Bondanella (1987), 210–3; Gori (1988), 16–25; Gili (1990); Dalle Vacche (1992), 27–52; Quartermaine (1995); Becker (1995).

19. See Gili (1990), 94–7, and Quartermaine (1995), 205–6.

20. Cardillo (1987), 153; Gili (1990), 99; Quartermaine (1995), 206–7.

21. Wood (1975), 184.

22. Cf. Higashi (1994), 202–3, and Nadel (1993) on Cecil B. DeMille's *The Ten Commandments* (1956). On the parallels with the present at work in *Ben-Hur* (1959), especially regarding the foundation of Israel, see Babington and Evans (1993), 201–2.

23. Babington and Evans (1993), 210–3.

24. For discussion of Kracauer's work, see Bergman (1971), xiii–xvi; Arcand (1974), 22; Sorlin (1980), 25–6; Elsaesser (1984); Allen and Gomery (1985), 159–67; Christensen (1987), 6–7; Ortoleva (1991), 43–53, and (1994), 319–28.

25. Lindgren (1963), 14–17; Calendoli (1967), 70–4; Solomon (1978), 15–6; Bernardini (1986), 35–40; de Vincenti (1988), 8–10; Brunetta (1991b), 14–5; dall'Asta (1992), 19–20. On the comparative development of American feature-length films see, for example, Gevinson (1988), 146–50; Pearson and Uricchio (1990); Higashi (1994), 1–33.

26. dall'Asta (1992), 31–2; Parigi (1994), 67–9.

27. Usai (1985), 54–5.

28. On the classical Hollywood style see, for example, Bordwell, Staiger, and Thompson (1985), esp. 1–308; Staiger (1986); Izod (1988), 53–7 and 86–7; Salt (1991), 49–54; Grindon (1994), 16–22.

29. Eckert (1978); Allen (1980); Doane (1989); Gaines (1989); Gaines and Herzog (1990); Stacey (1994), 176–223.

30. May (1980), 200–36; Izod (1988), 64–7 and 101–4; Hamer (1993), 118 and 121–2; Higashi (1994), esp. 142–78.

31. Thompson and Routt (1987), 35–6.

32. Thompson and Routt (1987), 36–43.

33. Solomon (1978), 134. Sample advertisements for such "Ben Hur" products are to be found in MGM's campaign books which were sent to theater managers to supply ideas for selling the film.

34. Wood (1975), 169.

35. Neale (1983), 34–6; Bordwell, Staiger, and Thompson (1985), 353–64; Belton (1992), esp. 183–210.

36. Neale (1983), 35. Cf. dall'Asta (1992), 31–2.

37. Houston and Gillett (1963); Wood (1975), 165–80; Sklar (1975), 294–6; Hirsch (1978), 29; Rondolino (1980), 65; Neale (1983), 34–6; Belton (1992); Babington and Evans (1993), 6–8.

38. Cf. on the Cold War rhetoric of Cecil B. DeMille's *The Ten Commandments* (1956), Whitfield (1991), 218–9; Nadel (1993); Higashi (1994), 202–3.

39. Babington and Evans (1993), 207. Cf. Belton (1992), 190–1.

40. Wood (1975), 184–5. Cf. Belton (1992), 194–5; dall'Asta (1992), 31–2.

41. See, for example, *Variety* and the *Los Angeles Times* for 17 September 1953.

42. Wood (1975), 173.

43. Houston and Gillett (1963); Wood (1975), 168–73; Neale (1983), 34–6; dall'Asta (1992), 31–2; Belton (1992), 210.

44. Cf. Higson (1989), 42–3, on strategies for the analysis of "national" cinema, and Pearson and Uricchio (1990), 243–4, on strategies for the analysis of Shakespeare on screen.

45. On the numerous evidentiary problems faced when researching film history see, for example, Sorlin (1980), 22–4, and Allen and Gomery (1985), 28–36.

46. On the methodological problems of writing film history see, for example, Nowell-Smith (1977); Rosen (1984); Elsaesser (1984); Beck (1985); Allen and Gomery (1985), 25–42; de Cordova (1988); Allen (1990); Straw (1991). Cf. Wyke (1996), 152–3.

47. Lowenthal (1985), 412.

Notes to Chapter 3

1. For a history of the rebellion led by Spartacus, and for the following analysis of the ancient sources, see Bradley (1989), esp. 136–9.

2. Florus 2.8.20. The translation is that of Yavetz (1988), 101.

3. See, for example, Bradley (1989), xi–xiii; Vogt (1974), 61.

4. Rubinsohn (1987), 1.

5. For Benjamin's views on the cult of republican antiquity instigated during the French Revolution, see Norman Vance (forthcoming).

6. Highet (1949), 390–9, and Bondanella (1987), 130–1.

7. Bondanella (1987), 143.

8. Saurin in Petitot (1803), 211–9.

9. Bradley (1989), xi; Yavetz (1988), 118.

10. Vogt (1974), 172; Finley (1983), 12–7. See also Canfora (1980), 23–30, for the slavery debates in France and America.

11. Calendoli (1967), 68–70; de Vincenti (1988), 12.

12. Lopez-Celly (1939), 10 and 14; Russo (1956), 75–6.

13. Page references are to the seventh edition of Giovagnoli's novel, published in Milan by Paolo Carrara in 1916.

14. On this passage, compare Russo (1956), 76–7.

15. Lovett (1982), 28.

16. Bondanella (1987), 137–41; Norman Vance (forthcoming).

17. Springer (1987), esp. 65–74.

18. Lovett (1982), 56; Treves (1962), 91; Bondanella (1987), 158–65.

19. Lopez-Celly (1939), 51–2.

20. Russo (1956), 74–5.

21. On Garibaldi's letter, see also Russo (1956), 77.

22. Analysis of the Latium film *Spartaco* of 1909 is precluded by the apparent lack of primary material concerning the film. Brunetta (1993), 154, remarks only that the film was based on Giovagnoli's novel. To my knowledge, no copy of the film survives.

23. Bernardini and Gili (1986); Bernardini (1991b); Brunetta (1991b); dall'Asta (1992), 19–20; and see chapter 2 above.

24. Cagnetta (1979), 15–34; Bondanella (1987), 165–6; Visser (1992), 7–8; Moatti (1993), 128.

25. Cardillo (1987), 25–37; Brunetta (1991a), 64–5; dall'Asta (1992), 31; Brunetta (1993), 143–6. See also chapter 2 above.

26. Brunetta (1993), 52–3.

27. Prolo (1951), 54.

28. Giovagnoli (1907), 28.

29. Giovagnoli (1916), plates on pages 353, 385, and 449. Giovagnoli had also bestowed Spartacus's armies with the iconography of modern revolutionary movements within the narrative proper (346). For the use of "liberty trees" in the rituals of the *risorgimento*, see Springer (1987), 68.

30. Webster (1960), 14–6.

31. See chapter 5.

32. See chapter 6.

33. My analysis of *Spartaco* (1913) is based on examination of the footage which survives in the George Kleine collection in the Library of Congress. Although few of the film's English intertitles remain, and one whole reel as well as parts of others are missing, it has been possible to piece together the plot of the film from the summary available in the publicity distributed by Kleine, and that provided by *Illustrated Films Monthly* 2 (1914), 97–104.

34. dall'Asta (1992), 27–9.

35. Compare dall'Asta (1992), 36–9, on the camera's voyeuristic play on the muscled body of Maciste in *Cabiria* (1914).

36. Farassino (1983), 42–4.

37. Martinelli (1983), 13. Perhaps some of the paintings Guaita brought to life included such famous gladiatorial scenes as Gérôme's *Ave Caesar, Morituri Te Salutant* (1859) and *Pollice Verso* (1874), both of which provided a recognizable iconography for the arena set designs in many early historical films.

38. This and other reviews are quoted in Martinelli (1993), 261–4, who also notes that *La vita cinematografica* dedicated several pages to photographs of Guaita and comments about him after he exhibited his muscular physique at the film's opening in Budapest.

39. On screen bodies as metaphors for the Italian body politic, see Dalle Vacche (1992), 27–52, on *Cabiria* (1914) and *Scipione l'Africano* (1937).

40. My description of the scene follows Brunetta (1993), 167–8.

41. This sequence of *Spartaco* does not survive in the copy at the Library of Congress, but is referred to in *Illustrated Films Monthly* and, more briefly, in the Kleine publicity.

42. Here the plot draws on that of Vidali's earlier film *Ione* or *Gli ultimi giorni di Pompeii*, where Glaucus is falsely accused of murder and thrown to the lions. The credibility of incorporating the historical figure of Spartacus into such a fantastical plot is perhaps sustained for film audiences by the repetition of the earlier film's narrative drive.

43. Crassus's daughter is called Emily in the summary provided by *Illustrated Films Monthly*. According to Martinelli (1993), 261–2, she is named Elena in the version of the film exhibited in Italy. Martinelli's summary of the plot does not include the final,

triumphant sequence found in the Kleine archive and assumes that both Noricus and Spartacus die in the arena.

44. The film's celebratory parallel between Spartacus and Garibaldi is also observed by Mayer (1994), 314.

45. Noted by Russo (1956), 78, and Cammarota (1987), 121–2.

46. Guarino (1979), 13–5; Yavetz (1988), 126.

47. Finley (1983), 40–4; Vogt (1974), 176–7.

48. Rubinsohn (1987), 1.

49. Guarino (1979), 13–5; Rubinsohn (1987), 5; Finley (1983), 57; Yavetz (1988), 127–8.

50. Gramsci (1975), 845, n.208. See Russo (1956), 77–8, and Cammarota (1987), 122.

51. As Russo (1956), 78.

52. The preface by Luigi Russo appeared in an edition of *Spartaco* published by Parenti in 1955, and reappeared as a self-contained article in 1956. See Russo (1956).

53. Rubinsohn (1987), 36, n.155.

54. Siclier (1962), 29–31; Brunetta (1982), 499–502; Liehm (1984), 90; Gori (1984), 79–85; Spinazzola (1985), 324.

55. Corsi (1991), 92. *Spartaco* (1952) was one such coproduction, made by API Film of Rome in collaboration with Rialto Film of Paris.

56. For the epic genre's capacity to exhibit the powers of cinema, see Neale (1983), 34–6, and dall'Asta (1992), 31–2.

57. Siclier (1962), 29–30; Spinazzola (1965), 274; Brunetta (1991a), 419.

58. Siclier (1962), 29–30.

59. Cagnetta (1979); Bondanella (1987), 172–206; Braun (1990); Visser (1992); Quartermaine (1995); Benton (1995); Fraquelli (1995).

60. Quoted in Gori (1984), 41, and Gori (1988), 12–3.

61. Quoted and translated in Dalle Vacche (1992), 44. Cf. Becker (1995) and Quartermaine (1995), and see chapter 2 above.

62. Siclier (1962), 29–30; Brunetta (1982), 405–6; Gori (1984), 79–84; Spinazzola (1985), 324.

63. My analysis of *Spartaco* (1952) is based on a version dubbed into English and lasting 85 minutes which is available from UK film distributors. The version originally distributed in Italy is said to have been 110 minutes long, cut by the state censors from Freda's 120 minutes. See the filmography in Martini and Della Casa (1993).

64. On such Italian films about the resistance, see Sorlin (1980), 189–206, and Bondanella (1988), 31–73.

65. Bondanella (1987), 181–2.

66. For the development of an armed resistance movement in Italy, see Forgacs (1990), 83–5, and Ginsborg (1990), 10–7.

67. For the Christian iconography in Rossellini's film, see Sorlin (1980), 200–1; Bondanella (1988), 41–2; Dalle Vacche (1992), 180–1, and still 37.

68. See Sorlin (1980), 189–206 and, more generally, Ginsborg (1990), 70.

69. See, especially, Dalle Vacche (1992).

70. On Girotti's varied roles, including his subsequent appearance as a failed *risorgimento* revolutionary in Luchino Visconti's *Senso* (1954), see Bondanella (1988), 23 and 95–100; Forgacs (1990), 91–3.

71. *Vie Nuove* 1 (1952), 18.

72. See Brunetta (1982), 405–6, and Gori (1984), 79–94.

73. Sassoon (1981), 8–28; Ginsborg (1990), 15; Forgacs (1990), 152–72.

74. Sassoon (1981), 59–72; Forgacs (1990), 103–6; Ginsborg (1990), 72–120.

75. Spartacus's opponent within the slave army is (more plausibly) entitled "Ocnomas" in Italian credits for the film. See Martini and Della Casa (1993), 77–8.

76. Sassoon (1981), 73–97; Ginsborg (1990), 42–8 and 199–200; Gundle (1991), 114; Dalle Vacche (1992), 123–4. My thanks to Joseph Castagna of Queens University, Kingston, for drawing my attention to the Togliatti/Secchia debates within the PCI.

77. See, for example, *Monthly Film Bulletin* 20.239 for December 1953 and *Variety* 30 June 1954.

78. Smith (1991), 204–6.

79. Reinhold (1984); Lowenthal (1985), 105–24; Bondanella (1987), 115–50; Vance (1989), 1–67; Anderson (1992), 95. See also chapter 2 above.

80. Dahl (1963), 40–61; McConachie (1992), 91–118; Mayer (1994), 20; Vance (forthcoming).

81. See especially Vance (1984), and Vance (1989), 31–3. Cf. Canfora (1980), 26–30, on the use of studies of ancient slavery in the American emancipation debates and the southern counterexample of the glories of a Greek-style democracy based on slavery.

82. Dahl (1963), 58–61; Vance (1989), 18 and 30; McConachie (1992), 91–118; Mayer (1994), 20.

83. See, for example, the Panther edition first published in Great Britain in 1959. All subsequent page references refer to this edition.

84. Cf. Vance (1989), 33.

85. Fast (1990), 275–7.

86. Sklar (1975), 256–68; Ceplair and Englund (1979); Smith (1989), 76; Leab (1993), 120–2.

87. Wittner (1978), 129–30; Whitfield (1991), 34–7 and 60–4; Elley (1984), 109; Fast (1990), 275–7. Cf. Biskind (1983), Vanderwood (1991), and Samuels (1991) on mainstream films of the 1950s and their stress on conformity and domesticity.

88. Vance (1989), 33; Smith (1989), 93 and n.148.

89. See Whitfield (1991), 20–2, and, for covert commentaries on race relations to be found in, for example, liberal Westerns of the 1950s, see Biskind (1983), 228–45. I am also indebted here to a paper on Howard Fast given by Alan Wald at a conference on Cold War culture held at University College, London, in 1994.

90. See Whitfield (1991), 43–5, and Biskind (1983), 326–7, on Cold War attitudes to homosexuality, and Vance (1989), 33, on its narrative function in Fast's novel.

91. Fast (1990), 286–95; Whitfield (1991), 180. Cf. Wald (for which see n.89 above).

92. Ceplair and Englund (1979), 250 and 419; Elley (1984), 109–12; Smith (1989); Whitfield (1991), 218–9; Cooper (1991), 18. See also *Limelight* 13 October 1960.

93. Bourget (1985), 58.

94. Nadel (1993), 416 and 419; Whitfield (1991), 218–9.

95. On the conservative ideological structures of *Ben-Hur*, see Babington and Evans (1993).

96. Cary (1974), 52; Hirsch (1978), 98; Babington and Evans (1993), 183; Whitfield (1991), 218–19. For Kubrick's claims to inspiration, see the *New York Times,* 2 October 1960.

97. Biskind (1983), 97; Elley (1984), 112; Whitfield (1991), 218.

98. Ceplair and Englund (1979), 418; Biskind (1983), 336–48; Smith (1989); Suid (1991), 220; Whitfield (1991), 205–30.

99. Vanderwood (1991).

100. See Biskind (1991).

101. Cooper (1974) and (1991); Bourget (1985), 59–60. Cf. the review of the rereleased *Spartacus* in *The Independent on Sunday*, 27 October 1991.

102. Houston and Gillett (1963); Sklar (1975), 294–6; Wood (1975), 168; Hirsch (1978), 29; Smith (1989); Babington and Evans (1993), 4–8. Cf. chapter 2 above.

103. Cooper (1991), 27.

104. Bourget (1985), 57–8.

105. Solomon (1978), 34–8; Hirsch (1978), 98; Elley (1984), 109–12; Bourget (1985), 58–9; Babington and Evans (1993), 191–2.

106. See Sklar (1985), 65, and cf. *Film Daily* 7 October 1960.

107. Whitfield (1991), 100–26.

108. Cf. Smith (1989), 76, who notes in passing a similarity between the sequence in *Spartacus* where the gladiators break out of their imprisoning school and the traditional, heroic accounts of breaking out of the confines of the blacklist.

109. *Los Angeles Mirror,* 20 October 1960. Cf. *Variety,* 12 December 1960, on the protests of the American Legion against the film, and a letter to the *Los Angeles Times* of 15 January 1961 denouncing the distribution to schools of a photoplay study guide to *Spartacus.*

110. See Adam Mars-Jones's review of the rereleased *Spartacus* in *The Independent,* 1 November 1991.

111. Wittner (1978), 190–2 and 198–201; Whitfield (1991), 20–3.

112. Babington and Evans (1993), 224–6.

113. Shohat (1991b), 232–3. Cf. Babington and Evans (1993), 224–6.

114. See Alexander Walker's review of the rereleased *Spartacus* in *The Evening Standard,* 31 October 1991. Cf. Derek Elley in *The Independent,* 25 October 1991.

115. Douglas (1988), 277.

116. Cooper (1974), 30. Cf. Elley (1984), 109–12.

117. Cooper (1974), 30. Elley (1984), 111; Hunt (1993), 71–2 and 74–7. It was fully restored for the 1991 rerelease of *Spartacus.*

118. See especially Hunt (1993) and Hark (1993).

119. See Hark (1993), 161–2, who, in her analysis of gender operations in *Spartacus,* draws on and responds to Laura Mulvey's work on the cinematic gaze.

120. Hark (1993), 152–3.

121. Hark (1993), 159–68; Hunt (1993), 65. See also Biskind (1983) on the roles of John Wayne in the 1950s.

122. Hark (1993), 160–1, who refers to a review by David Denby of the rereleased film.

123. Smith (1989), 92–3; Cooper (1991), 18; Whitfield (1991), 218–9.

124. Hirsch (1978), 98.

125. See Wood (1975), 183–4.

126. See the review of Adams Mars-Jones in *The Independent,* 1 November 1991. Cf. Elley (1984); Solomon (1978), 37; Hirsch (1978), 98; Babington and Evans (1993), 194.

127. Smith (1989), 92–3.

128. *Variety,* 7 October 1960.

129. Cf. Babington and Evans (1993), 55–6.

Notes to Chapter 4

1. Robert F. Hawkins, *New York Times*, 7 January 1962.

2. *Giornale d'Italia*, 4 November 1913. Quoted in Prolo (1951), 55.

3. Hughes-Hallett (1991), 21–143; Wyke (1992), 100–5; Hamer (1993), 1–23.

4. Plutarch, *Life of Antony* 25.1, and see Brenk (1992).

5. Hughes-Hallett (1991), 15–6 and 64–82; Wyke (1992), 106–12; Hamer (1993), xvi–xvii.

6. See especially Hughes-Hallett (1991) and Hamer (1993).

7. Pearson and Uricchio (1990).

8. For details of this film, and a survey of the silent era's film adaptations of Shakespeare, see Ball (1968).

9. Ball (1968), 47–8.

10. Ball (1968), 96. English titles and release dates are listed in Ball's index.

11. Ball (1968), 167.

12. *Giornale d'Italia*, 4 November 1913. Quoted in Prolo (1951), 55.

13. On Shakespeare's *Antony and Cleopatra* see, for example, Bloom (1990) and Hughes-Hallett (1991), 169–202. For its place among the other Roman plays, see Thomas (1989) and Martindale and Martindale (1990).

14. For the "killer-Cleopatra" of the nineteenth century, see Hughes-Hallett (1991), 252–311.

15. The motif is inherited from Dryden's *All for Love*, for which see Hughes-Hallett (1991), 212–4, and Martindale and Martindale (1990), 140–1.

16. The sequence of the triumph at Rome survives in the print at the Library of Congress but is missing from the print at the Cineteca archive—a clearly mutilated version with scarcely any intertitles. But, as if to elide the film's difference from Shakespeare's play, George Kleine's publicity for the American launch of *Marcantonio e Cleopatra* fails to conclude its plot summary with mention of the triumphal procession.

17. On Italy's use of the tradition of *romanità* in the period before the First World War, see chapter 2 above, and Cagnetta (1979), 15–33.

18. Quoted in Cagnetta (1979), 17. See also chapter 2 above.

19. Brunetta and Gili (1990), 9–13 and (1993), 160–77.

20. For discussion of the nineteenth-century "colonialist imaginary" and its structuring of film narratives, see esp. Shohat (1991a).

21. Hughes-Hallett (1991), 252–80.

22. Said (1985), 3. For the importance of the Napoleonic campaign see also Said (1985), 42–3 and 76–88.

23. Curl (1994), 132.

24. For the feminization of the Orient, more generally, see Said (1985), 188 and 206–8, and Shohat (1991a), 46–62.

25. Higashi (1994), 90, who extends Said's definition of orientalism to include its more theatrical forms. Cf. Stevens (1984) and Lant (1992), 96.

26. Lant (1992), 93–8. For the spectacle of Egypt generally, cf. Curl (1994), 187–206.

27. Hughes-Hallett (1991), 266–70.

28. Shohat (1991a), 45.

29. de Vincenti (1988), 25. The opening documentary sequence survives in the Cineteca print, but not in that of the Library of Congress.

30. Shohat (1991a), 49.

31. Quoted in Martinelli (1993), 42–5, along with a number of other reviews.

32. The translation is that of Mandelbaum (1981).

33. Cagnetta (1979), 22–5.

34. This intertitle, as well as the subsequent triumph in Rome, is missing from the Cineteca print of the film.

35. Ball (1968), 166.

36. Quoted in Ball (1968), 168, from *The Art of the Motion Picture* (New York, 1915).

37. Lant (1992) and Shohat (1991a), 49–51.

38. Prolo (1951), 56; Martinelli (1993), 46. On the eroticism of the Italian historical films of this period, see generally, Brunetta (1993), 169.

39. Renzi (1991), 121, and Lant (1992), 109.

40. Said (1985), 188 and 309; Shohat (1991a), 46–62 and 69–70; Hughes-Hallett (1991), 93.

41. Hughes-Hallett (1991), 263 and 346–8; Renzi (1991), 121.

42. Ball (1968), 239; Hughes-Hallett (1991), 330–1 and 340; Lant (1992), 109–10. No print of *Cleopatra* (1917) survives, but its content is deduced from extant stills, contemporary publicity, and reviews.

43. Lant (1992), 109–10.

44. Higashi (1994), 151–2.

45. May (1980), 200–36; Higashi (1994), 4–5 and 87–9; Black (1994), 26–8; Christie (1991), 20.

46. May (1980), 212–3; Higashi (1994), 100; Black (1994), 28; Christie (1991), 20.

47. Elley (1984), 93; Izod (1988), 87–8.

48. Hamer (1993), 119–21.

49. See Paramount's *Study Guide and Manual* (1934), 16, and compare question 47.

50. See Hays quoted in May (1980), 204–5. Cf. Izod (1988), 69–70; Black (1994), 27–34.

51. Izod (1988), 105–6; Black (1994), 1 and 39–83.

52. Black (1994), 65–70. See also chapter 5 below.

53. Izod (1988), 106; Black (1994), 149–97.

54. Izod (1988), 107; Black (1994), 72–80 and 174.

55. On the formation of Hollywood's oriental elsewhere see Shohat (1991a), 68–70.

56. Hamer (1993), 109–10.

57. Hughes-Hallett (1991), 315–6.

58. Hamer (1993), 148 n. 19, provides a useful list.

59. Quoted in Hughes-Hallett (1991), 319–20.

60. See Paramount's *Study Guide and Manual* (1934), 15, question 34.

61. Cf. Hamer (1993), 124–6. Lant (1992), 91–3 and n. 19, argues that the film's frame constructs the spectator's experience, as in early lantern shows, in terms of entering an Egyptian necropolis.

62. Higashi (1994), 3 and 108.

63. For the importance of ethnicity and immigration in both American society and Hollywood cinema, see Shohat (1991b), esp. 217–8.

64. Cf. Elley (1984), 93.

65. See chapter 2 above.

66. Cf. Shohat (1991a), 48–52.

67. Christie (1991), 20. For "objective correlatives" as a mode of filmic characterization, see also Dyer (1979), 124–6.

68. Hughes-Hallett (1991), 363. See Hughes-Hallett (1991), 362–4, and Hamer (1993), 128–30, for a more detailed analysis of the barge sequence.

69. As translated from a version of the film dubbed into Italian for television broadcasting.

70. Cf. Babington and Evans (1993), 113, on the representation of Mary Magdalene and her submission to Christ in DeMille's *King of Kings* (1927).

71. Compare the use of the myth that Amazon women were once defeated by Athenian men in the comedy *The Warrior's Husband,* which was produced by an associate of DeMille, Jesse L. Lasky, and released the year before *Cleopatra.*

72. Cf. Hamer (1993), 117–8.

73. For DeMille's lighting techniques see May (1980), 221; Higashi (1994), 15.

74. Higashi (1994), esp. 142–78; May (1980), 200–36; Eckert (1978), 7; Allen (1980), 488–9.

75. For Hollywood cinema's solicitation of a consumer gaze, see Doane (1989).

76. Eckert (1978); Allen (1980); Doane (1989); Gaines (1989); Gaines and Herzog (1990); Stacey (1994), 176–223. Cf. chapter 2 above.

77. See n. 74 above.

78. For a more extensive list, see Hughes-Hallett (1991), 88–92 and 102–43.

79. Higashi (1994), 90–1; Curl (1994), 211–20.

80. On the "metonymic" process generally, see Doane (1989), 24–7.

81. See Eckert (1978), 11–7; Gaines (1989); Doane (1989), 25–7.

82. Entitled *Last Minute News and Exploitation*, a copy of the press release is accessible at the British Film Institute.

83. Hamer (1993), 118 and 121–2.

84. Allen (1980), 487.

85. Doane (1989), 25.

86. See Hamer (1993), 123–4 and 132–3. Compare Gaines (1989) on *Queen Christina* released in the previous year.

87. The term is that of de Lauretis (1987).

88. On readings of femininity as masquerade, see Gaines and Herzog (1990), 23–7; Thumim (1992), 161–2; Stacey (1994), 26.

89. From the USC Film Library production files.

90. Luard (1989), esp. 1–17 and 514–48.

91. See USC Film Library, 20th Century-Fox collection 5042.17.

92. Hirsch (1978), 101.

93. See Beuselink (1988).

94. Baxter (1972), 160–4; Solomon (1978), 45–6; Elley (1984), 92–5; Smith (1991), 44–6; Hughes-Hallett (1991), 355–9. See *Newsweek,* 25 March 1963, for a contemporary account of the film's misfortunes.

95. Dyer (1979); Ellis (1982), 91–108.

96. The *Vogue* article catalogued on microfiche in the Academy of Motion Pictures is dated only as 1962.

97. See also Hughes-Hallett (1991), 341–2.

98. See Brodsky and Weiss (1963), 64, for a letter written by Weiss from New York expressing anxiety about the press reports.

99. Brodsky and Weiss (1963), 117.

100. See Hughes-Hallett (1991), 348–50 and 357–60.

101. See Wanger and Hyams (1963), 146–7.

102. Wanger and Hyams (1963), 148–9.

103. *New York Times,* 23 June 1963.

104. Dyer (1979), 28.

105. Whitfield (1991), 184–7; Dyer (1979), 49 and 51–2; Biskind (1983), 250–333; Nadel (1993), 422. Cf. Dyer (1986) on the function of Marilyn Monroe's star image in 1950s discourses about sex.

106. Dyer (1979), 22–3.

107. For which see Hughes-Hallett (1991), 357–60.

108. Those mechanisms were first analyzed in terms of the fetishistic and voyeuristic look by Mulvey (1975).

109. Cf. Hughes-Hallett (1991), 343–4.

110. Thumin (1992), 40.

111. Neale (1983), 35. Cf. Wood (1975), 168–72 and dall'Asta (1992), 31.

112. Wood (1975), 173 and 166–77. Cf. Houston and Gillett (1963); Belton (1992), 183–210; Babington and Evans (1993), 6–8. See also chapter 2 above.

113. See, for example, the account of the film's production in *Newsweek,* 25 March 1963, and cf. Biskind (1983), 336–7.

114. See Beuselink (1988), 6–7, for details of the cut scene.

Notes to Chapter 5

1. This chapter is an emended and much expanded version of Wyke (1994).

2. A copy of the campaign book is available in the USC Film Library production files.

3. On the rhetoric of the film's opening voiceover, see also Babington and Evans (1993), 181–5.

4. d'Amico (1946), 119.

5. For Sienkiewicz's claimed sources see Giergielwicz (1968), 127–8; d'Amico (1946), 120; Lednicki (1960), 55.

6. Warmington (1969), 127; Wallace-Hadrill (1983), 131; Sordi (1983), 31–3. Thus Suetonius's description of Nero's measures against the Christians, *Life of Nero,* 16, occurs within his list of the emperor's more praiseworthy acts.

7. The translation is that of Grant (1979), 365–6. For Tacitus's polemical portrait of Nero as the canonical tyrant, see Griffin (1984), 15, and, more recently, Rubiés (1994), 35–40. In addition see Walter (1957), 268–9, for an extensive list of the huge numbers of tragedies, operas, ballets, and pantomimes that were produced on the subject of Nero's tyranny from the sixteenth century onwards.

8. For the legend of *Nero redivivus, Revelation,* and the myth of the Antichrist, see Walter (1957), 257–62; Lawrence (1978), 54; Gwyn (1991), 452–3; Jenks (1991), 240–53.

9. See, respectively, McGinn (1979), 22–3, and Lawrence (1978), 60–3.

10. Lawrence (1978), 60–3.

11. Renan (nd), 178–9. For Renan's *Origines,* see Wardman (1964), 134–8; Chadbourne (1968), 71–2; Walter (1957), 261; Jenks (1991), 252–3.

12. In a letter of 1901, cited in Lednicki (1960), 55.

13. Highet (1949), 462–4; Lednicki (1960), 55.

14. See Turner (forthcoming); Mayer (1994), 1–20; Babington and Evans (1993), 177–205.

15. Page references are to the Continental Classic edition of *Quo Vadis?* translated by C. J. Hogarth and published in Great Britain in 1989.

16. Sienkiewicz's account of Lygia's torment in the arena seems to be based on a passage in the first epistle of Clement, which refers to Christian women being executed while dressed as the mythical Dirce. See Wiedemann (1992), 87, and Renan (nd), 170–2.

17. For discussion of the limited historical evidence, see Sordi (1983), 23–37; Frend (1984), 109.

18. d'Amico (1946), 121–2.

19. de Rossi, *Underground Christian Rome* (1864–1877) and *Inscriptiones Christianae* (1861–1888); Lanciani, *Pagan and Christian Rome* (1892) and, for example, collected letters to *The Athenaeum* in Cubberley (1988). See, more generally, Moatti (1993), 112–4; Barber (1990), 392.

20. See Marucchi's preface to the translation of *Quo Vadis?* by E. Salvadori. By 1923 the volume was already in its seventh edition.

21. Edmundson (1913), 47–51 and 118.

22. Edmundson (1913), 151–3.

23. Renan (nd), 305–6.

24. See d'Amico (1946), 125; Damiani (1946), 15–22; Highet (1949), 462–3; Giergiel-wicz (1968), 131; Hogarth in the preface to Sienkiewicz (1989), v–vii.

25. For the success of Sienkiewicz's novel and its wide cultural diffusion, see Begey (1946), 77–80; d'Amico (1946), 121–2; Robinson (1955), 24; Lednicki (1960), 11; Calen-doli (1967), 69; Giergielwicz (1968), 145; Martinelli (1993), 182; Mayer (1994), 18.

26. Cary (1974), 6; Elley (1984), 124.

27. Lindgren (1963), 17; Farassino (1983), 29; Elley (1984), 124; Hay (1987), 11 and 168; de Vincenti (1988), 9–10; Brunetta (1991b), 14–15; Mayer (1984–5) and (1994), 90–5.

28. For Nero in the Italian dramatic tradition, see Walter (1957), 268–70; Bondanella (1987), 103–5 on Monteverdi; Croce (1914), 152–4 on Cossa. On the sources and style of Maggi's *Nerone*, see Calendoli (1967), 70–4; de Vincenti (1988), 12–4; Bernardini and Gili (1986), 188; Brunetta (1993), 156–7.

29. Compare, more generally, Staiger (1986), 97.

30. Paolella (1956), 163–6.

31. The edition was published in 1914 by Fratelli Treves. See also Bernardini (1982), 149.

32. According to Cary (1974), 7, and see also 102.

33. See the descriptions of Ackerman (1972), 44–5 and 68–9, respectively. For the enormous popularity of these paintings in both Europe and America, see also Vance (1984), 112–3.

34. For the term "movement-image," see Deleuze (1986). On the relationship between early historical films and the visual arts, see Costa (1991), 16 and 50; Dunant (1994).

35. Verdone (1963); Farassino (1983), 30–1; de Vincenti (1988), 14–5; dall'Asta (1992), 32–3.

36. Cary (1974), 7; Bernardini (1982), 150; Elley (1984), 124.

37. For other reviews of Guazzoni's *Quo Vadis?* see Turconi (1963), 48–9, and Martinelli (1993), 175–82.

38. Hay (1987), 168.

39. dall'Asta (1992), 25 and 28–9. Cf. Brunetta (1991a), 64–5; Dalle Vacche (1992), 36.

40. Renan (nd), 549. See also Wardman (1964), 102.

41. Springer (1987), 3, 8, and 66–74. Cf. chapter 2 above.

42. Webster (1960), 3–9; Jemolo (1960), 81–3.

43. Cammarota (1987), 15–16, argues for such a reading of the film.

44. Webster (1960), 3–9; Jemolo (1960), 134–5.

45. Forgacs (1990), 50.

46. Cf. de Vincenti (1988), 26.

47. Calendoli (1967), 95; Cary (1974), 6–7; Liehm (1984), 9; Bernardini (1982), 149–50; Martinelli (1983), 9; Elley (1984), 124; Martinelli (1993), 183.

48. Cagnetta (1979); Canfora (1980), 76–146; Bondanella (1987), 172–81; Braun (1990), 344–50; Visser (1992); Quartermaine (1995); Benton (1995); Fraquelli (1995).

49. On relations between Church and state in Fascist Italy, see Webster (1960), 57–106, and Jemolo (1960), 182–209.

50. See Elsaesser (1984) on the valorization of vision and the look in Weimar cinema. On *Quo Vadis?* (1924), cf. Gili (1985), 24–5; Gori (1988), 17–8; dall'Asta (1992), 30.

51. On the film see further Chiti and Quargnolo (1957), 30–4; Martinelli (1981), 186–9; dall'Asta (1992), 153 and 159–60.

52. Angelini (1984), 2 and 18; Petrocchi (1984), 181; Calò (1989), 133. For a transcript of the sketch, see Angelini (1984), 103–18.

53. Calò (1989), 134–5; Angelini (1984), 17.

54. *Giornale d'Italia,* 14 November 1930, cited in Angelini (1984), 19.

55. The previous film version of the play was directed by Frederick Thompson and released in 1914 by Famous Players Lasky, the forerunner of Paramount.

56. Mayer (1994) provides a script of Barrett's *The Sign of the Cross*, discussion of the play, and of toga drama in general.

57. For DeMille's retrospective comments on his film, see Hayne (1960), 280 and 297, respectively. For DeMille's biblical films of the 1920s, see Maltby (1990); Babington and Evans (1993); Higashi (1994).

58. Quoted in Higham (1973), 216.

59. Mayer (1994), 16–7.

60. Mayer (1994), 7–15.

61. See Mayer (1994), 1–5 and 109–10 for the evangelical features of Barrett's play and its wide appeal. Cf. Maltby (1990) on DeMille's *The King of Kings*.

62. Hirsch (1978), 18.

63. See Wood (1975), 183–4 on such strategies in Hollywood histories of Rome. Cf. Babington and Evans (1993), 10, and chapter 2 above.

64. Higashi (1985), 33.

65. Babington and Evans (1993), 183–4, who also note that in this representation of contemporary America there is no place for the Jew or the black. Cf. Hirsch (1978), 62.

66. Higashi (1994), 126–7.

67. See the comments in *Variety* for 16 August 1944. A copy of the 1944 pressbook is available in the USC film archives.

68. Cf. Gili (1979), 133 and see Neale (1990), 48–9, on the role of such extra-cinematic discourses in the circulation of narrative images for films.

69. Sklar (1975), 161–2 and 176–8; Balio (1985), 255–6 and 268–9; Black (1994), 58–9.

70. As Higashi (1994), 115, on the visual style of earlier films by DeMille. Cf. Higashi (1985), 36–7 and 71–2; Hirsch (1978), 72; Black (1994), 65–70.

71. Wood (1975), 184–5. Cf. chapter 2 above.

72. Black (1994), 70.

73. Cary (1974), 105.

74. See the studio press releases collated in the campaign book for the distribution of *Quo Vadis* in 1951, and their reiteration in newspaper articles such as those in the *Los Angeles Times* of 22 May 1949 and the *New Yorker* of 10 July 1950. Many of the studio's press releases, and newspaper and magazine articles about *Quo Vadis*, are also accessible in the archives of the American Academy of Motion Pictures.

75. On the voiceover, see Babington and Evans (1993), 181–5.

76. According to a report in the *New York Times* for 7 May 1950.

77. For the *Mostra* see, for example, Bondanella (1987), 189–91, and Visser (1992), 15–17.

78. See, for example, Hay (1987), 222, and the still from a LUCE documentary on Mussolini reproduced on 227.

79. Bondanella (1987), 181–206; Visser (1992); Moatti (1993), 130–40; Quartermaine (1995). Cf. chapter 3 above.

80. Noted briefly by Giulio Cesare Castello in *Cinema* 105 (1953), 151.

81. Toynbee and Ward-Perkins (1956), xv, xix, and 127; Springer (1987), 78; Moatti (1993), 192.

82. Jemolo (1960), 266–7; Webster (1960), 109–18.

83. See, for example, the *New York Times* for 7 May 1950.

84. *Los Angeles Times,* 22 May 1949; *Films in Review,* April 1952.

85. *New York Times,* 14 May 1950.

86. Cf. Elley (1984), 125–6.

87. Wittner (1974), 34.

88. Whitfield (1991), 77–100; Wittner (1974), 123; Biskind (1983), 115–7; Nadel (1993), 416.

89. See Nadel (1993), 416–7; Whitfield (1991), 218; Higashi (1994), 202–3.

90. Cf. *Hollywood Citizen News,* 27 November 1951.

91. The letter is signed by Arthur H. DeBra and dated 28 November 1951. A copy can be found in the MGM archives at USC.

92. I am most grateful to Laura Gibbs-Wichrowska for providing me with a copy and a translation of this newspaper article.

93. On the HUAC hearings and the blacklist, see Ceplair and Englund (1979); Sklar (1975), 256–68; Wittner (1974), 86–110.

94. Babington and Evans (1993), 210–3. On the significance of the figure of Petronius, see also Elley (1984), 125, and a review of *Quo Vadis* in *Newsweek* for 19 November 1951, which compares Petronius to the columnist Walter Lippmann—a frequent critic of the excesses of "Red-baiting" undertaken by the likes of Senator Joseph McCarthy.

95. Sklar (1975), 261–2; Cogley (1985), 487; Balio (1985), 408–12; Lenihan (1993), 140–1.

96. For the Marshall plan as part of America's anti-Communist crusade in Europe, see Wittner (1974), 44–6; Ginsborg (1990), 115–6.

97. Compare the similar remarks made by the producer himself, quoted in the *Daily News* of 12 December 1950.

98. Cary (1974), 105–6. Cf., on the epic films of the 1950s more generally, Wood (1975), 168–73; Belton (1992), 70–4; Babington and Evans (1993), 7.

99. Doane (1989), 26–7. See also Eckert (1973), 11–21, and Gaines (1989).

Notes to Chapter 6

1. This chapter is an emended and much expanded version of Wyke (1996). I am most grateful to Pim Allison, Vittorio Martinelli, Riccardo Redi, and Christopher Wagstaff for their comments on an earlier version of this material.

2. The brochure advertises Anheuser-Busch Theme Parks.

3. Cf. Anderson (1992), 93, on the fascination which American visitors to Pompeii have exhibited towards the volcanic cataclysm.

4. For the history of the excavations at Pompeii, see Corti (1950); Mackendrick (1962); Leppmann (1966); Trevelyan (1976); Etienne (1992), 11–41; Conticello (1992) and (1994).

5. Leppmann (1966), 53, 61, and 76–7; Honour (1968), 14 and 46–7; Jenkyns (1980), 82; Bologna (1992), 79; Anderson (1992), 93; Etienne (1992), 16–8; Goalen (1995), 181–7.

6. Jenkyns (1980), 81–2 and 89; Conticello (1992), 3. On Romantic historiography generally, see Bann (1984), 2–4 and 134.

7. Corti (1950), 154–5; Leppmann (1966), 92–109; Reinhold (1984), 265–79; Anderson (1992), 93; Etienne (1992), 16.

8. Quoted from Dickens's *Pictures from Italy* (1845) in Etienne (1992), 164–5.

9. On the ancient sources, see Leppmann (1966), 27–47; Etienne (1992), 138–45. Cf. Corti (1950), 85.

10. This observation is made by Norman Vance in his forthcoming book on Rome in the nineteenth-century historical imagination. I am most grateful to him for showing me a draft of his chapter "Rome and European Revolutions."

11. Quoted from Twain's *The Innocents Abroad* (1875) in Etienne (1992), 165–9.

12. See, especially, Leppmann (1966).

13. See Leppmann (1966), 134–5; Etienne (1992), 19; Redi (1994), 63; Vance (forthcoming).

14. See, in particular, the final chapter of Lytton's novel and Leppmann (1966), 135–6.

15. Quoted in Ernst (1992), 82. Subsequent page references are to the Collins edition of Lytton's *The Last Days of Pompeii,* published in 1953.

16. Compare, more generally, on the relations between the historical novel and historical film, Jameson (1992), 258.

17. Bann (1984), 144–5.

18. Gell and Gandy (1817–1819), ix–x and xvi; Eigner (1978), 146–7; Jenkyns (1980), 82; Leppmann (1966), 133. Cf. Green (1982), 1–16, on the historiographic techniques of Scott and Flaubert.

19. Jenkyns (1980), 85.

20. Jenkyns (1980), 85.

21. Turner (forthcoming).

22. Mayer (1984–1985), 42.

23. Lowenthal (1985), 229–30. Cf. Jenkyns (1980), 85–6, and Green (1982), 58–72.

24. Mayer (1984–1985), 47–8. Cf. Green (1982), 58–72, on the use of ancient Carthage in Flaubert's *Salammbô* to address anxieties about the decline of contemporary France.

25. See McConachie (1992), 119–55; Dunant (1994), 85; Mayer (1994), 19–20; Redi (1994), 63; Vance (forthcoming).

26. Quoted in Jenkyns (1980), 317–8. Cf. Dunant (1994), 85.

27. Jenkyns (1980), 317–8; Wood (1983), 28–9, 110, and 120–1; Dunant (1994), 84; Pretjohn (forthcoming).

28. Wood (1983), 17–8; Kestner (1989), 214–5 and 280; Dunant (1994); Pretjohn (forthcoming).

29. Ash (1989); Kestner (1989), 18 and 272; Wood (1983), 28–9; Dunant (1994), 84. Contrast Pretjohn (forthcoming) on the Victorian paintings which suggest a discontinuity with antiquity.

30. Ash (1989); Wood (1983), 28–9 and 106; Dunant (1994), 82 and 90–1. Cf. Vance (1989), 68–9 and 112–3 on the dissemination of Gérôme in America.

31. Cf. more generally Costa (1991), 16, and Parigi (1994), 69–74.

32. For Pompeian pyrodramas, see Mayer (1984–1985) and (1994), 90–5.

33. Mayer (1984–1985), 42, and (1994), 90–9. Cf. Verdone (1963) and de Vincenti (1988), 14–5, on the influence of circus spectacles on historical film.

34. Martinelli (1994), 35. Cf. Bann (1984), 61–2, on the even earlier representations of Vesuvius's eruption in the dioramas of Daguerre.

35. Calendoli (1967), 70–4; de Vincenti (1988), 8–10; Bernardini (1986), 34–5; Brunetta (1991a), 14–5; Bernardini (1991), 24–6.

36. de Vincenti (1988), 11–2 n.17; Redi (1994), 63; Vance (forthcoming).

37. Leppmann (1966), 126–7; Calendoli (1967), 67–8; Bernardini (1986), 34; Martinelli (1994), 35–7; Parigi (1994), 67–74. Cf. Ghigi (1977), 733, on the operatic sources of early Italian cinema. I have not seen Maggi's film of 1908, although a print is available for viewing at the Nederlands Filmmuseum of Amsterdam.

38. The review is quoted more fully in Martinelli (1994), 37.

39. Brunetta (1993), 144 and 155; Martinelli (1994), 37.

40. On the importance of *Quo Vadis?* (1913) to the development of the genre of the historical film, see chapter 5 above.

41. Quoted in Cary (1974), 7.

42. Prolo (1951), 54; Martinelli (1993), 301–2, and (1994), 40–6.

43. Mackendrick (1962), 197; Leppmann (1966), 49–55; Trevelyan (1976), 39–44.

44. Trevelyan (1976), 85; Etienne (1992), 28–38.

45. Mackendrick (1962), 202; Leppmann (1966), 163–7; Etienne (1992), 38–41; Conticello (1994), 15–8.

46. de Vincenti (1988), 16–20.

47. In Wyke (1996), following a mistake commonly made in the secondary literature on silent Italian cinema, I credited the direction of the Ambrosio film to Mario Caserini. But the silent-film historians Vittorio Martinelli and Riccardo Redi have both informed me that the attribution to Caserini is incorrect, and that the Ambrosio remake of 1913 was actually directed by Rodolfi. Prints of the Ambrosio film exist in a number of archives, but the Pasquali film, to my knowledge, only survives in the British National Film Archive and is currently incorrectly listed as an Ambrosio film directed by Caserini.

48. These and other reviews of the two films are quoted in Martinelli (1993), 296–301 and 314–9.

49. In the Ambrosio version of 1913, Glaucus is designated an Athenian only at the film's opening and when his Pompeian friend demands his release from the arena. In contrast to the techniques of Lytton's novel, his Greekness has no narrative function in the film.

50. For the discourses of orientalism generally, see Said (1978). For the discussion that follows, compare chapter 4 above on the orientalism inscribed in *Marcantonio e Cleopatra* (1913).

51. Shohat (1991a), esp. 62–3.

52. Quoted in Martinelli (1993), 317–8. Cf. the admiring comments on the same scene in *Il giornale d'Italia* of 26 August 1913, also quoted in Martinelli (1993), 315.

53. Cagnetta (1979), 15–33; Canfora (1980), 39–40; Visser (1992), 7–8. Cf. chapter 2 above.

54. Brunetta (1990b), 9–13; (1991a), 64–5; (1993), 156–7 and 160–77. Cf. dall'Asta (1992), 25 and 31.

55. Calendoli (1967), 78; de Vincenti (1988), 25–6; Brunetta (1991a), 67–8, and (1993), 166–7; dall'Asta (1992), 40.

56. See the reviews cited in Martinelli (1993), 296–302 and 314–9.

57. 4 October 1913, quoted in Martinelli (1993), 301.

58. Paolella (1956), 421–4; Bernardini (1983), 26–7; Farassino (1983), 38; Hay (1987), 68; Brunetta (1991a), 128–36, and (1993), 238–59; Redi (1991), 55–64; dall'Asta (1992), 153; Redi (1994), 27–30.

59. Paolella (1956), 424; Hay (1987), 152; Bernardini (1983), 26–7; Gili (1985), 24–5; Brunetta (1991a), 93–4 and 145–6; dall'Asta (1992), 153; Brunetta (1993), 253–4; Martinelli (1994), 47; Redi (1994), 30–2.

60. See, on this opening sequence, Gori (1988), 18, and Parigi (1994), 74.

61. Solomon (1978), 54; Parigi (1994), 74.

62. Quoted in Bernardini and Martinelli (1979), 78; Martinelli (1981), 286–7; Redi (1994), 134.

63. Liehm (1984), 10.

64. See Parigi (1994), 74–6, on the fantastic design of the film's set for the house of Arbaces.

65. Trevelyan (1976), 97; Etienne (1992), 24–61; Conticello (1994), 18–25; Raffaelli (1994), 86.

66. Quoted in Martinelli (1981), 287, and Redi (1994), 134.

67. Raffaelli (1994), 87. See Bondanella (1987), 172–81, for the Fascist regime's strategic use of *romanità* in its first decade in power.

68. Brunetta (1983), 49–50, and (1993), 269–94. Cf. chapter 2 above.

69. Gili (1985), 24–5; Gori (1988), 18; Parigi (1994), 74; Martinelli (1994), 47.

70. Gili (1985), 24–5.

71. Leprohon (1972), 55–6; Solomon (1978), 54; Bernardini and Martinelli (1979), 76–7; Brunetta (1993), 272–4; Martinelli (1994), 47; Redi (1994), 34 and 132–4; Parigi (1994), 67.

72. For the classical models and anti-models deployed by the Founding Fathers, see Richard (1994), 53–122. Cf. chapter 2 above.

73. Anderson (1992), 95–7.

74. Anderson (1992), 93–101.

75. See Smith (1991), 137 and Martinelli (1994), 47.

76. Anderson (1992), 93.

77. Cf. Solomon (1978), 54; Elley (1984), 124; Smith (1991), 136–7; Martinelli (1994), 47–51.

78. Izod (1988), 84–94; McDonald (1982), 109; Christensen (1987), 27.

79. For the origins and development of the genre of the gangster film, see Bergman (1971), 6–17; Shadoian (1977); McDonald (1982); Jowett (1991), 57–75; Black (1994), 107–32.

80. As noted by Elley (1984), 20 and 124. Compare also the account of Warner Brothers' subsequent gangster film *The Roaring Twenties* (1939) in Rosen (1984), 24–5.

81. Bergman (1971), 3–6; Black (1994), 39–46 and Appendix A.

82. Black (1994), 39.

83. See esp. Black (1994), 149–291. Cf. Christensen (1987), 39–40; Izod (1988), 105–6; Neve (1992), 2.

84. Bergman (1971), 83–8; Christensen (1987), 27; Izod (1988), 106–8; Neve (1992), 15.

85. Both the letter and the circular can be found in the production file on *Last Days* in the UCLA film archive.

86. *Variety*, 23 October 1935.

87. On *Roman Scandals* as a film of social protest, see Thompson and Routt (1987). Cf. chapter 1 above.

88. Benton (1995), 125–7. Cf. Braun (1990), 352.

89. See *Motion Picture Herald*, 23 October 1935.

90. Ceplair and Englund (1979), 95; Neve (1992), 4.

91. Black (1994), 260–1. Cf. Bergman (1971), 111.

92. Cf. Martinelli (1994), 45–51.

93. See, for example, Leppmann (1968), 173–4.

94. Trevelyan (1976), 102; Etienne (1992), 182.

95. Cf. Martinelli (1994), 51–2.

96. Leppmann; (1968), 39–44; Trevelyan (1976), 101.

97. On the presentist strategies of *Fabiola* (1948), see Siclier (1962), 29–30; Brunetta (1982), 405–6; Gori (1984), 79–84; Spinazzola (1985), 324. Cf. also chapter 3 above on *Spartaco* (1952).

98. See, for further details of the film, Solomon (1978), 54–5; Brunetta (1982), 504; Elley (1984), 121; Smith (1991), 139–40; Martinelli (1994), 52.

Notes to Chapter 7

1. On *Le Mépris*, see Goldmann (1976), 74–8; Marie (1986), 25–36; Aumont (1990), 217–29; Rakovsky, Zimmer, and Lefèvre (1991).

2. Houston and Gillett (1963); Baxter (1972), 7–13 and 151–64; Wood (1975), 14–15 and 193–5; Hirsch (1978), 24 and 29–37; Biskind (1983), 336–48; Elley (1984), 24; Belton (1992), 210–14; Babington and Evans (1993), 6–8.

3. Elley (1976), 22; Elley (1984), 103–4; Bondanella (1987), 121–2; Babington and Evans (1993), 178; Winkler (1995), 140.

4. Elley (1976), 24; Bondanella (1987), 224–7; Babington and Evans (1993), 182.

5. Elley (1976), 21–2; Solomon (1978), 55–8; Bondanella (1987), 225; Winkler (1995), 143–6 and 148–52.

6. Wood (1975), 178. Cf. Elley (1976), 24, and Winkler (1995), 142.

7. *Motion Picture Herald,* 1 April 1964.

8. Luard (1982), 1–90.

9. Steigerwald (1995).

10. Solomon (1978), 58; Elley (1984), 108; Bondanella (1987), 227; Winkler (1995).

11. See, for example, *The Hollywood Reporter,* 23 March 1964; *BoxOffice,* 30 March 1964; *Motion Picture Herald,* 1 April 1964.

12. *New York Herald Tribune,* 27 March 1964.

13. Elley (1976), 18; Smith (1991), xix.

14. Wood (1975), 194; Hirsch (1978), 47; Elley (1984), 24; Bordwell, Staiger, and Thompson (1985), 378–85.

15. Dick (1981), 152–4; Curchod (1984), 31–2; Bondanella (1987), 239, and (1992), 239–40; Markulin (1993), 145–6. In my discussion of *Fellini-Satyricon*, I use the Italianate names allocated to Petronius's characters in the film.

16. Reproduced in translation in Fellini (1978), 17. For discussion of Fellini's comments, see Zanelli (1969), 21; Bondanella (1992), 239–40; Markulin (1993), 139–40; Verdone (1994), 76.

17. Dick (1981), 150; Bondanella (1992), 242–4; Markulin (1993), 146.

18. Rosenthal (1976), 80–3; Snyder (1978); Dick (1981), 147; Bondanella (1992), 241 and 245–6.

19. Cf. Dick (1981), 155–6, who discusses the play-acting that takes place during the banquet of Trimalchio sequence.

20. Zanelli (1969); Solomon (1978), 179; Dick (1981), 147; Bondanella (1992), 243–5.

21. On these statements by Fellini see, for example, Curchod (1984), 33–4; Bondanella (1988), 234.

22. Fellini (1978), 17.

23. Zanelli (1969), 23–9 and 34–5; McBride (1978), 155; Dick (1981), 148; Bondanella (1987), 239 and 242–6, (1988), 235–7, and (1992), 250–2; Markulin (1993), 139.

24. Moravia (1978), 163–5. Cf. Dick (1981), 146–7 and 157; Verdone (1994), 9.

25. Fellini (1978), 18–19.

Filmography

The filmography provides details only for those films that comprise the case studies of this book. Prints may be available in other archives additional to those listed here. A fairly comprehensive inventory of films set in antiquity can be found in Derek Elley's *The Epic Film: Myth and History* (1984). Fuller details for some of the silent Italian historical films can be found in Vittorio Martinelli's catalogues, which have appeared at regular intervals since the 1980s in the journal *Bianco e Nero*. Historical films of the sound era are catalogued in Gary A. Smith's *Epic Films* (1991).

Cleopatra (1917)
dr. J. Gordon Edwards.
pr. Fox Film Corporation.
with Theda Bara (Cleopatra), Fritz Leiber (Caesar), Thurston Hall (Antony), Albert Roscoe (Pharon), Dorothy Drake (Charmian), Henri de Vries (Octavius).
print: none extant.

Cleopatra (1934)
dr. Cecil B. DeMille.
pr. Cecil B. DeMille for Paramount.
with Claudette Colbert (Cleopatra), Warren William (Julius Caesar), Henry Wilcoxon (Mark Antony), Gertrude Michael (Calpurnia), Joseph Schildkraut (Herod), Ian Keith (Octavian), C. Aubrey Smith (Enobarbus).
print: National Film Archive at British Film Institute, London.

Cleopatra (1963)
dr. Joseph K. Mankiewicz.
pr. Walter Wanger for 20th Century-Fox.
with Elizabeth Taylor (Cleopatra), Richard Burton (Mark Antony), Rex Harrison (Julius Caesar), Pamela Brown (High Priestess), George Cole (Flavius), Hume Cronyn (Sosigenes), Cesare Danova (Apollodorus), Kenneth Haig (Brutus), Andrew Keir (Agrippa), Martin Landau (Rufio), Roddy McDowall (Octavian), Robert Stephens (Germanicus).
print: widely available on video release from CBS Fox Video, in 4-hour version and letter-box format.

Ione o gli ultimi giorni di Pompei (1913)
dr. Giovanni Enrico Vidali (e Ubaldo Maria del Colle).
pr. Pasquali, Turin.
with Suzanne De Labroy (Nidia), Ines Melidoni (Giulia), Cristina Ruspoli (Jone), Luigi
Mele (Glauco), Giovanni Novelli-Vidali (Arbace).
US title *The Last Days of Pompeii*.
print: National Film Archive at British Film Institute, London (incorrectly listed as
directed by Mario Caserini).

The Last Days of Pompeii (1935)
dr. Ernest B. Schoedsack.
pr. Merian C. Cooper for RKO.
with Preston Foster (Marcus), Dorothy Wilson (Clodia), Basil Rathbone (Pontius
Pilate), Alan Hale (Burbix), John Wood (Flavius as a man), David Holt (Flavius as a
boy), Louis Calhern (Prefect), Wyrley Birch (Leaster).
print: National Film Archive at British Film Institute, London; UCLA Film Archive,
Los Angeles.

Marcantonio e Cleopatra (1913)
dr. Enrico Guazzoni.
pr. Cines, Rome.
with Gianna Terribili Gonzales (Cleopatra), Amleto Novelli (Marcantonio), Ignazio
Lupi (Ottaviano), Matilde Di Marzio (la schiave Agar), Elsa Lenard (Ottavia), Ida
Carloni Talli (la strega), Ruffo Geri (il capo dei congiurati), Giuseppe Piemontese,
Bruto Castellani.
U.S./UK title. *Antony and Cleopatra*.
print: Cineteca Nazionale, Rome (with only a few intertitles, and ending missing);
Library of Congress, Washington, DC (English intertitles).

Nerone (1909)
dr. Luigi Maggi.
pr. Ambrosio Film, Turin.
with Lydia de Roberti (Poppea), Alberto A. Capozzi (Nerone), Mary Cleo Tarlarini
(Ottavia), Luigi Maggi (Epafrodite).
U.S. title. *Nero or the Burning of Rome* or *Nero or the Fall of Rome*.
print: Cineteca Nazionale, Rome; UCLA Film Archive, Los Angeles (includes some
tinted sequences); Library of Congress, Washington, DC.

Quo Vadis? (1913)
dr. Enrico Guazzoni.
pr. Cines, Rome.
with Amleto Novelli (Vinicio), Gustavo Serena (Petronio), Lea Giunchi (Licia), Amelia
Cattaneo (Eunice), Carlo Cattaneo (Nerone), Bruto Castellani (Ursus).
print: Cineteca Nazionale, Rome (with Spanish intertitles).

Quo Vadis? (1924)
dr. Gabriellino d'Annunzio and Georg Jacoby.
pr. Arturo Ambrosio for UCI.
with Emil Jannings (Nerone), Elena Sangro (Poppea), Alfons Fryland (Vinicio), Lillian
    Hall-Davis (Licia), Andrea Habay (Petronio), Raimondo van Riel (Tigellino), Rina
    de Liguoro (Eunica), Bruto Castellani (Ursus), Gino Viotti (Chilone Chilonide),
    Gildo Bocci (Vitellio).
print: Cineteca Nazionale, Rome.

Quo Vadis (1951)
dr. Mervyn LeRoy.
pr. Sam Zimbalist for MGM.
with Robert Taylor (Marcus Vinicius), Deborah Kerr (Lygia), Leo Genn (Petronius),
    Peter Ustinov (Nero), Patricia Laffan (Poppaea), Finlay Currie (Peter), Abraham
    Sofaer (Paul), Marina Berti (Eunice), Buddy Baer (Ursus).
print: widely available on video release from MGM/UA Home Video.

The Sign of the Cross (1932)
dr. Cecil B. DeMille.
pr. Cecil B. DeMille for Paramount Publix Corporation.
with Frederic March (Marcus Superbus), Elissa Landi (Mercia), Claudette Colbert
    (Poppaea), Charles Laughton (Nero), Ian Keith (Tigellinus), Tommy Conlon
    (Stephanus).
Print: UCLA Film Archive, Los Angeles; National Film Archive at British Film
    Institute, London (including additional prologue from 1944 re-release).

Spartaco or *Il gladiatore della Tracia* (1913)
dr. Giovanni Enrico Vidali.
pr. Pasquali, Turin.
with Mario Guaita Ausonia (Spartaco), Enrico Bracci (Crasso), Luigi Mele (Norico),
    Maria Gandini (daughter of Crassus), Cristina Ruspoli (sister of Spartacus).
U.S./U.K. title. *Spartacus* or *The Revolt of the Gladiators*.
print: Library of Congress, Washington, DC (entire reel 5 of 6 missing as well as other
    sections, with a few English intertitles).

Spartaco (1952)
dr. Riccardo Freda.
pr. Consorzio Spartacus—API Film (Rome) and Rialto Film (Paris).
with Massimo Girotti (Spartaco), Gianna Maria Canale (Sabina), Ludmilla Tcherina
    (Amitis), Carlo Ninchi (Mario Licinio Crasso), Yves Vincent (Ocnomas/Octavius),
    Vittorio Sanipoli (Rufo).
UK title. *Spartacus the Gladiator*, distr. International Pictures.
U.S. title. *Sins of Rome*, distr. RKO Radio Pictures.
print: dubbed and heavily cut version available for hire from Glenbuck, London.

Spartacus (1960)
dr. Stanley Kubrick.
pr. Edward Lewis. exec. pr. Kirk Douglas for Byrna Production.
distr. Universal-International.
with Kirk Douglas (Spartacus), Laurence Olivier (Crassus), Jean Simmons (Varinia),
Charles Laughton (Gracchus), Peter Ustinov (Batiatus), Tony Curtis (Antoninius),
John Gavin (Julius Caesar).
print: re-released by CIC Video in 1991, re-edited and in letter-box format.

Gli ultimi giorni di Pompei (1908)
dr. Luigi Maggi.
pr. Ambrosio, Turin.
with Umberto Mozzato (Glauco), Lidia De Roberti (Nydia), Mirra Principi (Jone),
Luigi Maggi (Arbace).
print: Nederlands Filmmuseum, Amsterdam.

Gli ultimi giorni di Pompei (1913)
dr. Eleuterio Rodolfi (often incorrectly credited to Mario Caserini).
pr. Ambrosio, Turin.
with Fernanda Negri Poulet (Nidia), Eugenia Tettoni Florio (Jone), Ubaldo Stefani
(Glauco), Cesare Gani-Carini (Apecide), Antonio Grisanti (Arbace).
U.S. title. *The Last Days of Pompeii.*
print: UCLA Film Archive, Los Angeles (some colored sequences); Library of
Congress, Washington, DC (two reels only); Cineteca Nazionale, Rome (only has
short segment).

Gli ultimi giorni di Pompei (1926)
dr. Carmine Gallone and Amleto Palermi.
pr. Amleto Palermi for Società Italiana "Grandi Films," Rome.
with Rina de Liguoro (Jone), Maria Korda (Nydia), Viktor Varkonyi (Glauco),
Bernhard Goetzke (Arbace), Emilio Ghione (Caleno), Bruto Castellani (Eumolpo).
U.S. title. *The Last Days of Pompeii.*
print: Cineteca Nazionale, Rome; National Film Archive at British Film Institute,
London (includes colored sequences).

Gli ultimi giorni di Pompei (1948, release delayed until 1950)
dr. Paolo Moffa with Marcel L'Herbier.
pr. Salvo D'Angelo for Universalia, Roma/Franco-London Film, Paris.
with Micheline Presle (Elena), Georges Marchal (Lysia), Marcel Herrand (Arbace),
Adriana Benetti (Nydia).
French title. *Les derniers jours de Pompei.*
U.S. title. *The Last Days of Pompeii.*
print: Cineteca Nazionale, Rome.

Gli ultimi giorni di Pompei (1959)

dr. Mario Bonnard (and Sergio Leone although not credited).

pr. Cineproduzioni Associate, Rome/Procusa Film, Madrid.

with Steve Reeves (Glauco), Christine Kaufmann (Jone), Anne Marie Baumann (Julia), Barbara Carroll (Nydia), Mimmo Palmara (Gallino).

U.S. title. *The last days of Pompeii*.

Print: Library of Congress, Washington, DC.

Bibliography

Ackerman, Gerald M. *Jean-Léon Gérôme (1824–1904)*. *Exhibition Ca0.talogue*. Dayton, Ohio: Dayton Art Institute, 1972.

Ades, Dawn; Benton, Tim; Elliott, David; and Whyte, Iain Boyd (eds.). *Art and Power: Europe under the Dictators 1930–45*. *Hayward Gallery Exhibition Catalogue*. Manchester: Cornerhouse Publications, 1995.

Allen, Jeanne. "The film viewer as consumer." *Quarterly Review of Film Studies* 5.4 (1980), 481–99.

Allen, Robert C. "From exhibition to reception: reflections on the audience in film history." *Screen* 31.4 (1990), 347–56.

Allen, Robert C., and Gomery, Douglas. *Film History: Theory and Practice*. New York: McGrawHill Publishing Co., 1985.

Anderson, Maxwell L. "Pompeii and America." In *Rediscovering Pompeii* 1992, 93–103.

Angelini, Franca (ed.). *Petrolini: la maschera e la storia*. Rome: Laterza, 1984.

Arcand, Denys. "The historical film: actual and virtual." *Cultures* 2.1 (1974), 13–26.

Ash, Russell. *Sir Lawrence Alma-Tadema*. London: Pavilion Books, 1989.

Aumont, Jacques. "The fall of the gods: Jean-Luc Godard's *Le Mépris* (1963)." In S. Hayward and G. Vincendeau (eds.), *French Film: Texts and Contexts*. London: Routledge, 1990, 217–29.

Babington, Bruce, and Evans, Peter William. *Biblical Epics: Sacred Narrative in the Hollywood Cinema*. Manchester: Manchester University Press, 1993.

Balio, Tino (ed.). *The American Film Industry*. Madison: University of Wisconsin Press, 1985. First edition published in 1976.

Ball, Robert Hamilton. *Shakespeare on Silent Film: A Strange Eventful History*. London: George Allen and Unwin, 1968.

Bann, Stephen. *The Clothing of Clio: A Study of the Representation of History in Nineteenth-century Britain and France*. Cambridge: Cambridge University Press, 1984.

———. *The Inventions of History: Essays on the Representation of the Past*. Manchester: Manchester University Press, 1990.

Barber, Robin. "Classical art: discovery, research and presentation, 1890–1930." In Cowling and Mundy 1990, 391–411.

Baxter, John. *Hollywood in the Sixties*. London: Tantivy Press, 1972.

Beard, Mary, and Henderson, John. *Classics: A Very Short Introduction*. Oxford: Oxford University Press, 1995.

Beck, Philip. "Historicism and historism in recent film historiography." *Journal of Film and Video* 37.1 (1985), 5–20.

Becker, Lutz. "Black shirts and white telephones." In Ades et al. 1995, 137–9.

Begey, M. B. "La fortuna di E.S. in Italia." In *Nel centenario* 1946, 75–83.

Belton, John. *Widescreen Cinema*. Cambridge: Harvard University Press, 1992.

Benjamin, Walter. *Illuminations*. London: Fontana, 1973.

Benton, Tim. "Rome reclaims its empire." In Ades 1995, 120–9.

Bergman, Andrew. *We're in the Money: Depression America and its Films*. New York: New York University Press, 1971.

Bernal, Martin. *Black Athena: The Afroasiatic Roots of Classical Civilization. Volume 1: The Fabrication of Ancient Greece 1785–1985*. London: Free Association Press, 1987.

———— *Black Athena: The Afroasiatic Roots of Classical Civilization. Volume 2: The Archaeological and Documentary Evidence*. London: Free Association Press, 1991.

Bernardini, Aldo. *Cinema muto italiano. Volume 3: Arte, divismo e mercato 1910–1914*. Rome-Bari: Editori Laterza, 1982.

————. "Il primo boom del cinema italiano (1911–1920)." In Turconi and Sacchi 1983, 13–44.

————. "Le cinéma muet italien, étapes et tendances." In Bernardini and Gili 1986, 33–45.

————. "Industrializzazione e classi sociali." In R. Renzi 1991, 22–33.

Bernardini, Aldo, and Gili, Jean A. (eds.). *Le cinéma italien de La Prise de Rome (1905) à Rome ville ouverte (1945)*. Paris: Centre Georges Pompidou, 1986.

Bernardini, Aldo, and Martinelli, Vittorio (eds.). *Il cinema italiano degli anni venti*. Rome: Cineteca Nazionale del Centro Sperimentale di Cinematografia, 1979.

Beuselink, James. "Mankiewicz's *Cleopatra*." *Films in Review* 39.1 (1988), 3–4.

Biskind, Peter. *Seeing is Believing: How Hollywood Taught Us to Stop Worrying and Love the Fifties*. London: Pluto Press, 1983.

Black, Gregory D. *Hollywood Censored: Morality Codes, Catholics and the Movies*. Cambridge: Cambridge University Press, 1994.

Bloom, Allan. *The Closing of the American Mind: How Higher Education has Failed Democracy and Impoverished the Souls of Today's Students*. London: Penguin Books, 1987.

Bloom, Harold (ed.). *Cleopatra*. New York: Chelsea House Publishers, 1990.

Bologna, Ferdinando. "The rediscovery of Herculaneum and Pompeii in the artistic culture of Europe in the Eighteenth Century." In *Rediscovering Pompeii* 1992, 78–91.

Bondanella, Peter (ed.). *Federico Fellini: Essays in Criticism*. New York: Oxford University Press, 1978.

————. *The Eternal City: Roman Images in the Modern World*. Chapel Hill and London: University of North Carolina Press, 1987.

————. *Italian Cinema: From Neorealism to the Present*. New York: Continuum, 1988.

————. *The Cinema of Federico Fellini*. Princeton, New Jersey: Princeton University Press, 1992.

Bondanella, Peter, and Degli–Esposti, Cristina (eds.). *Perspectives on Federico Fellini*. New York: G. K. Hall and Co., 1993.

Bordwell, David; Staiger, Janet; and Thompson, Kristin. *The Classical Hollywood Style: Film Style and Mode of Production to 1960*. London: Routledge, 1985.

Bourget, Jean-Loup. "La storia come repertorio di immagini: iconografia e iconologia di Kubrick." In Brunetta 1985, 55–60.

Bradley, Keith R. *Slavery and Rebellion in the Roman World, 140 B.C.–70 B.C.* Bloomington: Indiana University Press, 1989.

Braun, Emily. "Political rhetoric and poetic irony: the uses of classicism in the art of fascist Italy." In Cowling and Mundy 1990, 345–58.

Brenk, Frederick E. "Plutarch's Life 'Markos Antonios': a literary and cultural study." *Aufstieg und Niedergang der römischen Welt* 33.6 (1992), 4346–469.

Brodsky, Jack, and Weiss, Nathan. *The Cleopatra Papers: A Private Correspondence*. New York: Simon and Schuster, 1963.

Brunetta, Gian Piero. *Storia del cinema italiano dal 1945 agli anni ottanta*. Rome: Editori Riuniti, 1982.

———. (ed.) *Stanley Kubrick: tempo, spazio, storia e mondi possibili*. Parma: Pratiche Editrice, 1985.

———. "L'évocation du passé. Les années d'or du film historique." In Bernardini and Gili 1986, 55–60.

———. "No place like Rome: the early years of Italian cinema." *Artforum* Summer (1990a), 122–5.

———. "L'ora d'Africa del cinema italiano." In Brunetta and Gili 1990b, 9–37.

———. *Cent'anni di cinema italiano*. Rome: Editori Laterza, 1991a.

———. "Filogenesi artistica e letteraria del primo cinema italiano." In Renzi 1991b, 7–21.

———. *Storia del cinema italiano: il cinema muto 1895–1929. Volume 1*. Rome: Editori Riuniti, 1993. First edition published in 1979.

———. "Cinema e fascismo: la soluzione del sette per cento." In Turconi and Sacchi. 1983, 47–81.

Brunetta, Gian Piero, and Gili, Jean A. *L'ora d'Africa del cinema italiano 1911–1989*. Trent: LaGrafica-Mori, 1990.

Cagnetta, Mariella. *Antichisti e impero fascista*. Bari: Dedalo Libri, 1979.

Calendoli, Giovanni. *Materiali per una storia del cinema italiano*. Parma: Edizioni Maccari, 1967.

Calò, Anna Maria. *Ettore Petrolini*. Florence: La Nuova Italia Editrice, 1989.

Cammarota, M. D., Jr. *Il cinema peplum*. Rome: Fanucci Editore, 1987.

Canfora, Luciano. *Ideologie del classicismo*. Turin: Piccola Biblioteca Einaudi, 1980.

Cardillo, Massimo. *Tra le quinte del cinematografo: cinema, cultura e società in Italia 1900–1937*. Bari: Edizioni Dedalo, 1987.

Cary, John. *Spectacular! The Story of Epic Films*. London: Hamlyn, 1974.

Ceplair, Larry, and Englund, Steven. *The Inquisition in Hollywood: Politics in the Film Community, 1930–1960*. Berkeley: University of California Press, 1979.

Chadbourne, Richard M. *Ernest Renan*. New York: Twayne Publishers, 1968.

Chiti, Roberto, and Quargnolo, Mario. "La malinconica storia dell'U.C.I." *Bianco e Nero* 18.7 (1957), 21–35.

Christensen, Terry. *Reel Politics: American Political Movies from Birth of a Nation to Platoon*. Oxford: Blackwell, 1987.

Christie, Ian. "Cecil B. DeMille: grand illusions." *Sight and Sound* ns 1.8 (1991), 18–21.

Cogley, John. "HUAC: the mass hearings." In Balio 1985, 487–509.

Conticello, Baldassare. "Rediscovering Pompeii." In *Rediscovering Pompeii* 1992, 3–25.

———. "Scienza, cultura e cronaca a Pompei nella prima metà del nostro secolo." In Redi 1994, 15–25.

Cooper, Duncan. "A second look: Spartacus." *Cineaste* 6.3 (1974), 30–1.

———. "Who killed Spartacus?" *Cineaste* 18.3 (1991), 18–27.

Cornell, T. J., and Lomas, Kathryn (eds.). *Urban Society in Roman Italy*. London: University College Press, 1995.

Corsi, Barbara. "Le coproduzioni europee del primo dopoguerra: l'utopia del fronte unico di cinematografia." In Ellwood and Brunetta 1991, 88–95.

Corti, Egon Caesar Conte. *The Destruction and Resurrection of Pompeii and Hercula-neum*. London: Routledge and Kegan Paul, 1950.

Costa, Antonio. "La traduzione filmica di un romanzo storico: 'Il Gattopardo' da Lampedusa a Visconti." In Costa et al., *Cinema e Storia*. Venice: Quaderni di circuito-cinema 34 (1989), 3–13.

————. *Cinema e pittura*. Turin: Loescher Editore, 1991.

Cowling, Elizabeth, and Mundy, Jennifer (eds.). *On Classic Ground: Picasso, Léger, de Chirico and the New Classicism 1910–1930*. London: Tate Gallery Publications, 1990.

Croce, Benedetto. *La letteratura della nuova Italia. Volume 2*. Bari: Laterzi, 1914.

Cubberley, Antony L. (ed.). *Rodolfo Lanciani: Notes from Rome*. Rome: British School at Rome, 1988.

Curchod, Olivier. "Le sourire et la fresque: la représentation de l'antiquité dans Fellini-Satyricon." *Positif* 276 (1984), 30–7.

Curl, James Stevens. *Egyptomania. The Egyptian Revival: A Recurring Theme in the History of Taste*. Manchester: Manchester University Press, 1994.

Dahl, Curtis. *Robert Montgomery Bird*. New Haven: Twayne Publishers, 1963.

dall'Asta, Monica. *Un cinéma musclé: le surhomme dans le cinéma muet italien (1913–1926)*. Translated from Italian by Franco Arnò and Charles Tatum Jr. Belgium: Édi-tions Yellow Now-Banlieues, 1992.

Dalle Vacche, Angela. *The Body in the Mirror: Shapes of History in Italian Cinema*. Princeton, New Jersey: Princeton University Press, 1992.

Damiani, Enrico. "Henryk Sienkiewicz." In *Nel centenario* 1946, 15–22.

d'Amico, M. "Il 'Quo Vadis?'" in *Nel centenario* 1946, 117–27.

de Cordova, Richard. "Film history as discipline." *Camera Obscura* 18 (1988), 146–54.

de Lauretis, Teresa. *Technologies of Gender: Essays on Theory, Film, and Fiction*. London: Macmillan Press, 1987.

Deleuze, Gilles. *Cinema 1: The Movement-Image*. London: The Athlone Press, 1986.

de Tommaso, Piero. *Nievo e altri studi sul romanzo storico*. Padua: Liviana Editrice, 1975.

de Vincenti, Giorgio. "Il kolossal storico-romano nell'immaginario del primo Nove-cento." *Bianco e Nero* 49.1 (1988), 7–26.

Dick, Bernard F. "Adaptations as archaeology: *Fellini Satyricon* (1969)." In Andrew S. Horton and Joan Magretta (eds.), *Modern European Filmmakers and the Arts of Adap-tation*. New York: The Crossroad Publishing Co., (1981), 145–57.

Doane, Mary Ann. "The economy of desire: the commodity form in/of the cinema." *Quarterly Review of Film and Video* 11 (1989), 23–33.

Douglas, Kirk. *The Ragman's Son: An Autobiography*. New York: Pocket Books, 1988.

Dunant, Caroline. "Olympian dreamscapes: the photographic canvas. The wide-screen paintings of Leighton, Poynter and Alma-Tadema." In Jacky Bratton, Jim Cook and Christine Gledhill (eds.), *Melodrama: Stage Picture Screen*. London: British Film Insti-tute, 1994, 82–93.

Durgnat, Raymond. "Epic." *Films and Filming* 10.3 (1963), 9–12.

Dyer, Richard. *Stars*. London: British Film Institute, 1979.

————. *Heavenly Bodies: Film Stars and Society*. London: British Film Institute and Macmillan, 1986.

Eckert, Charles. "The Carole Lombard in Macy's window." *Quarterly Review of Film Studies* 3.1 (1978), 1–21.

Edmundson, George. *The Church in Rome in the First Century: An Examination of Var-ious Controverted Questions Relating to its History, Chronology, Literature and Tradi-tions*. London: Longmans, 1913.

Eigner, Edwin M. *The Metaphysical Novel in England and America: Dickens, Bulwer, Melville, and Hawthorne*. Berkeley: University of California Press, 1978.

Eliot, T. S. *What is a Classic? An address delivered before the Virgil Society on the 16th of October 1944*. London: Faber and Faber, 1945.

Elley, Derek. "The fall of the Roman Empire." *Films and Filming* 22.5 (1976), 18–24.

———. *The Epic Film: Myth and History*. London: Routledge, 1984.

Ellis, John. *Visible Fictions: Cinema, Television, Video*. London: Routledge, 1982.

Ellwood, David W., and Brunetta, Gian Piero (eds.). *Hollywood in Europa: industria, politica, pubblico del cinema 1945–1960*. Florence: La Casa Usher, 1991.

Elsaesser Thomas. "Film history and visual pleasure: Weimar cinema." In Mellencamp and Rosen 1984, 47–84.

Elsner, Jas, and Masters, Jamie, eds. *Reflections of Nero: Culture, History and Representation*. London: Duckworth, 1994.

Ernst, Wolfgang. *Historismus im Verzug: Museale Antike(n) Rezeption im Britischen Neoklassizismus (und jenseits)*. Dortmund: Zeitdruck GbR Kolander and Poggel, 1992.

Etienne, Robert. *Pompeii: The Day a City Died*. Translated by Caroline Palmer. London: Thames and Hudson, 1992. First published 1986.

Farassino, Alberto, and Sanguineti, Tatti. (eds.) *Gli uomini forti*. Milan: Mazzotta, 1983.

———. "Anatomia del cinema muscolare." In Farassino and Sanguineti 1983, 29–49.

Fast, Howard. *Spartacus*. London: Panther Edition, 1959. First published in the United States in 1951.

———. *Being Red*. Boston: Houghton Mifflin Company, 1990.

Fellini, Federico. "Preface to *Satyricon*." In Bondanella 1978, 16–9. Reproduced from Dario Zanelli (ed.), *Fellini's Satyricon by Federico Fellini*. Translated by Eugene Walter. New York: Ballantine Books, 1970, 43–6.

Ferro, Marc. *Cinema and History*. Translated by Naomi Greene. Detroit: Wayne University Press, 1988. First published in French 1977.

Fink, Guido. "To be or to have been: Italian cinema, time and history." *Cultures* 2.1 (1974), 116–38.

Finley, Moses I. *Ancient Slavery and Modern Ideology*. Middlesex: Penguin, 1983.

Fledelius, Karsten. "Campi e strategie dell'analisi storica del film." In Gori 1994, 15–39.

Foreman, Walter C. "Fellini's cinematic city: *Roma* and myths of foundation." In Bondanella and Degli-Esposti 1993, 151–65. Reprinted from *Forum Italicum* 14 (1980), 78–98.

Forgacs, David. *Italian Culture in the Industrial Era 1880–1980: Cultural Industries, Politics and the Public*. Manchester: Manchester University Press, 1990.

Fraquelli, Simonetta. "All roads lead to Rome." In Ades 1995, 130–6.

Frend, W.H.C. *The Rise of Christianity*. London: Darton, Longman and Todd, 1984.

Gaines, Jane. "The Queen Christina tie-ups: convergence of show window and screen." *Quarterly Review of Film and Video* 11 (1989), 35–60.

Gaines, Jane, and Herzog, Charlotte (eds.). *Fabrications: Costume and the Female Body*. New York: Routledge, 1990.

Galinsky, Karl. *Classical and Modern Interactions: Postmodern Architecture, Multiculturalism, Decline and Other Issues*. Austin: University of Texas Press, 1992.

Gamel, Mary-Kay. "An American tragedy: *Chinatown*." In Winkler 1991, 209–31.

Gell, Sir William, and Gandy, John P. *Pompeiana: The Topography, Edifices, and Ornaments of Pompeii. Volumes 1 and 2*. London: Rodwell and Martin, 1817–1832.

Gevinson, Alan. "The birth of the American feature film." In Usai and Codelli 1988, 132–55.

Ghigi, Giuseppe. "Come si spiegano le fortune del 'pepla' su cui sembra che torni a puntare." *Cineforum* 17.2 (1977), 733–46.

Giergielewicz, Mieczyslaw. *Henryk Sienkiewicz*. New York: Twayne Publishers, 1968.

Gili, Jean A. "Film storico e film in costume." In Riccardo Redi (ed.), *Cinema italiano sotto il fascismo*. Venice: Marsilio Editori, 1979, 129–44.

———. *L'Italie de Mussolini et son cinema*. Paris: Editions Henri Veyrier, 1985.

———. "I film dell'Impero fascista." In Brunetta and Gili 1990, 39–112.

Ginsborg, Paul. *A History of Contemporary Italy: Society and Politics, 1943–1988*. Harmondsworth: Penguin, 1990.

Giovagnoli, Raffaello. *Spartaco: racconto storico illustrato del secolo VII dell'èra romana*. Milan: Paolo Carrara, seventh edition 1916. First edition published in 1874.

——— (ed. et al.). *Garibaldi nel primo centenario della sua nascita*. Rome: Comitato Parlamentare, 4 July 1907.

Goalen, Martin. "The idea of the city and the excavations at Pompeii." In Cornell and Lomas 1995, 181–202.

Goldmann, Annie. "Deserts of belief. Bunuel—Pasolini—Godard." *The Australian Journal of Screen Theory* 1 (1976), 67–78.

Gori, Gianfranco Miro. *Alessandro Blasetti. Il castoro cinema 108*. Florence: La Nuova Italia, 1984.

———. *Patria diva: la storia d'Italia nei film del ventennio*. Florence: La Casa Usher, 1988.

———. (ed.) *La storia al cinema: ricostruzione del passato, interpretazione del presente*. Rome: Bulzoni Editore, 1994.

Grant, Michael (trans.). *Tacitus. The Annals of Imperial Rome*. Middlesex: Penguin, 1979.

Green, Anne. *Flaubert and the Historical Novel*. Cambridge: Cambridge University Press, 1982.

Griffin, Jasper. "Virgil." In Richard Jenkyns (ed.), *The Legacy of Rome: A New Appraisal*. Oxford: Oxford University Press, 1992, 125–50.

Griffin, Miriam T. *Nero. The End of a Dynasty*. London: B. T. Batsford, 1984.

Gramsci, Antonio. *Quaderni del carcere. Volumi 1–4*. Edited by Valentino Gerratana. Turin: Giulio Einaudi Editore, 1975. First published 1948–1951.

Grindon, Leger. *Shadows of the Past: Studies in the Historical Fiction Film*. Philadelphia: Temple University Press, 1994.

Guarino, Antonio. *Spartaco: analisi di un mito*. Naples: Liguori Editore, 1979.

Gundle, Stephen. "Il PCI e la campagna contro Hollywood (1948–1958)." In Ellwood and Brunetta 1991, 113–32.

Gwyn, W. B. "Cruel Nero: the concept of the tyrant and the image of Nero in western political thought." *History of Political Thought* 12.3 (1991), 421–55.

Hall, Edith. Review of *Black Athena*, vol. 2, in *The Higher*, 13 September 1991.

Hamer, Mary. *Signs of Cleopatra: Histories, Politics, Representation*. London: Routledge, 1993.

Hark, Ina Rae. "Animals or Romans: looking at masculinity in *Spartacus*." In Steven Cohan and Ina Rae Hark (eds.), *Screening the Male: Exploring Masculinities in Hollywood Cinema*. London: Routledge, 1993, 151–72.

Hawkins, Harriett. *Classics and Trash: Traditions and Taboos in High Literature and Popular Modern Genres*. Hemel Hempstead: Harvester-Wheatsheaf, 1990.

Hay, James. *Popular Film Culture in Fascist Italy: The Passing of the Rex*. Bloomington: Indiana University Press, 1987.

Hayne, Donald (ed.). *The Autobiography of Cecil B. De Mille*. London: W. H. Allen, 1960.

Heath, Stephen. "Contexts." *Edinburgh Magazine* 2 (1977), 37–43.

Higashi, Sumiko. *Cecil B. DeMille: A Guide to References and Resources*. Boston: G. K. Hall, 1985.

———. *Cecil B. DeMille and American Culture: The Silent Era*. California: University of California Press, 1994.

Higham, Charles. *Cecil B. De Mille*. New York: Dell, 1973.

Highet, Gilbert. *The Classical Tradition: Greek and Roman Influences on Western Literature*. Oxford: Clarendon Press, 1949.

Higson, Andrew. "The concept of national cinema." *Screen* 30.4 (1989), 36–46.

Hirsch, Foster. *The Hollywood Epic*. New Jersey: A. S. Barnes, 1978.

Hobsbawm, Eric, and Ranger, Terence. *The Invention of Tradition*. Cambridge: Cambridge University Press, 1983.

Honour, Hugh. *Neo-Classicism*. Middlesex: Penguin, 1968.

Houston, Penelope, and Gillett, John. "The theory and practice of blockbusting." *Sight and Sound* 32 (1963), 68–74.

Hughes-Hallett, Lucy. *Cleopatra: Histories, Dreams and Distortions*. London: Vintage paperback edition, 1991. First published 1990.

Hunt, Leon. "What are big boys made of? *Spartacus, El Cid* and the Male epic." In Pat Kirkham and Janet Thumin (eds.), *You Tarzan: Masculinity, Movies and Men*. London: Lawrence and Wishart, 1993, 65–83.

Izod, John. *Hollywood and the Box Office 1895–1986*. Hampshire: Macmillan Press, 1988.

Jameson, Fredric. "Nostalgia for the present." In Jane Gaines (ed.), *Classical Hollywood Narrative: The Paradigm Wars*. Durham, NC: Duke University Press, 1992, 253–73.

Jemolo, A. C. *Church and State in Italy 1850–1950*. Translated by David Moore. Oxford: Blackwell, 1960.

Jenks, Gregory C. *The Origins and Early Development of the Antichrist Myth*. Berlin: de Gruyter, 1991.

Jenkyns, Richard. *The Victorians and Ancient Greece*. Oxford: Blackwell, 1980.

Jowett, Garth. "Bullets, beer and the Hays Office: *Public Enemy* (1931)." In O'Connor and Jackson 1991, 57–75.

Kennedy, Duncan. "Tradition and appropriation: T.S. Eliot and Virgil's *Aeneid*." *Hermathena* 158 (1995), 73–94.

Kerr, Paul (ed.). *The Hollywood Film Industry*. London: Routledge and Kegan Paul, 1986.

Kestner, Joseph A. *Mythology and Misogyny: The Social Discourse of Nineteenth-century British Classical-subject Painting*. Madison: University of Wisconsin Press, 1989.

Knox, Bernard. *Backing into the Future: The Classical Tradition and its Renewal*. New York: W. W. Norton and Co., 1994.

Kracauer, Siegfried. *From Caligari to Hitler: A Psychological History of German Film*. Princeton, New Jersey: Princeton University Press, 1947.

Lant, Antonia. "The curse of the Pharaoh, or how cinema contracted Egyptomania." *October* 59 (1992), 87–112.

Lawrence, John M. "Nero Redivivus." *Fides et Historia* 11.1 (1978), 54–66.

Leab, Daniel J. "Hollywood and the Cold War, 1945–1961." In Toplin 1993, 117–37.

Lednicki, Waclaw. *Henryk Sienkiewicz: A Retrospective Synthesis*. The Hague: Mouton and Co., 1960.

Lenihan, John H. "Hollywood laughs at the Cold War, 1947–1961." In Toplin 1993, 139–59.

Leppmann, Wolfgang. *Pompeii in Fact and Fiction*. London: Elek Books, 1966.

Leprohon, Pierre. *The Italian Cinema*. Translated by Roger Greaves and Oliver Stallybrass. London: Secker and Warburg, 1972.

Liehm, Mira. *Passion and Defiance: Film in Italy from 1942 to the Present*. Berkeley: University of California Press, 1984.

Lindgren, Ernest. "1908–1914: the years of the industrial revolution." *Bianco e Nero* 1–2 (1963), 14–19.

Lopez-Celly, Furio. *Il romanzo storico in Italia: dai prescottiani alle odierne vite romanzate*. Bologna: Licinio Cappelli-Editore, 1939.

Lovett, Clara M. *The Democratic Movement in Italy 1830–1876*. Cambridge: Harvard University Press, 1982.

Lowenthal, David. *The Past is a Foreign Country*. Cambridge: Cambridge University Press, 1985.

Luard, Evan. *A History of the United Nations. Volume 1: The Years of Western Domination, 1945–1955*. London and Basingstoke: Macmillan Press, 1982.

————. *A History of the United Nations. Volume 2: The Age of Decolonization, 1955–1965*. London and Basingstoke: Macmillan Press, 1989.

Lytton, Lord Edward Bulwer. *The Last Days of Pompeii*. London: Collins, 1953. First published 1834.

McBride, Joseph. *"Fellini: a Director's Notebook."* In Bondanella 1978, 152–60.

MacCabe, Colin. *High Theory/Low Culture: Analysing Popular Television and Film*. Manchester: Manchester University Press, 1986.

McConachie, Bruce A. *Melodramatic Formations: American Theatre and Society, 1820–1870*. Iowa City: University of Iowa Press, 1992.

McDonald, Neil. "Portrayals of capitalism, class and crime in the early American sound film." In Anne Hutton (ed.), *The First Australian History and Film Conference Papers*. Perth: History and Film Association of Australia, 1982, 89–111.

McGinn, Bernard. *Visions of the End: Apocalyptic Traditions in the Middle Ages*. New York: Columbia University Press, 1979.

Mackendrick, Paul. *The Mute Stone Speaks: The Story of Archaeology in Italy*. London: Methuen, 1962.

Maltby, Richard. *"The King of Kings* and the Czar of all the rushes: the propriety of the Christ story." *Screen* 31.2 (1990), 188–213.

Mandelbaum, Allen. *The Aeneid of Virgil. A Verse Translation*. Toronto: Bantam Books, 1981. First published in 1961.

Marie, Michel. "Un monde qui s'accorde à nos désirs." *Revue Belge du Cinéma* 15 (1986), 25–36.

Markulin, Joseph. "Plot and character in Fellini's *Casanova*: beyond *Satyricon*." In Bondanella and Degli–Esposti 1993, 139–50. First published in 1982.

Martindale, Charles. *Redeeming the Text: Latin Poetry and the Hermeneutics of Reception*. Cambridge: Cambridge University Press, 1993.

Martindale, Charles, and Martindale, Michelle. *Shakespeare and the Uses of Antiquity: An Introductory Essay*. London: Routledge, 1990.

Martinelli, Vittorio. "Il cinema muto italiano 1923–31." *Bianco e Nero* 4–6 (1981).

————. "Lasciate fare a noi, siamo forti." In Farassino and Sanguineti 1983, 9–27.

————. "Il cinema muto italiano: 1914." *Bianco e Nero* 1–2 (1992).

————. "Il cinema muto italiano: 1913." *Bianco e Nero* 1–4 (1993).

————. "Sotto il vulcano." In Redi 1994, 35–62.

Martini, Emanuela, and Della Casa, Stefano (eds.). *Riccardo Freda. Bergamo Film Meeting 1993*. Bergamo: Stamperia Stefanoni, 1993.

May, Lary. *Screening out the Past: The Birth of Mass Culture and the Motion Picture Industry*. Chicago: University of Chicago Press, 1980.

Mayer, David. "Romans in Britain 1886–1910: Pain's 'The Last Days of Pompeii'." *Theatrephile* 2.5 (1984–1985), 41–50.

———. *Playing out the Empire: "Ben-Hur" and Other Toga Plays and Films, 1883–1908. A Critical Anthology.* Oxford: Clarendon Press, 1994.

Mellencamp, Patricia, and Rosen, Philip (eds.). *Cinema Histories, Cinema Practices.* University Publications of America, *American Film Institute Monograph Series* 4, 1984.

Moatti, Claude. *In Search of Ancient Rome.* Translated by Antony Zielonka. London: Thames and Hudson, 1993. First published in 1989.

Moravia, Alberto. "*Fellini Satyricon*: color and the classics." In Bondanella 1978, 161–8.

Mulvey, Laura. "Visual pleasure and narrative cinema." *Screen* 16.3 (1975), 6–18.

Nadel, Alan. "God's law and the wide screen: *The Ten Commandments* as Cold War 'Epic'." *Publications of the Modern Languages Association of America* 108.3 (1993), 415–30.

Neale, Stephen. *Genre.* London: British Film Institute, 1983.

———. "Questions of genre." *Screen* 31.1 (1990), 45–66.

Nel centenario di Enrico Sienkiewicz (1846–1946). Rome: Libreria dell'800 Editrice, 1946.

Neve, Brian. *Film and Politics in America: A Social Tradition.* London: Routledge, 1992.

Nowell-Smith, Geoffrey. "On the writing of the history of the cinema: some problems." *Edinburgh Magazine* 2 (1977), 8–12.

———. "On history and the cinema." *Screen* 31–2 (1990), 160–71.

O'Connor, John E., and Jackson, Martin A. (eds.). *American History/American Film: Interpreting the Hollywood Image.* New York: Continuum Publishing Company, 1991. First edition published in 1979.

Ortoleva, Peppino. *Cinema e storia: scene dal passato.* Turin: Loescher Editore, 1991.

———. "Testimone infallibile, macchina dei sogni: il film e il programma televisivo come fonte storica." In Gori 1994, 299–331.

Paolella, Roberto. *Storia del cinema muto.* Naples: Giannini, 1956.

Parigi, Stefania. "La rievocazione dell'antico." In Redi 1994, 67–84.

Pearson, Roberta A., and Uricchio, William. "How many times shall Caesar bleed in sport: Shakespeare and the cultural debate about moving pictures." *Screen* 31.3 (1990), 243–61.

Petitot, M. (ed.). *Théâtre François. Volume 4.* Paris: P. Didot l'aîné, 1803.

Petrocchi, Giorgio. "Nerone mancato centurione." In Angelini 1984, 173–82.

Pretjohn, Liz. "Fiction and fact in Victorian paintings of Roman antiquity." Paper delivered at University of Bristol *Reception of Rome* Conference in June 1994, forthcoming.

Prickett, Stephen. "'Hebrew' versus 'Hellene' as a principle of literary criticism." In G.W. Clarke (ed.), *Rediscovering Hellenism: The Hellenic Inheritance and the English Imagination.* Cambridge: Cambridge University Press, 1989, 137–59.

Prolo, Maria Adriana. *Storia del cinema muto italiano.* Milan: Poligono Società Editrice, 1951.

Quartermaine, Louisa. "'Slouching towards Rome': Mussolini's imperial vision." In Cornell and Lomas 1995, 203–15.

Raffaelli, Sergio. "Didascalie tra vecchio e nuovo." In Redi 1994, 85–95.

Rakovsky, Antoine; Zimmer, Jacques; and Lefèvre, Raymond. "Sur *Le Mépris* de Jean-Luc Godard." *La revue du cinéma* 469 (1991), 54–66.

Redi, Riccardo. "Da 'Quo Vadis' a 'Pompei'." In Redi 1994, 27–34.

——— (ed.). *Gli ultimi giorni di Pompei.* Naples: La Macchina dei Sogni A.C. and Electa Napoli, 1994.

Rediscovering Pompeii. Exhibition Catalogue. Rome: "L'Erma" di Bretschneider, 1992.

Reinhold, Meyer. *Classica Americana: The Greek and Roman Heritage in the United States.* Detroit: Wayne University Press, 1984.

Renan, Ernst. *Histoire des Origines du Christianisme. Volume 4. = Oeuvres Completes. Volume 25.* Paris: Calmann-Levy, no date.

Renzi, Lisetta. "Grandezza e morte della 'femme fatale'." In Renzi 1991, 121–30.

Renzi, Renzo (ed.). *Sperduto nel buio: il cinema muto italiano e il suo tempo (1905–1930).* Bologna: Cappelli Editore, 1991.

Richard, Carl J. *The Founders and the Classics: Greece, Rome, and the American Enlightenment.* Cambridge: Harvard University Press, 1994.

Robinson, David. "Spectacle." *Sight and Sound* 25 (1955), 22–7 and 55–6.

Rondolino, Gianni. *Vittorio Cottafavi: cinema e televisione.* Bologna: Cappelli Editore, 1980.
———. "Il cinema." In Gori 1994, 159–82.

Rose, Peter W. "Teaching Greek myth and confronting contemporary myths." In Winkler 1991, 17–39.

Rosen, Philip. "Securing the historical: historiography and the classical cinema." In Mellencamp and Rosen 1984, 17–34.

Rosenstone, Robert A. (ed.) *Revisioning History: Film and the Construction of a New Past.* Princeton, New Jersey: Princeton University Press, 1995.

Rosenthal, Stuart. *The Cinema of Federico Fellini.* South Brunswick and New York: A. S. Barnes and Co., 1976.

Rubiés, Joan-Pau. "Nero in Tacitus and Nero in Tacitism: the historian's craft." In Elsner and Masters 1994, 29–47.

Rubinsohn, Wolfgang Zeev. *Spartacus' Uprising and Soviet Historical Writing.* Translated by J. G. Griffith. Oxford: Oxbow Books, 1987.

Russo, Luigi. "Lo "Spartaco" di R. Giovagnoli." *Belfagor* XI (1956), 74–9.

Said, Edward W. *Orientalism.* London: Penguin, 1985. First published 1978.

Salt, Barry. "Il cinema italiano dalla nascita alla Grande Guerra: un'analisi stilistica." In Renzi 1991, 49–58.

Samuels, Stuart. "The age of conspiracy and conformity: *Invasion of the Body Snatchers* (1956)." In O'Connor and Jackson 1991, 203–17.

Sassoon, Donald. *The Strategy of the Italian Communist Party: From the Resistance to the Historic Compromise.* London: F. Pinter, 1981.

Shadoian, Jack. *Dreams and Dead Ends: The American Gangster/Crime Film.* Cambridge: MIT Press, 1977.

Shohat, Ella. "Gender and culture of empire: toward a feminist ethnography of the cinema." *Quarterly Review of Film and Video* 13.1–3 (1991a), 45–84.
———. "Ethnicities-in-relation: toward a multicultural reading of American cinema." In Lester D. Friedman (ed.), *Unspeakable Images: Ethnicity and the American Cinema.* Urbana: University of Illinois Press, 1991b, 215–50.

Siclier, Jacques. "L'age du péplum." *Cahiers du cinéma* 22.131 (1962), 26–38.

Sienkiewicz, Henryk. *Quo Vadis?* Translated by C. J. Hogarth. Gloucester: Alan Sutton, 1989. First published in book form in 1896.

Sklar, Robert. *Movie Made America: A Cultural History of American Movies.* New York: Vintage Books, 1975.
———. "Kubrick e l'industria del cinema negli Stati Uniti." In Brunetta 1985, 63–74.

Smith, Gary A. *Epic Films: Casts, Credits and Commentary on over 250 Historical Spectacle Movies.* Jefferson: McFarland and Co., 1991.

Smith, Jeffrey P. "'A good business proposition': Dalton Trumbo, *Spartacus*, and the end of the blacklist." *Velvet Light Trap* 23 (1989), 75–100.

Snyder, Stephen. "Color, growth and evolution in *Fellini Satyricon*." In Bondanella 1978, 168–87.

Solomon, Jon. *The Ancient World in the Cinema*. South Brunswick: A. S. Barnes, 1978.

Sordi, Marta. *The Christians and the Roman Empire*. Translated by Annabel Bedini. London: Croom Helm, 1983.

Sorlin, Pierre. *The Film in History: Restaging the Past*. Oxford: Blackwell, 1980.

Spinazzola, Vittorio. "Significato e problemi del film storico-mitologico." *Cinema Nuovo* July–August (1965), 270–9.

————. *Cinema e pubblico: lo spettacolo filmico in Italia 1945–1965*. Rome: Bulzoni Editore, 1985.

Springer, Carolyn. *The Marble Wilderness: Ruins and Representation in Italian Romanticism, 1775–1850*. Cambridge: Cambridge University Press, 1987.

Stacey, Jackie. *Star Gazing: Hollywood Cinema and Female Spectatorship*. London: Routledge, 1994.

Staiger, Janet. "Mass-produced photoplays: economic and signifying practices in the first years of Hollywood." In Kerr 1986, 97–119.

Steigerwald, David. *The Sixties and the End of Modern America*. New York: St. Martin's Press, 1995.

Stevens, Mary Anne (ed.). *The Orientalists: Delacroix to Matisse. European Painters in North Africa and the Near East*. London: Royal Academy of Arts and Weidenfeld and Nicolson, 1984.

Storey, John. *An Introductory Guide to Cultural Theory and Popular Culture*. Hemel Hempstead: Harvester-Wheatsheaf, 1993.

Straw, Will. "The myth of total cinema history." In Ron Burnett (ed.), *Explorations in Film Theory: Selected Essays from Ciné-Tracts*. Bloomington: Indiana University Press, 1991, 237–46.

Suid, Lawrence. "The Pentagon and Hollywood: *Dr. Strangelove or: How I Learned to Stop Worrying and Love the Bomb* (1964)." In O'Connor and Jackson 1991, 219–35.

Taplin, Oliver. *Greek Fire*. London: Jonathan Cape, 1989.

Thomas, Vivian. *Shakespeare's Roman Worlds*. London: Routledge, 1989.

Thompson, Richard J., and Routt, William D. "'Keep young and beautiful': surplus and subversion in *Roman Scandals*." In Tom O'Regan and Brian Shoesmith (eds.), *History on/and/in film. Selected Papers from the Third Australian History and Film Conference*. Perth: History and Film Association of Australia, 1987, 31–44.

Thumin, Janet. *Celluloid Sisters: Women and Popular Culture*. Basingstoke: Macmillan, 1992.

Toplin Robert Brent (ed.). *Hollywood as Mirror: Changing Views of "Outsiders" and "Enemies" in American Movies. Contributions to the Study of Popular Culture 38*. Westport, Connecticut: Greenwood Press, 1993.

Toynbee, Jocelyn, and Perkins, John Ward. *The Shrine of St. Peter and the Vatican Excavations*. London: Longmans, 1956.

Trevelyan, Raleigh. *The Shadow of Vesuvius: Pompeii AD 79*. London: Michael Joseph, 1976.

Treves, Piero. *L'idea di Roma e la cultura italiana del secolo XIX*. Milan-Naples: Riccardo Ricciardi Editore, 1962.

Turconi, Davide. "I film storici italiani e la critica americana dal 1910 alla fine del muto." *Bianco e Nero* 1–2 (1963), 40–54.

Turconi, Davide, and Sacchi, Antonio (eds.). *Bianconero rosso e verde: immagini del cinema italiano 1910–1980*. Florence: La Casa Usher, 1983.

Turner, Frank M. *The Greek Heritage in Victorian Britain*. New Haven: Yale University Press, 1981.

———. "Rome versus Greece: the politics of culture." Paper delivered at University of Bristol *Reception of Rome* Conference in June 1995, forthcoming.

Usai, Paolo Cherchi. *Giovanni Pastrone. Il castoro cinema 119*. Florence: La Nuova Italia, 1985.

Usai, Paolo Cherchi, and Codelli, Lorenzo. *Sulla via di Hollywood 1911–1920*. Pordenone: Edizioni Biblioteca dell'Immagine, 1988.

Vance, Norman. *The Victorians and Ancient Rome*. Oxford: Blackwell, forthcoming.

Vance, William L. "The Colosseum: American uses of an imperial image." In Annabel Patterson (ed.), *Roman Images. Selected Papers from the English Institute n.s.8*. Baltimore: John Hopkins University Press, 1984, 105–40.

———. *America's Rome. Volume 1: Classical Rome*. New Haven: Yale University Press, 1989.

Vanderwood, Paul J. "An American Cold Warrior: *Viva Zapata!* (1952)." In O'Connor and Jackson 1991, 183–201.

Verdone, Mario. "Preistoria del film storico." *Bianco e Nero* 1–2 (1963), 20–5.

———. *Federico Fellini*. Milan: Il Castoro Cinema/Editrice il Castoro, 1994.

Vidal, Gore. *Screening History*. London: Abacus, 1993; Harvard University Press, 1992.

Visser, Romke. "Fascist doctrine and the cult of the Romanità." *Journal of Contemporary History* 27 (1992), 5–21.

Vogt, Joseph. *Ancient Slavery and the Ideal of Man*. Translated by Thomas Wiedemann. Oxford: Blackwell, 1974.

Wallace-Hadrill, Andrew. *Suetonius: The Scholar and his Caesars*. London: Duckworth, 1983.

Walter, Gerard. *Nero*. London: George Allen and Unwin, 1957.

Wanger, Walter, and Hyams, Joe. *My Life with Cleopatra*. London: Transworld Publishers, 1963.

Wardman, H. W. *Ernest Renan: A Critical Biography*. London: The Athlone Press, 1964.

Warmington, B. H. *Nero: Reality and Legend*. London: Chatto and Windus, 1969.

Webster, Richard A. *The Cross and the Fasces: Christian Democracy and Fascism in Italy*. Stanford: Stanford University Press, 1960.

White, Hayden. *Metahistory: The Historical Imagination in Nineteenth-Century Europe*. Baltimore: Johns Hopkins University Press, 1973.

Whitfield, Stephen J. *The Culture of the Cold War*. Baltimore: John Hopkins University Press, 1991.

Wiedemann, Thomas. *Emperors and Gladiators*. London: Routledge, 1992.

Williams, David. "Medieval movies." *The Yearbook of English Studies* 20 (1990), 1–32.

Winkler, Martin W. (ed.). *Classics and Cinema*. Lewisburg: Bucknell University Press, 1991.

———. "Cinema and the fall of Rome." *Transactions of the American Philological Society* 125 (1995), 135–54.

Wittner, Lawrence S. *Cold War America: From Hiroshima to Watergate*. New York: Praeger Publishers, 1974.

Wood, Christopher. *Olympian Dreamers: Victorian Classical Painters 1860–1914*. London: Constable, 1983.

Wood, Michael. *America in the Movies: Or "Santa Maria, it had Slipped my Mind."* London: Secker and Warburg, 1975.

Wyke, Maria. "Augustan Cleopatras: female power and poetic authority." In Anton Powell (ed.), *Roman Poetry and Propaganda in the Age of Augustus*. London: Bristol Classical Press, 1992, 98–140.

———. "Make like Nero! The appeal of a cinematic emperor." In Elsner and Masters 1994, 11–28.

———. "Cinema and the City of the Dead: reel histories of Pompeii." In Colin Mac-Cabe and Duncan Petrie (eds.), *New Scholarship from BFI Research*. London: British Film Institute, 1996, 140–56.

———. "Herculean Muscle! The classicizing rhetoric of bodybuilding." *Arion* 4.3 1997.

Yavetz, Zvi. *Slaves and Slavery in Ancient Rome*. New Brunswick, New Jersey: Transaction Books, 1988.

Zanelli, Dario. "Dal pianeta Roma." In Zanelli (ed.), *Fellini-Satyricon by Federico Fellini*. Bologna: Cappelli Editore, 1969, 13–79.

Ziolkowski, Theodore. *Virgil and the Moderns*. Princeton, New Jersey: Princeton University Press, 1993.

Index